The Devil and Uncle Will

TO TOM & DEBBIE

IF YOU EVER HAD ANY BUSINESS
WITH UNCLE WILL I AM NOT
RESPONSIBLE FOR HIS DEBTS

Best wishes & merry Christmas

[signature]

The Devil & Uncle ill

by Harold Miles

Humana Press • Clifton, New Jersey

© 1991 The Humana Press Inc.
Crescent Manor
PO Box 2148
Clifton, New Jersey 07015

Printed in the United States of America.

Library of Congress Cataloging in Publication Data

Miles, Harold.
     The devil & Uncle Will / by Harold Miles
        286 pp.
      ISBN 0-89603-197-7
      I. Title.
     PS3563.I3718D4   1991   90-49274
     813'.54—dc20   CIP

Contents

Acknowledgments

Profoundest thanks to my sweet wife,
Mary, for encouraging the writing of this book.

To Ms. Susan Brownlow, the most patient and probably the best secretary that anybody ever had, for her work in this effort.

To Mr. Gary Solomon for his editing expertise and perhaps making something out of nothing.

Uncle Will 'n Me

Suddenly I find myself rapidly approaching old age without having put to paper the story of one of the most incredible people I've ever known—my Uncle Will.

Actually, he was my great uncle, my maternal grandmother's older brother, but I always called him Uncle Will. During most of his life Uncle Will terrorized both the family and the community. He was a drunkard, a liar, and a cheat. By his own admission he also killed two men and went to prison for a third murder of which he claimed no recollection. Yet, with me, he could be the kindest, most gentle human being a boy could ever hope to know.

And, oh, what a wondrous storyteller he was! I would sit literally spellbound for hours, especially during the years just prior to his passing, listening to him recount tales of his early days as a brash, arrogant young man.

I take many of the secrets Uncle Will told me during this time as something of a death-bed confession. At the time he related them, he was a wizened old man with emphysema so advanced that he could hardly breathe. In fact, he'd often talk himself out completely and then sit for long stretches without any sound escaping his lips other than the rattle of his labored breathing.

Uncle Will came from fundamentalist Baptist stock who believed literally that St. Peter was the keeper of the Pearly Gates and Gabriel was his bosom buddy. Together, they guarded the entrance to Heaven, and in order to get through the Gates to stand in the presence of the Almighty, you first had to get by them.

"Up there," he once said, gesturing toward the heavens, "is every mean, stinkin', low-down thing I ever did. Someday I'm gonna have to explain it all, and boy, I won't be done by the time you get there."

In the years since his death I've often wondered why he chose me, a mere lad at the time, to be his confessor and hear all the sins he'd committed. Somewhere in the Holy Scriptures it says, "Every head shall bow, every knee shall bend, and every tongue confess." Perhaps Uncle Will's revelations were spoken for that purpose—to purge his soul of any blight that might keep him out of the Pearly Gates.

Still, sometimes I can see him in my mind's eye, standing before the Almighty with a glint in his eye, trying to slip one last fib over on Him as he chuckles to himself, "Hell, it don't hurt to give it a try."

Such was Uncle Will.

Harold Miles

Bury'n Uncle Will

On a warm November morning in 1948, only a few months after my eighteenth birthday, they called from the hospital at Bowdon, Georgia, to tell me Uncle Will was dead. When I arrived, an orderly ushered me to a small side room where Will lay curled in a fetal position, his ragged white mane almost covering the pillow. The icy embrace of death was profoundly evident.

I sat silently staring a long while at my uncle, wondering what his final hours had been like. He almost certainly had spent them alone. After all, most of the family still hated him for things he'd done in his younger days. But had he spent his last hours in peace? That's what I wanted to know most of all.

During his later years, when emphysema began to sap his very life's breath, peace of mind was the thing he sought more than any other. I remembered once while we were sitting astride a log on the bank of the Tallapoosa River, he suddenly pointed a finger heavenward and said, "Nephew, I know up there somewhere is writ every mean, stinking thing I ever did. Some day I am going to have to explain them to the almighty himself. Chances are, I'll still be trying to do that when you get there and I'm old enough to be your grandpa. I powerfully dread that day." As I sat there in the room with his body, I voiced a quiet prayer that he'd finally found it.

1

We buried him two days later in the cemetery at nearby Indian Creek Church, the resting place of most of my other relatives. I don't recall the minister's name. For all I know, they may have had to bribe him to come. I do recall, though, that Uncle Will's brother Jim showed up barefooted and in overalls, with no shirt. It was obvious to anyone who stood next to him that Jim wasn't wearing underwear, either. That certainly raised some eyebrows.

The church could not hold the crowd that attended the service that day. It overflowed into the front yard. The only one I saw shed a tear, however, was my grandmother, and I remembered with some bitterness Uncle Will's prophecy that most folks would come to his funeral just to be sure he was dead.

My clearest memory of the funeral is the preacher's struggle to say something kind about that enigma of a man resting in the coffin at the front of the sanctuary.

He began, as was traditional, by listing aloud the names of Uncle Will's survivors and next of kin, taking his time to do so. I'm sure he'd have loved to call it a day and go home after finishing that task, but he knew he needed to conduct the service properly. That was when his troubles began.

He opened his mouth to begin the eulogy, but nothing came out. For what seemed like an eternity, he stood there searching for the right words. The silence was deafening. I thought he'd been struck dumb. Despite the embarrassment of the moment, though, there wasn't a person in that congregation who didn't feel great sympathy for the man. Had they been in his shoes, they knew that they, too, would have been at a loss for words.

Finally, gratefully, he uttered a brief phrase in a voice that was little more than a croak.

"Will is dead," he whispered hoarsely.

Whether out of obligation or simply in joyous recognition of that fact, someone on the far side of the church answered, "Amen!"

Bolstered by that show of support, the preacher regained sufficient composure to repeat, a bit more forcefully, "Will is dead!" This time he got two Amens.

Now he was on a roll. "Will preached his own funeral every day of his life!" he exclaimed. From the sound of it, nearly everyone present voiced an Amen to that, and that was good enough for the man of God. He dropped his head quickly to voice a brief prayer for the souls of all who had gone on before, then closed with, "Amen. Mr. Undertaker to the front, please." He didn't mention Uncle Will's soul in the prayer.

As was customary in those days, those of us in the immediate family filed forward to view the body first, followed by the congregation. After everyone returned to their seats, the family had a final opportunity to say goodbye to Will before the coffin was closed and taken to the cemetery.

There, without further ado, we laid Uncle Will to rest.

By the time I reached home that evening, clouds had gathered and begun to sprinkle the area with rain. With chores still to do, I grabbed a bucket and went to milk the cow.

As the rain drummed softly on the tin roof of the

barn, my mind was drawn back to the many times during the past two years when Uncle Will and I sat and talked into the early hours of the morning. Somehow it seemed to me that he'd been trying to put his house in order. I believe he had a powerful desire to convince me that maybe, just maybe, he wasn't all bad. Still, he knew he had a lot to answer for.

I sat silently on the milking stool for a long time, reliving a host of memories from the days Uncle Will was a vigorous man to now, when he lay in the cemetery a few miles away. I thought of the men he'd killed, of the people he'd lied to and stolen from. I recalled all the times he cheated me. I remembered the moments he inspired great hope in me, only to leave me frustrated and angry. I should've hated him, but didn't. In fact, I couldn't stop the flow of warm tears. You either loved Uncle Will or you hated him. There was no in-between. I loved him, tho I didn't fully understand why.

Perhaps it was because he showed me a vulnerability few people ever saw. In the years just before he died, we spent hour after hour together discussing both the future and the past. He told me stories about his life that startled and amazed me. He expressed concerns about the afterlife that saddened and disturbed me.

Most of all, he exhibited a depth of soul I hadn't known existed until then. All of those images—from the moment I first laid eyes on him until I watched him being lowered into the grave—came to life that night as I sat alone in the barn and cried.

Will was dead, but I knew six feet of Georgia clay could not shield him from that encounter he so dreaded.

Meetin' Uncle Will

I first met Uncle Will just before I turned three, on a day Daddy hitched up our one-horse wagon and carried me and several of my cousins to visit great-grandmother Rebecca. It's my first memory of seeing her, and from that moment on I knew her as old, mostly blind, and mean.

A ten-year-old neighbor girl, Cleo Smith by name, accompanied us on our trip that day. Cleo lived with her grandfather, and, although I was oblivious to it at that age, rumor had it that she was the illegitimate child of one of the man's daughters. The daughter had left town in disgrace shortly after giving birth, or so the story went, leaving Cleo in the care of her grandfather.

Upon arriving at Grandma's house, we were ushered in to see her, and I'll never forget that moment as long as I live. It was 1933, and the world was in the depths of the Great Depression. Inside the house, in a darkened room with the shades drawn, sat a withered, decrepit woman old enough to be Methuselah's great-grandmother. Instead, she was my great-grandmother. She, like the rest of us in that tiny band, lived a tenuous existence. It was only through the mercy and good graces of her two sons, Will and Jim, that she survived at all.

Ma used tobacco, and the room reflected that habit. Huge chunks of tobacco hung suspended from nails driven in the ceiling, and Ma herself reeked of tobacco and asafetida.

It was a terrifying experience to enter that dimly lit room, and doubly so when we were introduced and shoved up close so Ma could see us through her cataract-laden eyes. When the neighbor girl's name was announced, Ma reached out two gnarled claws that had once been hands, drew the girl toward her until their noses almost touched, and said, "You're that little bastard gal that Clem Smith is raisin', ain't ya?"

I was too young to know what those words meant, but Cleo wasn't. She tore loose of Ma's grip with a great sob and lunged wildly toward the door. A great injustice had been done in that moment, of that I was certain, though I didn't understand how or why.

The rest of the children quickly dispersed into the sunshine, where we ran into Uncle Will. It was the first time I'd ever seen him, and I was awestruck.

Even in his late forties, Uncle Will was still an imposing figure. He stood nearly six-foot-six and, though quite slender, loomed huge to a child my age. He also had a lively, happy air about him that was contagious to anyone around him.

That day he wore a lightweight dress suit, along with bright red suspenders and a felt hat. The outfit set him apart impressively from Granddaddy, Daddy, and the ragtag assemblage of youngsters dressed in worn-out blue denim overalls. The automobile he stood leaning against was eye-popping as well: a bright green Model A touring car with the top down. It was the most beautiful car I'd ever seen in my life.

Uncle Will's wife, Beth, whom I'd also never met, was almost six-feet tall herself, but not nearly as friendly. She tried to persuade him to go inside and see Ma, but he was too busy talking to us children and smoking cigars to pay heed to her. As he stood jawing with those of us gathered around him, he suddenly bent down, grabbed me under the arms, and boosted me up to eye level.

"Who are you, boy?" he asked. "I ain't never seen you before."

"I'm Irene's boy," I replied softly.

"Why, I didn't even know Irene was married," he laughed. "Seems like she oughta still be a child. Guess I've been out of state longer than I thought."

"Out of state." That phrase had a wonderful ring to it. It conjured up images of far-away, exotic lands where everyone owned cars like the sparkling green beauty Uncle Will was driving.

After looking me over another second or two, Uncle Will set me back down with a thud, but not before I glimpsed something in his car I'd never seen before. Between the front and back seats lay a pile of tin cans. All the food we preserved at home was kept in glass jars sealed with a band of rubber. I had no idea what the cans in Will's car were good for. I just found them shiny and attractive, so I asked if I could have one.

"Boy," Uncle Will responded, "take all ya want. They're empty." When the other children saw what I had, they huddled around and begged me to share with them, making me for a brief moment the most popular person in the yard.

7

In those days, what toys children had, they made themselves. Store-bought toys were a thing of the future. Usually when my cousins went anywhere, they carried along a tightly wound ball made of yarn from an old sock, in hopes of playing ball. After studying the tin cans I'd given out, several of the older ones punched holes in the tops with a nail and threaded yarn from their sock-balls through them several times, leaving a length of eight to ten feet of yarn hanging from the holes. Next, they took the cans and laid them in the back of the wagon.

I had no idea what they planned to do until we headed home later that day. Then, they sat on the tailgate, dropped the cans on the road below, and dragged them rattling and banging behind the wagon. It was great fun for everybody—except Daddy, who after a piece made us draw them in because the noise was driving him crazy.

As we neared home I began telling one of the older boys about my introduction to Uncle Will earlier in the day. I mentioned the strong and unusual odor I'd noticed on Will's breath while I hung in mid-air staring at him, and I asked what the odor might have been.

"You don't know nothin'," the boy replied. "That was liquor." Uncle Will had been drunk, he went on to say. Since Mama and Daddy didn't keep spirits in the house and didn't drink, I'd never smelled alcohol before. As I got to know Uncle Will better through the years, however, it was an odor with which I became very well acquainted.

Sawmillin'
and the Marsh Hen

I didn't see Uncle Will very often during the three or four years following our first meeting. That could have been because he came and went from the area regularly. One moment he'd be living on a farm a few miles away, and the next thing we knew, he'd upped and moved somewhere else in search of greener pastures. When our paths did cross, however, I always thoroughly enjoyed sitting and talking with him about this and that, and he seemed to feel the same way.

One week in the spring of 1937, I went to stay with my grandparents for several days. I was excited about the visit because Uncle Will now owned and operated a steam-driven sawmill on the banks of Indian Creek right across from where they lived, and I was hoping to get a chance to see him again.

Finding a way to visit Uncle Will wasn't going to be easy, though, because Granddaddy didn't much like me spending time with him. Granddaddy considered Uncle Will a good-for-nothing who tried to bully and intimidate other people. And truth be told, Granddaddy was scared to death of Uncle Will's violent temper.

Uncle Will didn't have much use for Granddaddy, either. From what I could understand, Uncle Will thought his sister—Granddaddy's wife—had married beneath herself, and he didn't make any bones about telling everybody so. I do know that Grandmother was much more educated than Granddaddy.

No one in the family really liked Uncle Will except Daddy, and that probably had more to do with Daddy's easygoing nature than anything Uncle Will did to deserve it. Mama, in particular, despised him because of his drinking and his foul mouth. In fact, the sparks seemed to fly any time the two of them were in the same room together. To make matters worse, Uncle Will knew how to get under Mama's skin with an off-color story or a string of cuss words, and he often appeared to set her off on purpose.

There were also whispered conversations about his cheating and conniving, stealing, welching on bills, and even about him serving time in prison for killing a drinking buddy of his. Of course, when children entered a room where such talk was going on, the conversation immediately shifted to other things, but children hear a lot more than their parents realize.

As big a man as he was physically, Uncle Will's reputation as a black-hearted scoundrel was even bigger. Yet in my brief encounters with him, he was so wonderful and likable that I always looked forward to seeing him, and this time was no different.

One day after dinner when Granddaddy was busy, I slipped across the creek bridge and over to Uncle Will's sawmill. I'd heard the mill running that morning and thought I'd watch Uncle Will and his men work for a while, but when I got there the mill was shut down. Uncle Will was the only one around.

There he sat on a pine log atop the mill carriage, sharpening by hand the big five-foot circular saw used to cut the lumber. As I watched silently, he worked on one tooth at a time, filing it deftly until it felt sharp to the touch, then pulling the saw forward to the next tooth and repeating the exercise. It was a slow and tedious process, but he didn't seem to mind. In fact, he was humming a soft tune as he worked.

After several minutes, I walked on up to him and said, "Hey, Uncle Will, whatcha doin'?"

He stopped, looked down at me over the top of the half-sized glasses he was wearing, and answered, "Hey there, boy. I didn't hear ya come up. Whatcha doin' here, runnin' away from home?"

"No, sir, I'm stayin' with Grandmother and Granddaddy this week. I heard the mill runnin' this mornin', so I came over to see if ya needed a hand."

"I suspect ya need to grow another foot or so before you'll be much help around the mill," he replied with a chuckle. "I'll tell ya what ya can do, though," he said. "You can take that jar," pointing to a half-gallon fruit jar nearby, "and bring me a drink of water from the spring. I've worked up a powerful thirst sharpenin' this saw, and I'm only a third finished. We hit a nail in a tree we cut in the swamp. I can't figure how a nail got in a tree like that, unless somebody drove a spike in it to hang their clothes on at a baptizin',' but it damn near ruined my saw. I had to send my help home 'cause we couldn't cut nothin'."

I grabbed the jar and hurried to the spring and back, then watched as Uncle Will drank from it. Next he took a corncob pipe and a can of Prince Albert out of the bib of his overalls, filled the pipe with tobacco, and lit it in a way I'd never seen before. He pulled a kitchen match out of his overall pocket and, raising his right leg up to tighten the fabric, struck the match across the blue denim.

I was awestruck.

"Could ya do that again, Uncle Will?" I asked. "I never did see nothin' like that before." Obligingly, he reached into the same pocket, drew out another match, and raked it across the tight denim fabric, causing the matchhead to burst into flames. I stood silently and stared at the match until it burned itself out.

"Ya know what, young fella?" Uncle Will spoke as if to break the spell. "I betcha I've got somethin' else you'd like to see. There's an old marsh hen sittin' on a nest up the creek a ways. We've cut around a half-acre of good timber so we don't bother her. If ya wanna see, I'll show ya her nest, but ya gotta be awful quiet, 'cause we don't wanna disturb her."

Never in my life had a grownup been willing to take time out for me like that, and it made me feel great. How Granddaddy could possibly dislike this wonderful man, I couldn't understand.

After Uncle Will set aside his tools, we left the mill and headed up an old dry run. Uncle Will stooped low as he led the way through the thick swamp and up a couple of short embankments until we were within fifty feet of the creek. From there we crawled slowly and quietly on our stomachs up to the edge of the creek.

"Look over there and you can see her," he whispered, pointing toward a thick clump of alder bushes. "She's on the nest."

I laid there staring intently at the spot he had indicated, but the hen was so well-camouflaged that I couldn't distinguish her from the bushes. "I don't see anything," I whispered back.

"Just watch that spot and you'll see her move pretty soon," he answered softly. Sure enough, after studying the bushes for a minute or two, I saw a bird about the size of a good frying chicken rustle slightly in her nest. She was mostly brown, with flecks of white scattered throughout her feathers. It was thrilling to see such a beautiful creature, and even more so because this big man had taken time off from his work to bring me here.

It's difficult to express the magic of that afternoon, but lying there on the embankment with Uncle Will's hand resting on my back as he waited for me to spot the marsh hen is probably the moment he stole my heart. Despite all the pain he would cause me later on, I never forgot the joy and excitement of that day.

About that time, I heard Granddaddy call my name from across the creek. Without thinking, I answered back. When I did, the marsh hen bounded off the nest and flittered away through the trees. I immediately started apologizing to Uncle Will for doing such a stupid thing, but he patted me on the shoulder and said, "That's okay, boy. She'll get a drink of water and then come back to the nest once it's quiet again. But we better move on so we don't upset her no more."

With that, we crawled back through the undergrowth and made our way down to the sawmill. After saying a quick goodbye to Uncle Will, I took off in a dead run for Granddaddy's house

"Where ya been, boy?" he asked when I arrived. "We was gettin' worried about ya." I knew he'd be mad if I said I'd been with Uncle Will, so I only told him what he wanted to know.

"I been watchin' a marsh hen nestin' in some bushes down on the creek," I answered.

"A marsh hen? I ain't seen one of them in years. Ya sure you're not makin' this up?"

"No, sir," I replied with complete honesty. "I spotted her in some alder bushes along the creek. Would ya like to see her?"

"I don't have time, boy," he answered as he turned and walked back toward the fields. A sense of relief swept over me, because the nest was on the other side of the creek, and if I'd had to show it to him, he would have known I'd been visiting with Uncle Will.

That whole spring I visited my grandparents as often as possible. Then when they weren't watching, I would slip across the creek to see Uncle Will. Any time he could, he would take a break and go with me to the edge of the creek, where we'd lie quietly and watch the little hen for what seemed like hours. Occasionally she would leave the nest to stretch her wings, gliding so silently through the undergrowth that it was like she was riding on a cushion of air. Except for Granddaddy, I never told another soul about it, and as far as I know, neither did Uncle Will. It was just our little secret, and that made it all the more special.

One day as we were watching the hen, Uncle Will whispered, "I sure hope those chicks hatch soon. I gotta cut those trees around her nest or I'm gonna lose the sawmill." I left there with a heavy heart, thinking about him having to disturb the nest before the baby birds were hatched. When we got back to the mill I asked, "Uncle Will, are you gonna be able to hold off long enough for those chicks to hatch?"

"Don't you fret, boy," he responded assuringly, "I'm not gonna destroy the only brood of marsh hens I've seen in fifteen or twenty years. I won't touch those trees until that hen's got a family, I promise ya that." That eased my mind a great deal.

A few days later we made our way to the nest again. By now we had a pretty good trail worked out, and the going was fairly easy. Just as we got in position to observe the hen, she came marching by us with eleven chicks chirping and following along behind her. That was the last time I ever saw her or the chicks, and I've never seen a marsh hen again. In fact, I don't even know if that's the proper name for the thing. That's just what we called it.

The next day, Uncle Will's crew moved in and started cutting down those big poplars, sawing them into lumber to make furniture.

Cuttin' Pigs
and Pickin' Strawberries

I suppose in all of my dealings with Uncle Will, at least during my early years, the only one that turned out to be pure pleasure was the season we watched the marsh hen raise her brood.

As soon as she left the nest, Uncle Will cut out the timber, picked up his portable sawmill, and moved on. It was probably the better part of a year before I saw him again. In the meantime, I continued the process of growing up.

Actually, I was one of the lucky number who did survive childhood. In the years before antibiotics, a lot of children died in infancy, as witnessed by the many gravestones of children in the cemeteries of the day. Growing up was quite an ordeal when any disease you got could be fatal.

During my first year in school, there was an outbreak of pinkeye. As soon as Mama heard about it, she went to town and bought some new medicine that was supposed to cure or prevent it. When she got home she picked up the family eyedropper, loaded it with medicine, and ordered my baby sister and me to lay our heads in her lap while she administered this magical elixir. We were highly skeptical of having anything dropped in our eyes, however, and we so informed her. We didn't oppose Mama on many things, but we absolutely refused to let her drop some unknown solution in our eyes.

Finally, after realizing that this was one war she wasn't going to win, she called out to Daddy and said, "Come in here and let me put these drops in your eyes to show the kids that it won't hurt 'em." Daddy dutifully did as he was instructed and lowered his head down on her knee.

There was only one problem. Unknown to either him or Mama, the last thing that medicine dropper had been used for was to administer Lugol's Solution, a liquid high in iodine content that was used to treat goiter and other ailments. Around our house it had probably been used to remove a wart or something similar. At any rate, residue from the solution was apparently still in the glass tube of the medicine dropper, and when Mama squirted her magic pinkeye cure into Daddy's eye, she also washed the Lugol Solution down into it.

I've seen rocket launchings at Cape Canaveral that caused fewer fireworks than that medicine did when it hit Daddy's eye. Although he was generally a man of gentle temperament, he flew into one of the wildest, most awe-inspiring fits I've ever seen. In a flash he yelled, leaped up, and proceeded to bang into and knock over nearly every piece of furniture in the house, including the kitchen table and all the chairs. The terrifying racket sent our big white cat diving for refuge into the butter churn, but when Daddy kicked that over, the cat flew up the open fireplace and out the chimney. A second later he landed spead-eagle on the slick, tin roof and slowly slid toward the edge, groping desperately but unsuccessfully all the way for a clawhold. When he finally plunged over the side and past the window a moment later on the way to the hard ground below, he was as black as a quarter past twelve.

All of this commotion happened in the twinkling of an eye, so to speak, with the cat landing with a thud outside and Daddy laying under the bed, pounding the floor and moaning loudly over the administration of the supposedly "painless" medication.

When he finally came to his senses and crawled out from under the bed, Mama examined his eye and found that the drops had burned a brown spot about as big as an english pea on the white of his eye. Needless to say, he put a stop to the pinkeye treatment right then and there. As best I remember, I never received the treatment, nor did I ever contract pinkeye.

It was nearly three weeks before we could coax the cat back into the house.

The following spring, Mama herself came down with a mysterious illness that confined her to bed for several months. She couldn't cook or do any of the housework, so after much discussion between her and Daddy, she decided to take my little brother and sister and go stay with Grandmother and Granddaddy until she recovered. Meanwhile, I remained at home to wash and cook for Daddy.

At that early age (I was almost eight), about all I knew how to cook was vegetables. You simply cleaned the vegetables, tossed them in a pot with a chunk of fat meat and a little salt, and boiled them until they were done. I had mastered that. Otherwise, I was a complete novice, although I'd watched Mama make corn bread from time to time. From what I remembered, she sifted some corn meal, sprinkled in a little baking soda and a pinch of salt, then mixed it with buttermilk into a big pone, and put it in the stove to cook.

Mama cooked supper ahead of time on the day she left, so we were safe for twelve hours. My duties didn't begin until the following day.

The next morning, Daddy rose early to cook our breakfast, and I must say it was pretty poor fare. He was not any great shakes at cooking, and it showed. When he left to go to the field, he told me to have dinner cooked when he returned home at noon. "Ya forgot to fill the stove box up with dry wood, and it rained last night," he said. "The wood's gonna be wet, so ya better gather some up and put it in the oven to dry it out. If ya don't, ya won't be able to cook dinner. You can also take some coals out and put 'em around the wash pot so you'll have somethin' to build a fire with when ya do the wash." Having given me those meager instructions, he left and headed out to work in the field.

Now, to an eight-year-old, the hours from daylight to noon seem endless, so I wasn't in any particular hurry to do what Daddy said. So I went outside, picked up some smooth rocks, and shot my slingshot a while. Before I knew it, it was well past mid-morning and I suddenly realized I'd forgotten to keep the fire going. I rushed back into the house, but sure enough, it was out. There wasn't a dry twig or piece of lighter wood to be found anywhere, so I threw several sticks of wet stove wood into the ashbed in the bottom of the fire box, hoping by some miracle that they'd blaze up. Then I went back out to play a while longer until the fire got hot.

We didn't own a clock, but I could pretty well guess the time of day by looking at the sun, and it was moving up in the sky a lot faster than I'd have liked, especially since I hadn't done any of the things I was supposed to do toward getting dinner ready. Nevertheless, I tried to reassure myself that the wood would catch fire at any minute. As if to urge it on, I went ahead and made the corn bread and put it in the stove, which was ice cold.

Anybody who's ever set corn bread batter out for long knows it starts cracking open like a mudhole drying out after a summer rain, but I was certain the fire would catch on shortly, so I went back out into the yard and played some more. After checking the sun a while later, I saw it was close to dinner, and rushed back to check the firebox. I figured I could do the wash-ing that afternoon, but I best have Daddy some dinner cooked when he came home. Unfortunately, that green, wet stovewood looked exactly like it had when I put it in the ashbed earlier. The only flames I felt were the flames of panic beginning to spread like a wildfire through me.

I snatched open the stove door to look and see how the corn bread was doing, knowing full well it probably wasn't doing a whole lot in that frigid stove, but I was wrong. It was definitely beginning to crack. In fact, some of the crevices running across it looked like the Grand Canyon. In desperation, I started searching for something dry. The only thing I could find was our wooden kitchen matches, and I poured a pile of them under the end of the stove wood and lit it, half depleting our meager supply of matches. They blazed up brilliantly for about half a minute, then went out—just like my hopes.

By now I was beginning to greatly fear the prospect of what Daddy might do when he saw how poorly I'd followed his directions. I rushed down to the barn to see if I could find anything dry there, but there was nothing. As I hurried back to the house, I looked up at the top of the hill and saw Daddy coming home after a hard morning in the fields. He was riding our old mule, something he only did when he was very tired, and I knew that didn't bode well for me. Even though he was a gentle man and never fussed much, you'd best do what he told you to do, especially when he was tired, and I hadn't done that at all.

When he got to the house, he carried the mule straight to the barn to take off the gear and feed her. Meanwhile, I frantically searched all over the house for anything that would burn. There was a cookbook and the Holy Bible, the only two books we had in the house. I seriously considered using the Holy Bible to light the wood, but I knew Daddy would kill me if I did that. I thought about the cookbook, but Mama would kill me for using that. So, for the first time in my young life I knelt down in the floor, brought my hands together up under my chin, and began earnestly beseeching the Almighty to save me from what was shortly to come.

After begging without any luck whatsoever for the good Lord to make me disappear in a puff of smoke, the thought suddenly occurred to me that I might prevail on Daddy's sympathy simply by letting him catch me in an attitude of prayer when he opened the back door. When he came in a minute or two later, however, he only noticed that the little table on which we ate was bare. "Harold, ya don't even have the table set," he said. Little did he realize that was one of the smaller problems I had at that moment. When I didn't answer, he opened the door to the stove and saw my pitiful effort at corn bread. By now the cracks were almost to the bottom of the pan, it had been sitting out so long.

After a moment collecting his thoughts, he looked down at me and said, "What else was ya plannin' to cook?"

"Turnip greens," I answered meekly.

"Where are they?"

"I haven't picked 'em yet."

"Well, do ya think ya can have me some supper cooked by sundown?" he asked with controlled anger.

"Yes, sir, I know I can."

"It's best ya do," he warned, then he turned and walked out to the barn, waited a few minutes for the mule to finish eating, and headed back to the field.

After Daddy left I started thinking about this prayer business. It hadn't seemed to work very well for me in my time of need. After all, God didn't set that stove wood on fire like I'd asked Him. However, I had to admit that neither did He let Daddy whip me, so maybe my prayer was answered and I just didn't know it. Prayer had always been explained to me as something like asking favors of God, and since I didn't get the tar beat out of me, maybe it worked, only in a different way from what I expected. At any rate, I didn't have much faith that it would save me a second time if I didn't have supper ready. By then the sun had dried a field of broom sage. I gathered an armful and was able to get the wood going in the stove, then built a fire around the wash pot and started washing clothes.

I had a heck of a time with the wash. In those days we boiled the clothes in an old black, cast-iron pot, then laid them out on what we called a battlin' block, which was a round chunk of wood standing on its end, and beat the water and dirt out of them with the battlin' stick. I was so short at the time that I had to stand on a block of unsplit stove wood in order to hold my Daddy's overalls up off the ground. I had to stand on this same block to pour the water I drew from the well into the rinse tubs. We didn't have a lot of clothes, either clean or dirty, but that day I washed what we did have in order to stay in Daddy's good graces. By the time he got home I had the turnip greens and corn bread cooked, and all the wash done. Daddy didn't say much, because that kind of work was just expected of me, but neither did he turn me over his knee, so I was satisfied.

The next morning, I didn't have to cook breakfast because Daddy did it again. His biscuits neither looked nor tasted like Mama's, and his sawmill gravy resembled a high-grade glue. It stuck to all of the dishes, as well as to the roof of my mouth, but it was still better than having to cook it myself because I didn't understand all the intricacies of cooking gravy.

It seemed more lonely around the house the second day, maybe because the novelty of being "on my own" had already worn off, but I had an added chore to keep me busy—churning milk. We had to churn the milk every day to make butter, cheese, and other products. To me, it was always the most tedious, drawn-out job in the house, but there was no one else to blame if it didn't get done, so I went to it.

trap, I decided that I'd just have to wait for Daddy to rescue me when he came home that night. The prospect of hanging there for hours with my hands over my head unnerved me a bit, though, and I started screaming my head off in an effort to attract attention from anybody who might be within earshot. I yelled until I was so hoarse I could barely whisper, then just hung there, slowly twisting 'round and 'round, thinking about how this must be the most awful predicament a fellow could get himself into.

Just then, things got worse. A bee appeared and took a great interest in my nose. Since I couldn't move my arms, all I could do was wrinkle up my nose and blow at him whenever he got near. Finally, I decided to put forth every ounce of effort I had in one last horrendous scream, but only a tiny little croak came out, and suddenly I was eyeball-to-eyeball with an enormous bee.

The most terrifying part of my dilemma was that I didn't know how to tell the difference between a carpenter bee and a bumblebee. I knew a bumblebee stung and a carpenter bee did not, but which was this?

As I hung there totally helpless, staring that bee in the eye, he advanced a quarter of an inch up my nose and appeared to get his stinger in position. I squenched my eyes tightly, steeling myself for that painful jab, but it never came. Eventually I opened my eyes slightly and watched as he probed my skin with his tongue or whatever a bee carries up front. Then I had visions of him boring a hole in my head like I'd seen carpenter bees do in the eaves of the house, and that created even greater fear within me.

In that desperate moment, I once again discovered how prayer seems to be an ever-present need for people. I wondered if the Lord would be receptive to my pleas, coming as they were so close on the heels of the previous day's peril, or if He'd have anybody on duty at that hour of the afternoon, but I sent my petitions heavenward anyway, and miracle of miracles, about that time I heard a car rattling down the road in the distance.

I figured the driver could see me if he just glanced to the right when he passed our house, and that's what I prayed for. In a few minutes, the car slowed down and turned into our front yard, then came chugging around the corner into the back yard. I couldn't immediately see who was driving because I was facing the opposite direction and had very little control over which way I turned. After the car stopped, I heard the slam of the door and footsteps coming my way. Finally I caught a glimpse of a figure out of the corner of my eye. Lo and behold, there stood Uncle Will, grinning like a Cheshire cat.

"So your Daddy's found a way to keep ya outa mischief, has he, young fella?" he said with real mirth in his voice. I told him Daddy didn't have anything to do with it, but he just laughed. The more I said, the more he was tickled. Finally, he lifted me up to take the strain off the rope, unfastened the loop, and set me on the ground.

"Where's your Daddy, boy?" he asked. I told him he was over in the back field plowing and that I was looking after the house and tending to all of the chores. "It appears you're one of the things that needs tendin', if ya ask me," he chuckled. Then he stated his business.

"I've just rented a crop from Ben Nixon, and he's got

27

a great big strawberry patch. I need somebody to pick the berries that's low to the ground. I come over to ask your Daddy if he'd let ya help me with the harvest." I told him that Mama was sick and that I doubted that Daddy would let me go, since I was the only help he had, but he replied, "Well, let's go see what he says."

We walked to where Daddy was plowing, and Uncle Will told him how desperate he was to get those strawberries out, because they'd only last a couple of weeks and he had a ready market for them. He said he could get fifteen cents a pint for them and that he'd pay me a nickel a pint for picking them, which was an unheard-of amount of money. I guess Daddy recalled what fine care I was taking of him, because he decided that maybe, just maybe, he could get along without me, and I headed off with Uncle Will to make my first fortune.

The next morning Uncle Will got me up at day-break, just like at home, and told me that strawberries were best when picked while the dew was still on them. After a quick breakfast I hurried out to the fields and went to work picking the most luscious-looking strawberries I'd ever seen. Uncle Will gave me fifty or more wooden, slatted pint baskets and announced that for each one I filled, I'd get a whole nickel.

Visions of great wealth danced in my head, and I clearly remember picking twenty pints on the first day alone. The next morning Uncle Will loaded them in the Model A and headed for Bowdon while I continued to pick more. I'd earned a whole dollar the first day, though I wouldn't get paid 'til I finished the job, and I was determined to do better the second time around.

And I did! That day I picked twenty-four pints, worth another $1.20. Even if a grown man could get a job—which wasn't easy in those days—he couldn't earn that kind of money. I was literally delirious with joy.

That evening, however, Mother Nature put a crimp in my plans by sending a deluge that lasted most of the night.

The next morning when I went outside, the fields were standing full of water. "Ya won't be able to pick strawberries at least 'til noon," Uncle Will said after surveying the situation, "but come on over to the barn. I've got some chores we can do while the fields are drying."

I didn't really want to help him with the chores. I wanted to get back in the field, where in only two days' time I'd already earned $2.20. A fella like me who was independently wealthy shouldn't have to go out to the barn and do chores, though. Just let me back in that gold mine of a strawberry patch.

A few minutes later I learned that the chore he needed help with was castrating pigs. He had a 450-pound sow that was nursing eight six-week-old babies, and it was time to castrate the five males. My job was to hold them while he did the surgery. The pigs had worked the hog lot into a veritable sea of mud, leaving only one small dry corner up near the barn. Uncle Will led the way to that dry spot, bent down on one knee, and said, "Catch one of them little boars and bring him to me."

That is much easier said than done. For one thing, most sows get rather upset when you do harm to their pigs, and a mad sow can be dangerous. For another thing, I didn't understand why Uncle Will wanted to do the work inside the hog lot. It made more sense to me to move to the other side of the fence, away from the sow. If I were going to have to hold that little pig while it squealed and cried, I didn't want to have to worry about its mama taking out the seat of my britches.

I knew better than to question an adult, though, so I got half a dozen ears of corn, waded across the knee-deep muck, and laid them in the feed trough to distract the sow. The pigs stuck close to her as she moved over to eat, but the first chance I got I grabbed one of them, checked to make sure it was a boy, and trudged over to the dry ground where Uncle Will was waiting. While I held the pig's head between my knees and exposed his rear end, Uncle Will made a quick slash on one side with his knife, popped the testicle out, scraped the cord, and whacked it off. The pig was apparently so shocked he couldn't squeal immediately, but by the time Uncle Will did the second side, he let out a terrible shriek.

I turned to see how the old sow was taking it, but she only raised her head up a moment, decided it was nothing serious, and went back to eating. Uncle Will stuffed a little paste made of turpentine and lard into the slits he'd made, then turned the little pig loose to return to its mother.

It'd all gone more smoothly than I expected, but we still had four pigs to go, so I waded back through the mire and grabbed another one. The old sow was only half finished eating her corn, and when her baby started squealing, she again didn't pay much attention. With things proceeding as well as they were, I began to have visions of finishing the task quickly and lying around the rest of the morning until it was time to pick strawberries again. So convinced, I went after number three.

The old sow was just finishing the last ear of corn as I latched on to the third victim, but she made no move to stop me. However, when Uncle Will made his first cut on this one, it let out an ear-splitting cry, and I looked back at the old sow just in time to see her headed at us like a bull charging a red flag. "Look out!" I yelled to Uncle Will. In a flash he laid two hands on top of the fence and bolted over it, with me right behind.

The sow nuzzled her baby, snorted angrily at us, then nuzzled her baby some more. A few minutes later when she'd calmed down a bit, Uncle Will said, "Boy, we've gotta finish what we started with that pig, 'cause if we don't get antiseptic on him, he'll die."

"How 'bout you gettin' over in there, grabbin' him real quick and handin' him over the fence to me?" I said. "Then I'll hold him 'til you can get back out and finish operatin'."

He scowled. "Boy, there ain't no use in both of us gettin' mud all over us. Now, climb back in there—and be sure ya get the right one."

"That old sow ain't gonna give me time to look her pig over and make sure I get the right one," I replied. "Let me run to the house for a bucket of slop to feed her, and while she's eating I'll jump in there and pick him out." He nodded his assent, and I ran to get the feed.

While I was gone, Uncle Will pulled a cotton basket out of the corner of the barn and set it outside the fence where we were going to do our work. I coaxed the old sow over to the trough and set her to eating, then

31

quickly inspected the pigs to be sure I got the right one and raced over to Uncle Will with it. He stopped me as I started to climb out of the pen, however. "Get the other two, too," he said. "I'll put 'em here in the basket and we can finish the job outside the fence," which is exactly what I thought he should have done to begin with, though I'd never have had the nerve to tell him so.

By the time we completed our task, there were still a couple of hours until I could return to the fields, but instead of spending them in rest and relaxation, I found myself doing several other unseemly chores for my uncle.

Finally around noon, after reminding me to wash my hands so I wouldn't mess up those beautiful strawberries, Uncle Will sent me back out on my quest for financial independence. I worked until dark that day and picked sixteen pints. That made a grand total of sixty pints, meaning I was now due the unbelievable sum of three dollars! I was feeling as rich as Rockefeller.

From the looks of things, I thought I'd be able to finish up the next day. That way I could collect all my money and head home to help Daddy with the cooking and washing sooner than expected. When I reached the house, Uncle Will was thinking the same thing. "Try your best to finish by dinner tomorrow," he said. "It'll be Friday, and I need to take 'em into town and sell 'em durin' the afternoon 'cause they won't keep too well over the weekend. As soon as I get my money, I'll pay ya."

The next morning I got out bright and early and started picking strawberries as fast as I could. I must have set some sort of world record, too, because before midday I'd picked twenty more pints, bringing my wages to exactly four dollars. Uncle Will came out to the field, put the baskets in his Model A, and said, "Go in and let Beth feed ya and wash your clothes. As soon as I get back from Bowdon, I'll carry ya home."

In the back of my mind I vaguely remembered stories about Uncle Will not paying his debts, and I didn't want to be left holding the bag, not after all the plans I'd made for spending my hard-earned cash. I thought maybe if I went with him, I'd have a better chance of getting paid before something else happened to the money, so I said, "Let me go to Bowdon with ya."

He had a ready answer for that, though. "You're too filthy," he said. "Why, I wouldn't even take ya back to your Daddy lookin' like that. You go take a bath, and Beth will wash up your clothes for ya. You can sit in your underwear while she does."

"I ain't got no underwear," I replied.

"Well, ya can wrap up in a sheet while she washes your clothes and hangs 'em outside on the line. That way they'll be dry by the time I get back, and I can pay ya and get ya on home before dark."

There wasn't much I could do 'cept follow his instructions, and besides, he was right about how I looked. I was muddy from head to toe. In fact, I hadn't had a bath since the night I'd come home with him. So, hc took the strawberries and headed for Bowdon, and I went into the house to bathe and let Aunt Beth wash my clothes. She tossed out a pair of Uncle Will's old overalls that were ten times too big for me, "This will hide your nakedness while your clothes dry. Now, get ya a wash pan and clean yourself up."

I did as I was told, then tied on Uncle Will's overalls as best I could to "hide my nakedness," as Aunt Beth put it, and went outside to play the rest of the afternoon.

When the sun got well over into the sky and Uncle Will still hadn't returned, I began to feel some uneasy stirrings inside. I went into the house and asked Aunt Beth what she supposed had happened to him. "Lord, child, you know as much as I do," she said. "There ain't no tellin what he's gotten himself into." That answer, as you might imagine, wasn't a whole lot of comfort.

About a half hour before sundown, Uncle Will finally came chugging up in the Model A, and I ran excitedly out to greet him. "Get in," he said sort of short and snappy. I slid into the front seat of the car, and he slapped two coins in my palm. "That's all I got left," he said.

"Uncle Will, you owe me four dollars," I replied. "This is only seventy-five cents."

"Let me tell ya what happened, boy. I got down to Bowdon, sold those strawberries, and put your money right here," he said, pointing to the small opening on his overalls. "No sooner did I walk outa the store, though, than ol' man Nixon came by. 'Will,' he says, 'since I own the land you're workin', ya owe me half the money ya got for them strawberries.' Well, boy, I hadn't figured on that. I didn't think the owner of the farm had any right to garden produce, but there he was, and I had the money, and I had to pay him half of everything ya picked. So what I gave ya is all I've got left."

"But you owe me four dollars," I argued, "and even if we only got half, that's more'n seventy-five cents."

"Boy, I'm gonna give you a lesson about me," he responded. "I got paid a total of twelve dollars for all of them strawberries, and I had to give ol' man Nixon six. He came and took the bread right outa me and Beth's mouth, and boy, when he did that I wanted a drink of liquor so bad I'd have walked a rotten log through hell to get it. So, I went down to the bootlegger and bought a gallon of liquor, which cost $5.25, and that's the reason I ain't got but seventy-five cents left. The next time I see ya I'll give ya the other dollar and a quarter, but I ain't got it today."

When he finished talking, I wanted to cry, but I didn't figure that would do any good. Besides, seventy-five cents was more cash money than I'd ever had in my life, and I'd earned it with my own two hands.

A few minutes later Uncle Will deposited me at the front door, then tore off up the road because he knew Daddy wouldn't like him hauling me around when he was drunk. I ran into the house and showed Daddy the money I'd earned. He looked at it and said, "That's good, son."

I told him how I'd actually earned four dollars and how I only wound up with seventy-five cents. Daddy just smiled knowingly and said, "Will is one of those folks that likes to bore with a big auger. But things never seem to turn out the way he plans, so what you're sayin' don't surprise me none. Beth did feed ya good, though, didn't she?"

"Yes sir," I replied.

"Well, she's a fine cook." That was all he said.

Blowin' Stumps
and Stealin' Turnips

On the farm, there's little time to celebrate success or mourn failure because the wolf of hunger demands we prepare for next season. Thus, the disappointment of my first business venture with Uncle Will passed quickly as spring turned to summer and summer to fall.

Fall was always one of my favorite times of year. After the infinitely long, hot Georgia summers, the cool days and chilly nights were a welcome and refreshing change. One thing I particularly enjoyed, when I could talk Mama and Daddy into letting me, was going squirrel hunting with Uncle Will.

Every now and then he would stop by with his old double-barrel shotgun, say a few words to Daddy, then holler out, "C'mon, boy, let's go shoot us some supper." As soon as I could finish up what I was doing, off we'd head to stalk the gray squirrel. Years later after serving fourteen months in Korea where people with rifles were hunting *me*, I lost my taste for the sport, but as a child I thoroughly enjoyed the thrill of the hunt.

The woods still frightened me at times, especially during the late afternoon when shadows began to fall. Occasionally as we made our way through the trees and undergrowth, Uncle Will would suddenly stop and whisper, "Shhhh!" sending a shiver down my spine for fear we'd come upon a lion or tiger or other man-eating beast. Fortunately, we never did.

I was also overwhelmed by the sheer size of the forest. It seemed so deep and never-ending that I seldom entered it without fearing I'd lose my way and never come out again. Today those same forests seem small, and I realize how age and maturity change our perception of things.

At any rate, on one of our expeditions in late October of that year, we ran onto a little patch of turnip greens in the middle of the forest. The plants were up already, but the leaves were only about as big as a mouse's ear. Uncle Will mumbled something about it being a "wild" patch of greens, but it was obvious from the way the ground had been plowed that someone had sown the plants, and I suspect that Uncle Will knew who that someone was. However, he apparently made a mental note about the location of the clearing, because three or four weeks later we came upon the same field. This time the turnip greens were ready to harvest. In fact, you could see where some of them had already been cut, but there were still plenty of turnips as big as oranges.

Uncle Will turned right and left as if surveying the land, but probably just checking to see if anyone was around, then said, "Boy, we ain't shot nothin' all day, so we may as well get a mess of greens to take home. Grab ya up an arm full of those turnips, and be quick at it."

About the time I'd picked all the turnips I could hold, I turned to where Uncle Will was standing and

37

saw something that nearly made my knees buckle. There, not three feet behind him, was a huge fellow with a shotgun resting on his shoulder. Uncle Will saw me literally freeze in my tracks as I stared at the man behind him, but just as he started to turn around, the man said in a deep, booming voice, "Howdy, Will!" I swear Uncle Will jumped three feet straight up in the air before finally coming to earth and stuttering, "Uh, how-, howdy, Jess."

I stayed where I was, shakin' and almost unable to breathe as I waited to see what would happen, but when the other man made no move to threaten or challenge Uncle Will, I finally started easing my way to where they stood.

Uncle Will smoked Prince Albert tobacco in the can and rolled his own cigarets. After the initial shock of having this mountain of a man get the drop on him, he leaned his gun up against a tree, pulled out a cigaret leaf as nonchalantly as possible, and tapped some tobacco from the can onto the leaf. His hands were trembling so bad, however, that he tore the leaf in two and scattered all the tobacco on the ground.

"A little bit nervous today, ain't ya, Will?" the man asked with a slight chuckle, as if he was enjoying making Uncle Will sweat. "How 'bout a tailor-made?" Uncle Will took the cigaret the man offered, but by now he was shaking so hard he couldn't light it. That scared me, because I'd never seen anyone get the best of Uncle Will. The stranger finally took the cigaret out of Uncle Will's fingers, lit it, and handed it back to him. They stood there without talking for what seemed an eternity before the man named Jess said, "Well, I hope ya enjoy your mess of turnip greens, Will. Be sure and tell Beth I said howdy." Then he turned and meandered across the field with his shotgun over his shoulder.

As soon as he disappeared from sight, Uncle Will snapped, "Let's go, boy," and we made a beeline out of there. Uncle Will didn't utter a word the whole way until we reached the spot where I always peel off for home, then he said, "There'll be no talk of this, understand?"

"Yes, sir," I replied solemnly, still shaken by the experience.

That was nothing compared to the escapade Uncle Will involved me in the next spring, however. He came over and asked Daddy if I could come help him on his farm for a few days. After some serious negotiation, the details of which I was not made privy to, Daddy finally agreed that I could go spend the week and help Uncle Will do whatever he needed.

In the fall of the previous year, Uncle Will had traded with Eli Wilson to sharecrop for the years 1938 and '39. As was the custom in those days, you traded in the fall of the year for next spring and summer's crop. As soon as you gathered the crop from the farm where you were living, you moved on to your new farm if you'd made a deal with someone else.

Uncle Will rarely stayed more than one year on any farm. Something always happened to sour the deal, it seemed. Either the landlord didn't like Uncle Will, or Uncle Will didn't like the landlord. Whatever the cause, it resulted in Uncle Will and Aunt Beth sharecropping on a new spread nearly every year.

During this particular year, Indian Creek formed the back property line of Uncle Will's farm. Cole Palmer, a fellow he thoroughly detested, rented the farm just across the creek. In fact, the center of the creek was the boundary separating the two spreads. Both farms had one hundred acres and both farms were essentially square, which meant they had about a 2200-foot common boundary at the center of Indian Creek. For the most part, the creek ran relatively straight east and west. However, near the middle of that long property line the creek formed a loop which, if viewed from the air, would resemble a huge teardrop with the drop lying on Uncle Will's place. Since the center of the creek was the property line, this little meander effectively subtracted a fine piece of bottom land from Uncle Will's farm and added it to that of the man he despised, Cole Palmer.

Uncle Will was not about to let nature have the last say-so on this situation, though. Instead, he decided to take the loop out of the creek, and make it flow straight again, thus returning the choice bottom land to his own property. Of course, he didn't tell Daddy, Eli Wilson, or anyone else about his plans. I didn't even know what he was doing until after the fact.

When we got to his farm that day, Uncle Will showed me exactly what he wanted me to do. He'd bought or in some way acquired a ton of dynamite. My job was to set out the explosives in a straight line from one side of the beginning of the teardrop to the other, a span of about 500 feet. To do so, I took an iron bar about an inch and a half in diameter and hammered it three or four feet into the soft ground, then pulled it out and dropped a half-pound stick of dynamite down into the hole I'd made. Uncle Will wanted a hole placed every twelve inches, and he cut me a branch of that length to help me measure the work properly.

Meanwhile, Uncle Will walked ahead and, where trees fell along the line he wanted the new creek bed to run, he circled the tree with explosives like I was doing behind him.

By the end of the day, I'd placed one string of dynamite across that 500-foot stretch of land, just like Uncle Will had ordered.

However, the bed of the creek was probably twenty feet wide, and Uncle Will never did anything halfway, so the following morning he set me to placing two more rows of dynamite sticks parallel to the first, one on each side about ten feet away. Between the three rows, he apparently figured, they would blast a twenty-foot-wide swath. The two additional rows took nearly a full day to finish, and we headed home for supper knowing that tomorrow was going to be quite a day.

The next morning after all the chores were done, we went back to work on the creek, and by noon we had everything but the detonation charge set. The way Uncle Will explained it, all he had to do was add a fuse and cap to one stick of dynamite. Then when that stick exploded, it would ignite the stick next to it, and so on down the line.

Before lighting the fuse, however, we planted a row of dynamite across both ends and the middle, just for good measure. After checking our handiwork a final time, he put a cap on one stick of the explosive and cut a piece of fuse about five feet long. The printing on the fuse said, "Burning time: one foot per minute," and I found myself praying that would give us plenty of time to get clear of the spot, based on what Uncle Will had said was going to happen. When we were sure everything was ready, he took a kitchen match out of his pocket and held it to the fuse's end. In a split second it started spewing like a Fourth of July sparkler.

"We best get to high ground!" Uncle Will said, and took off in a trot up a nearby hill with me right behind him. About 300 yards above the creek, we sat down under the shade of a big oak tree and looked back in the direction of the dynamite. Five minutes can be an awful long time when you're waiting for a spectacle like he described to happen. After two or three minutes, Uncle Will broke the silence with a wry word of warning. "Boy, you ain't never heard nothin' like what you're fixin' to hear," he promised. "But I'll tell you somethin' else. That explosion ain't gonna be nothin' compared to the one you're gonna hear when Cole Palmer finds out I transferred seven acres of his bottom land over to me. There's gonna be hell to pay when he gets wind of that."

About that time, the most deafening explosion I've ever heard in my life began and continued for an eternity. It seemed to go on and on, like thunder rolling across the sky from horizon to horizon. A great black cloud of dirt filled the air, and trees that were eighty feet tall spun around overhead like toy tops. So massive was the destruction that I felt sure I was getting a first-hand preview of Armageddon.

Despite the terrible din, however, thirty minutes after the explosion, we were pulling the alder bushes out of that bottom land and getting it ready to work. Meanwhile, people began to arrive from surrounding areas to investigate Uncle Will's big blast. One neighbor came right out and asked, "What'd ya do that for, Will?" Uncle Will flashed him a sly little grin, the way he did when he knew something nobody else knew, and replied, "I'm just tryin' to drain this swamp so I can make use of the land, that's all." It was obvious to me, and I was just a kid, that Uncle Will had changed the property line, but apparently the man didn't notice. If he did, he didn't say anything about it.

Throughout the afternoon a steady stream of visitors dropped by to see what all the ruckus was about. After what Uncle Will had said about the explosion we were going to hear when Mr. Cole discovered his scheme, I was in a state of nervous agitation all afternoon, but none of the people who came to visit seemed to realize exactly what we'd done.

When we returned to Uncle Will's house about sundown, however, a long black car was parked out front. Inside it sat two men in dark suits who looked to be all business. As Uncle Will and I approached the vehicle, he chuckled smugly, "Well, the word is out." Then he turned to me and said, "Boy, you go feed the mule while I see what these fellas want," adding with a smile and a big wink, "as if I don't know."

An hour later when I finished taking care of the mule and doing the other chores, Uncle Will was still sitting out in the car talking with the two strangers, so

I went on into the house. Inside, Aunt Beth was nervous as a cat. She kept pacing back and forth and peeping out the window regularly to see what was happening.

After a while I went on home, not knowing how the issue was settled. Later I learned that my silver-tongued Uncle had somehow convinced the authorities that he'd actually done Cole Palmer a favor by draining the fertile bottom land and putting it to good use. When I told Daddy what Uncle Will had done, he just shook his head from side to side and muttered, "Someday Will's gonna get his come-uppance, and there won't be a soul around to help him when he does. No, sir, not a soul."

Holy Rollin'

As long as I knew Uncle Will, he always had a healthy respect for the Almighty and a healthy disrespect for organized religion. Aunt Beth once told me that Uncle Will attended church regularly with her when they were courting, but that something happened through the years—she didn't know what—to turn him against the hard-nosed, hell-fire-and-brimstone religion practiced in those parts. He still accompanied her to church now and then, but I think it was just to see if anything had changed since the last time he darkened the doors.

One incident in particular stands out in my mind. I'd gone to stay a few days with Aunt Beth and Uncle Will to help with one of Uncle Will's "projects." It'd been a wet and stormy week, but on Thursday the weather let up a bit, prompting Aunt Beth to insist that we all go down to the church that evening for revival services. I knew I didn't have a choice, but I expected Uncle Will to put up a fuss and refuse. To my surprise, however, he agreed to go along after only a mild protest.

The tiny sanctuary was packed with people when we arrived, and they'd opened all the doors and the windows to let what breeze there was blow through. We sang a few hymns to start things off, then the preacher stepped to the podium. He was a traveling evangelist from somewhere in Alabama, and his solid white suit and thick, snowy-white hair certainly fit the part. A kerosene lamp had been placed on a shelf behind the pulpit when it began to turn dark, and it cast a spooky glow.

The old preacher, with his white suit and mane, cut quite a figure as he marched back and forth across the pulpit in that flickering lamplight.

As he launched into his sermon, the wind gradually began to rise outside, causing the lamp to flutter even more and give him an almost ghostly appearance. On and on he went for nearly an hour, growing louder and stronger in his pronouncements about the great day of judgment, when everyone would be held accountable for their deeds. On and on the wind blew outside, growing fierce and angry until it seemed the little church building would surely be blown away.

About the time the man of God was telling how the Almighty would call down a curse on the head of the assembled unrepentant sinners, a gust of wind whipped through the room and snuffed out the lamp. For a split second there was total darkness, then a huge bolt of lightning lit up the sky like high noon, followed by a clap of thunder that sounded like a hundred cannons exploding at once. Almost instantaneously, a staccato roll of hailstones began pounding on the tin roof above, causing everyone to shift nervously in their seats.

Despite the unsettling racket, the preacher didn't miss a beat. In fact, he began shouting even louder, pacing back and forth across the pulpit like a man possessed, praising this wonderful demonstration of the Almighty's great power. Meanwhile, the lightning flashed again and again, illuminating the graveyard outside and causing the white marble tombstones to look like saints marching to judgment. It was an awe-inspiring, fearful sight for sure.

Sensing what was transpiring in the crowd, the preacher began calling our attention to the terrifying wrath of the Lord. After another clap of thunder echoed a loud "amen," he called all the sinners who hadn't been saved to come forward to receive the Holy Ghost. In a twinkling the whole congregation, even those who'd been members for years, raced down to the altar. People were confessing things they hadn't even done, and those who'd already been saved were begging to reenlist. Aunt Beth was there, and so was I.

After thirty minutes of intense prayer and hosannah-shouting recommitment, the storm began to subside, and the preacher announced that everybody who'd come forward would be baptized Sunday afternoon in the old wash-hole at Indian Creek. He also pointed out to the mob standing there that the ones who'd been saved at his last tent revival meeting might as well show up for a second dunking, because they wouldn't have come forward if they hadn't done something wrong.

I missed the baptizing, and I don't guess I ever officially became a member of the church, but for one brief moment I had sure become a believer.

As we turned to make our way back to our seats, I was shocked to see Uncle Will still sitting there like Ole Ebo hisself with his arms crossed near the back of the church, right where he'd been when the storm began. Of all the people at services that night, he was the only one who hadn't responded to the altar call. I was scared for him at the time, afraid he'd become so hardened that God's own storming couldn't soften his heart. But even then, I suspicioned he had great courage.

In another incident the following summer, two men and women drove up one Friday in an old Model A convertible to ask Daddy if they could hold religious services in the little grove of oak trees just above our house. The fellow who did all the talking explained that he was a traveling evangelist and that the other three played guitar and banjo for the hymn singing. Now Mama, Daddy, and most of my kin were all Primitive, Hard-Shell Baptists who allowed no musical instruments in the church, and to their way of thinking, people who used instruments were "Holy Rollers." Still, Daddy was the kind of man who felt that everyone was entitled to worship as they saw fit, and he gave them permission to use the grove. He did, however, ask the preacher why he'd picked our particular community to grace with his services. The preacher answered that because it looked like a prosperous area, he thought it'd be a good place to raise money for poor foreign missions, as well as for his own ministry.

"You're welcome to use the oak grove, Preacher," Daddy said, "but I can tell ya right now that ya ain't gonna raise any money around here. It's been an awful year for crops, and if ya robbed everybody within ten miles, ya wouldn't get ten dollars, much less any contributions for 'foreign missions.'"

"You're wrong, my friend," the preacher replied. "When these people hear the word of God, they'll open their hearts and pocketbooks. But even if we don't raise any money, maybe we can save some souls."

The man and his partners apparently spent the rest of the day going from door to door in the community, telling everybody they'd be holding services and playing music near our place, because by the next morning quite a crowd had gathered. In those days nobody had a radio, and any sort of musical entertainment would draw a crowd, even if it meant having to listen to preaching. Mama and Daddy didn't go, but they didn't object when Uncle Will stopped by and asked if I wanted to tag along with him. I was surprised that he'd show his face at a camp meeting like this, but as I say, music was a powerful drawing card.

At about ten o'clock, the musicians started playing, and they kept on almost nonstop for an hour. The sound of the guitars and banjo carried well in the shimmering heat of the August morning, and the crowd continued to grow because of it.

Finally around eleven o'clock the preacher, dressed in a brilliant white suit and panama hat, called the meeting to order. He opened with prayer, then led the congregation in a couple of hymns. A great spiritual alertness seemed to be present as the service began. People clapped their hands and swayed from side to side in time with the music. It was interesting to see our neighbors acting so relaxed and carefree, and I think Uncle Will was getting a kick out of it, too, as we sat at the edge of the crowd.

Most folks brought their own chairs, which they lined up several rows deep in a circle around a clearing in the oak grove, giving the preacher a true theatre in the round. After another prayer asking God to loosen his tongue and let him speak, he jumped out into the center of the clearing and started preaching. He talked so fast and yelled so loud that it took me a while to figure out what he was saying, but as I sat and listened, it soon became obvious that he had three main things on his mind—not necessarily in this order.

First, he was deeply worried that people who lived in distant lands might never hear about Jesus Christ. Second, he was afraid that some people who were present at the meeting didn't know Jesus Christ. And third, he seemed greatly concerned that he and his little evangelical band might not have enough money for gasoline to get them to the next town. He spent a major portion of his time trying to make sure that when he got ready to leave, he could buy enough gas to move on and save more souls.

Nevertheless, he was a powerful preacher, and pretty soon he'd worked the crowd into a frenzy. Every time he'd finish a sentence, the whole congregation would yell, "Amen! Tell it like it is, preacher, tell it like it is!" Suddenly, while the service was at a fever pitch, he turned to one of his associates and shouted, "Sister Grace, pass the collection plate!" Sister Grace grabbed up a three-gallon foot-tub and started into the crowd. From time to time you could hear a clink as somebody dropped a coin in the old tub, but it certainly didn't sound like money was flowing as freely as the Spirit.

When she finished working the crowd, Sister Grace brought the tub to the preacher. He stopped preaching just long enough to count the contents, then screeched, "Brothers and sisters, this great crowd has only contributed thirty-eight cents to our cause! You can do better than that, brothers and sisters. Now, I'm gonna ask Sister Grace to pass back through the crowd. As she does, I want you to remember all of those lost souls here and across the sea. Folks, help us to save those souls!"

Sister Grace went back through the congregation again, and occasionally I'd hear a coin land in the bottom of that big metal tub. Meanwhile, the preacher continued to work the crowd into a white-hot glow of religious fervor. When Sister Grace returned from her second round of collecting, however, she only had $1.08. The preacher gently scolded the congregation for their lack of commitment to the Lord's cause, then brought his sermon to a close. Before dismissing us, though, he announced that he and his crew would be back on Sunday. There'd be music from nine to eleven, he said, followed by another message from the Lord.

After everyone had left, Daddy walked up and asked the preacher how the service had gone. He replied that he thought a lot of people had received divine inspiration that morning, and said he expected a much bigger crowd the next day.

"How about the contributions?" Daddy asked.

"We got $1.08," answered the preacher, trying not to sound disappointed.

"I told ya if ya robbed everybody in the area, ya wouldn't get ten dollars."

The preacher's face clouded up a bit. "Well, maybe

you're right, Brother Miles," he said, "but we're gonna give it one more shot tomorrow."

In the Primitive Baptist Church, services are held only once a month, but they last through both Saturday and Sunday. Most churches describe their meeting time as the third Sunday and the Saturday before. Since it wasn't our weekend to meet, I got all my chores done Sunday morning and went with Uncle Will to the camp meeting again. "I wonder what they got up their sleeve this time to get that tub filled?" he said as we walked to the grove.

"Are you gonna put something in?" I responded.

"Hell, no, I ain't gonna put nothin' in," he snapped. "I got a lot better things to do with my money than support some travelin' circus." I'd never heard religious services called a "circus" before, but in looking back, it wasn't far from the truth.

As promised, the music started at nine, and by ten o'clock quite a crowd had gathered. The musicians asked everyone to join in singing songs, and the preacher said a few words to get them all pepped up. He also had everyone move their chairs back a little from where they were the day before in order to give him more room. "I need plenty of space when the Lord gets me going," he said with a wink.

At the appointed hour for the sermon to begin, the musicians stopped, moved out of the circle, and set a small sturdy wooden table there about three feet square. On top of the table, they placed the old foot-tub used to collect money the previous day. Then the preacher walked around that circle looking everybody dead in the eye. He introduced himself again for those who were new and explained that he had a mission to save lost souls for Jesus Christ. "All children who are twelve years old and older, raise your hand," he yelled across the group. Many hands in the crowd shot up. "How many of ya have been saved and joined the church?" he continued. Only one or two hands stayed up in response to that question.

"Does anybody know what it means to be twelve years old?" Apparently no one did, for he got no response. "Twelve years old is the age of accountability. If any of these children died tonight," he said, now speaking more to the adults than to the kids, "they'd go straight to hell and burn forever."

A murmur rippled through the crowd when he said that. I still didn't understand what the age of accountability was—I'd never even heard the phrase— but I was only nine, so I appeared to be safe from whatever the man was talking about.

"It grieves my soul," the preacher went on, "to think about these little children suddenly dyin' and goin' to hell because they haven't been baptized in the name of our Saviour, but that's the way it is. God makes the rules, not me. All I do is tell ya about 'em."

The preacher then walked around the circle several times, looking straight at people and asking if they'd been saved. Some said yes, some no. When an old person would admit they hadn't been saved, he'd get a grave look on his face. "Brother, you're flirtin' with the Devil!" he'd say harshly. Each time he traveled around that little circle, the speed and volume of his speech would increase a bit, like an automobile shifting gears. Eventually he became almost unintelligible, though I caught enough of his meaning to know that he was describing, in living color, that eternal lake of fire where all the condemned were going to spend eternity. He made it sound mighty uncomfortable, too.

Like the day before, people slowly began to get worked up. The longer and faster the preacher talked and the more he sweated, the more Amens he got. Just as he had the crowd going full tilt, however, he suddenly dropped to the ground like he'd been shot. He lay still for a full five seconds as everyone groaned in fear. I didn't know what was going on, and I don't think many of them did, either. Then his foot twitched a little. "He's gettin' the Spirit!" a woman on the front row shouted excitedly. His other foot twitched, and somebody else yelled,

"He's gettin' the Spirit!" Then his head jerked, and he rose as if levitated and started running around in circles like a man possessed. "I've got the Spirit, the Holy Ghost!" he shouted over and over.

Finally, he slapped the foot-tub off the table and did a couple of cartwheels across it. I'd never seen such goings-on. We didn't even do things like that on the playground at school. There was a woman feeding a baby with a bottle on the front row of the circle, and as the preacher passed by her in his mad frenzy, he snatched the bottle out of the baby's mouth and stuck it in his own. For three trips around the circle, he sucked on that bottle, then on the fourth time around he popped the nipple back in the baby's mouth, turned two more cartwheels across the table, and screamed, "The Living God lives!"

With the crowd nearly delirious now, the preacher leaped up on the table and ordered Sister Grace to come forth and pass "the offerin' plate"— i.e., the foot-tub— around. As she did so, he slowed his rhetoric to a normal speed and begged the audience to contribute so he and his little band of Christians could spread the word of the Lord.

From the sound of things, the people were more cooperative that morning than the previous day. One old man even took a crumpled dollar bill out of his overalls and dropped it in the tub, causing the preacher to break forth into a loud, "Praise the Lord!"

When Sister Grace finished working the crowd, she brought the money back and set it on the little table at his feet. It totaled $4.28, four times as much as the day before but still not enough to satisfy the preacher. "Brothers and sisters, at the beginnin' of this service I asked how many children had reached the age of accountability, and there was twenty-five or thirty hands held up," he said gravely. "The Lord might call any one of those children home tonight, and I feel I'd be remiss in my obligations to Him if I didn't make a further plea.

"I'm gonna have Sister Grace pass back through the congregation one more time, and for every quarter —just one-fourth of one dollar—that's placed in the offerin' plate, I'm gonna take one of these lost children down to Indian Creek and baptize 'em. I'm gonna take time out from my busy schedule to do that because I don't want to bear on my soul the damnation of any child that stands before me today, and I don't want you to, either. Just twenty-five cents could save a child from hell."

He handed the bucket to Sister Grace, who started back through the crowd as he began preaching again at a breakneck pace, telling us about all the terrible things that would happen if we spent eternity in that lake of fire where there was weeping and wailing and gnashing of teeth. When Sister Grace returned, however, she had only two quarters in the bucket. Upon seeing the results of his efforts, the preacher quickly lost the Spirit and drew the meeting to a close. "Only two people were concerned about the souls of their children," he proclaimed. "Those two, plus anyone who wishes to watch, should meet me down on the banks of Indian Creek in thirty minutes for the baptizin'. That'll give me and my associates time to tie up some loose ends."

The people dispersed quickly, with a few heading for the creek and the others going on home. After they were gone, Daddy came walking up through the little hardwood grove and asked the preacher how his collections had gone this time. The preacher told him he got nearly five dollars in the two days.

"I guess ya believe me now," Daddy said.

"Poor folks need the Lord just as much as anybody else," snapped the preacher. "We've got to go down to Indian Creek and baptize two lost souls."

As we stood there watching, he and his helpers gathered up their belongings, piled into the touring car, and drove away. However, they turned towards

Jonesville, away from Indian Creek. Daddy yelled and tried to tell them they were going in the wrong direction, but before we knew it they were long gone.

"Must not have heard me," Daddy said.

"Could be they didn't wanna hear," Uncle Will replied dryly.

Uncle Will and I decided we ought to walk the quarter mile to the creek and tell the folks waiting there that the preacher didn't head that way. When we arrived, about twenty people, including the two kids who were supposed to be baptized, were standing on the creek bank waiting for their sacrament. Uncle Will told one of the kids' fathers that the preacher had gone toward Jonesville and didn't appear to be coming back. The father in turn climbed up on a stump and made the announcement to the rest of the group. After milling around a few more minutes, we all headed home.

"Whatta ya think happened to the preacher?" I asked Uncle Will as we walked along.

"I guess five dollars didn't buy enough of his time to baptize two sinner babies," he replied. "Most of these preachers are just in business—got no more religion than any damn fool. And I gar'ntee you, nephew, most of 'em will have front seats in hell."

Pimento Plantin'
and Pickin'

In the spring of 1941, a fellow from the Hill Brothers Cannery came to West Georgia trying to sell farmers on the idea of growing pimentos rather than cotton. He talked glowingly about how much less labor and how much more money we could expect with pimentos compared to cotton. If anybody was ever on the lookout for an easier, faster way to make a living, it was Uncle Will, and he decided right away to become a pimento magnate. Daddy wasn't completely sold on the idea, though, and he stayed with cotton.

There was only one stipulation in the contract Uncle Will had to sign with Hill Brothers that he didn't like. The contract guaranteed forty dollars a ton for all pimentos accepted by the company, but the wording implied that Hill Brothers had the right to reject any or all of the pimentos you grew for them. That meant you could find yourself in the position of not being able to sell what you'd grown, whereas you knew there was always a market for cotton, however small the price.

Despite that possibility, Uncle Will felt pimentos had several advantages over cotton, one of which was that Hill Brothers furnished the plants. According to the salesman, the six-inch plants would come in large burlap bags, packed with red, gooey mud around the roots and ready to plant.

The weekend he received his shipment from the cannery, Uncle Will came over to the house to pick me up. Daddy had already agreed to let me help get the pimentos planted, with the usual promise that Uncle Will would pay for my services if the crop was successful. That was a big "if," considering Uncle Will's track record. As far as I was concerned, though, it had to be better than planting cotton. Sowing cotton was one of the worst jobs on earth, so I was more than willing to go along and help with pimentos.

Uncle Will always liked to do things in a big way, and this was no exception. He'd signed up to plant fifteen acres of pimentos, which for a one-horse farmer was about the same as someone with an income of $12,000 today trying to send ten kids to college. Uncle Will was a man who didn't want to be confused with facts, though. "Let's get down to business" was his motto.

The pimento plants came with instructions to plant one every eighteen inches in parallel rows three feet apart. That came to 10,500 plants per acre, or a total of 157,500 plants in fifteen acres. Each of the little boogers had to be handled separately, too. You had to scratch a little hole in the soil with your fingernail, drop in the plant, then pack the soil around the roots so it would get the nourishment it needed to live.

Besides the nearly 160,000 pimentos Uncle Will ordered, the company sent an additional 20,000 plants with instructions to substitute them for any ones that didn't look healthy. That meant having to make almost 180,000 decisions about whether to use one plant or another, which was overwhelming! After all, I'd never seen a pimento plant before. How did a healthy one look compared to a sick one? They all looked alike to me, except that some were a bit bigger than others.

Imagine for a moment that you're a twelve-year-old boy looking over a fifteen-acre field where you're about to begin setting out 160,000 plants. Imagine further that you work nearly an hour and finish one row across one acre. You look at what you've done, then at what's left to do. It could easily become discouraging, especially when you're working alone like I was initially. Uncle Will, you see, claimed to have other business to attend to, so he sent me out to "get things started" on my own.

By nighttime three days later, I'd worn out the knees of my overalls, rubbed my knees raw, and barely completed one-thirtieth of the job. In my mind I calculated that at a rate of one-thirtieth per every three days, I'd finish the job in ninety days. However, in ninety days it would be September, which was when we were supposed to harvest the crop. Even with my limited intelligence, things seemed to be out of kilter.

When I mentioned my concerns to Uncle Will at supper, he told me not to worry because I'd soon be getting some help with the task. Sure enough, two days later Aunt Beth started going to the field with me. She'd work four or five hours in the morning, go home to fix dinner and take care of some things around the house, then come back in the afternoon and work until almost dark. By the end of the second week we had all the pimentos planted—without any assistance from Uncle Will. When they loaded me in the wagon to carry me home on Saturday afternoon, I looked over that field of little pimento stalks with a sense of pride and accomplishment in being part of so monumental an undertaking. But I never wanted to do a job like that again.

From time to time during that summer, Uncle Will dropped by to tell us how great the pimento crop looked. At the ten tons per acre projected by the company, his fifteen acres would yield 150 tons of pimentos, and he didn't see how he could come out with less than eight to ten thousand dollars clear profit. And let me tell you, eight to ten thousand dollars would buy a house, an automobile, and a new wardrobe for the whole family in those days. We're talking big bucks.

Of course, all of this was in the future, but he told Mama and Daddy every time he came to see us that he'd pay me just as soon as he sold his first ton of pimentos. Not only that, he said, but since they were good enough to grant him credit for the whole summer and had already agreed to let me help him harvest the pimentos when they were ripe, he was going to pay me the unheard-of sum of three dollars a day as long as I worked for him. He even promised to let me ride into town with him when he went to sell the crop.

Upon hearing that, visions of great wealth began to dance in my head. The way it looked, the harvest season was going to last at least a month, and at three dollars a day, I'd earn ninety dollars or more. That'd make me probably the richest boy in the state of Georgia, certainly the richest one in all Carroll County.

Finally, one Sunday in early August, the great moment arrived. Uncle Will came over and told Daddy he wanted me to work for him the whole month. Daddy replied that school started in two weeks, but said I could help until then. That satisfied Uncle Will, and off we went to make our fortune. When we reached his place, I saw the pimentos for the first time since Aunt Beth and I had set them out that spring, and what a magnificent sight! In various stages of ripeness, they created a palette of beautiful colors, from emerald green to fiery amber. But more than that, each one meant money to me.

Before the dew was off Monday morning, Uncle Will and I were out picking pimentos. Anybody who thinks picking cotton is hard ought to try picking pimentos. They weigh a lot more and are a lot harder to handle than cotton. You also have to be careful to pick them at just the right stage. The man from Hill Brothers came by that morning and showed us exactly the ripeness he wanted, and we proceeded to work until it was too dark to see. On Tuesday we did the same, and by the end of the day we had a wagon full of the most beautiful pimentos you've ever seen.

I doubt there are many people who've ever seen a wagonload of pimentos. Come to think of it, I doubt there are many people who'd want to. But we had one, and as Uncle Will promised, we hitched up the old mule before daylight Wednesday morning and headed for Carrollton. It was a rough ride over those washboard roads in a wagon without springs, but I hardly noticed because I'd already earned six dollars. All we had to do was sell those pimentos.

At 10:30 we pulled into the Hill Brothers receiving station in Carrollton. As we sat there waiting our turn behind a dozen other wagons, I tried to figure what we had coming. Uncle Will said he thought we picked about 2500 pounds of pimentos. At forty dollars a ton, that came to about fifty dollars, six of which would be mine.

It was close to dinnertime when we finally pulled up to the shed to unload our pimentos on the three-foot-wide conveyer belt inside. Four workers standing along the length of the conveyer belt then inspected the pimentos as they rolled past, occasionally taking a few off the belt and placing them on another belt that went elsewhere in the building. They didn't seem to be discarding many of the pimentos, which was encouraging.

When we finished unloading the wagon, the cannery manager said, "Drive around and pick up your culls." Uncle Will thought, as I did, that those few they'd plucked out and put on the other conveyer belt were the culls, and in his most generous tone he answered, "Oh, just give 'em to the poor. It didn't look like there was many of 'em, anyway."

"The ones we put on the other conveyer were the good ones," the manager replied.

"Oh," Uncle Will muttered, his chin dropping almost to his chest.

We drove around to the other side of the dock, and to be honest with you, it looked like we had more pimentos to take home than we'd brought. The man at the far end told Uncle Will the company had kept 170 pounds for a total of $3.40, and he paid him right on the spot. That was barely enough to pay me for one day's work, and I'd almost finished three days by now, not counting the work I'd done in the spring that I expected to get paid for as well. It looked like a personal disaster for both of us. I knew Uncle Will had no way of making money except with that pimento crop; neither did I.

With heavy hearts, we began loading the pimentos back on the wagon. I wanted to cry but didn't let myself. I knew I probably would later on, but I didn't want those cannery folks to see me, so I shoveled pimentos and choked back the tears.

When we were ready to leave, Uncle Will took hold of the reins and yelled to the mules to get along. Instead of turning for home, however, he headed out of town the opposite direction. After a mile or so he pulled off at an old house, drove around to the back, jumped down, and went inside. A few minutes later he came out carrying something in a brown paper sack. I had no idea what it was, but as soon as he climbed back up beside me, I smelled whiskey on his breath, and I knew why we'd gone so far out of our way.

We rode back through Carrollton and were well on our way home before either of us said a word. Finally I looked over at Uncle Will and asked, "What are we gonna do with those pimentos?"

"Feed 'em to the hogs," he replied.

"The hogs won't eat 'em. I tried to feed 'em some the other day."

"Well, then, we'll feed 'em to the cows."

"The cows won't touch 'em either. Even that old steer you're raising for beef don't like 'em, and he's always hungry."

"Well..." Uncle Will said, staring straight ahead at nothing in particular.

"Besides," I continued, "I ain't just talkin' about this wagon load. This is just the first pickin'. What are we gonna do with fifteen acres of 'em?"

"Boy, you're gonna get paid just what I promised ya," Uncle Will responded. "I talked to the Hill Brothers representative, and he said we picked 'em a little too green, that's all. They just need to be a bit riper. If we're careful next time, they'll take a lot more of 'em."

I immediately felt better, and I guess Uncle Will did, too, because he took the top off the whiskey bottle and took another swig of it. I was still worried about what Aunt Beth would say when we got home. She was expecting us to bring $40 or more, and we only had $3.40, less whatever Uncle Will paid for the liquor. What's worse, she was going to be madder than a wet hen that he was drunk.

It was almost dark when we pulled up in front of the house. Uncle Will had finished his bottle about twenty minutes earlier and tossed the sack, bottle and all, over into the bushes as we drove along the road. "Put the mules up and feed 'em," Uncle Will said as we came to a stop. Then he tumbled off the front of the wagon and passed out on the ground, dead drunk.

Aunt Beth heard us drive up and quickly came outside. It was dark, however, and she didn't see Uncle Will's fall. She walked over to my side of the wagon and asked, "Well, how'd everything go?" I didn't have the heart to say anything. All I wanted to do was feed the mules and go to bed, so I hopped down to take the gear off of them while she walked around to the other side of the wagon and discovered Uncle Will for herself. She bent over him, took one whiff of his breath, and knew immediately. I didn't have to tell her anything.

When I finished feeding the mules and came out of the barn, Aunt Beth called me to help her drag Uncle Will into the house. After getting him to the bedroom, we had supper in silence.As we were clearing the table a few minutes later, I finally spoke.

"Why does Uncle Will always do this?"

"Whatta ya mean?" Aunt Beth replied, "lose money, or get drunk?"

"Get drunk. We didn't get paid what we wanted, but the man said all we had to do was let the pimentos get a little riper before we pick 'em."

"Will's a sick man, boy," she said.

"Has he ever thought about seein' a doctor?"

"The doctor came out to see him a few months ago. He'd read some things about how gettin' drunk is a medical problem, not just a moral problem, and he wanted to talk to us and see if he couldn't help Will out.

"About an hour before the doctor got here, I hid all of Will's liquor," Aunt Beth continued. "He got to pacin' the floor all nervous-like and talkin' about backin' out on the whole deal. He said if I'd just let him have one little drink to settle his nerves, he'd be more agreeable to meetin' with the doctor, so I finally gave him a drink about fifteen minutes before the doctor got here. After that his spirits improved considerably, and by the time the doctor sat down across the table from him, Will sure was feelin' his oats.

"'Will, I've come to the conclusion that you're an alcoholic,' the doctor told him. Will grinned and said,

'I want a second opinion,' but the doctor ignored him.

"'Will, you've gotten to where nobody has any faith in ya. You've lost the trust of your wife and your neighbors. Ya don't do anything ya promise folks you'll do. Ya don't pay your debts.'

"You could tell that hit Will pretty hard, 'cause tears welled up in his eyes and he started cryin'. 'Doc,' he said, 'I came out of a poker game the other night. I was drunk, had lost every dime I had, and fell down on my knees and said, "God, are you gonna destroy me?"'

"The doctor looked at him and said, 'Ya don't need God's help to destroy yourself. You're doin' a good job of that on your own.' Then he went on. 'Will, some people can drink and some people can't. I don't know why that's so, and I don't think anybody else does, either. But you've been tryin' for thirty-five years to learn how to drink liquor, and you've had absolutely no success at all. As smart a man as you are, ya should've figured out by now that it's just somethin' ya can't do, so why don't ya stop it now ?'

"Will raised his right hand, looked the doctor in the eye, and sobbed, 'Doctor, I swear I'll never touch another drop of the stuff again.' It wasn't but a day or two until he was drunk again, though."

Aunt Beth had never shared anything much of a personal nature with me before, and since she seemed in a talking mood, I decided to ask a question that'd been burnin' away inside for a long time.

"Did ya ever wish you'd never married Uncle Will?" I said as nonchalantly as possible. She jerked her head up and stared me square in the eye, and for a moment all I could think of was an old saying Mama had about 'fools rushing in.' I figured that's what I'd done. But eventually she answered.

"I've thought about it, boy. I can't deny that. Will's lived a rough life, and he's made it rough on me, too. The way I was raised up, though, if you make your bed hard, you still sleep in it, and I figure that's me. I made my bed hard the day I promised to marry Will. He just sorta swooped down real unexpected-like and popped the question. I don't know if ya know it or not, but he rescued me from bein' an old maid. I was 35 years old when I married Will, and except for him, I didn't have many prospects. Sometimes I think I mighta been better off if I'd said no.

"There's been several times when I've thought about pickin' up lock, stock, and barrel and goin' back to Alabama where I'm from, but the idea of goin' back to Pa's house with my tail between my legs like a whipped dog cuts against my grain. I almost get in the notion to leave when Will gets in one of his mean streaks, or when he loses a bale of cotton gamblin', but then I think of the embarrassment of goin' home and askin' Pa to let me move back in. I reckon he wouldn't fuss none, but I just somehow ain't got the heart for it. So I guess I'll just tough it out with Will as long as I can.

"Besides," she continued, "I really think Will is a good man at heart. He means to do right, but he's got some sorta sickness when it comes to gamblin' and drinkin'. It just gets the best of him every time, and he can't stop it. I know that sounds like I'm makin' excuses for him, but I really believe Will wants to do right. If I didn't believe that, I couldn't live with him another day. I'd just put my pride aside and go back to Pa's house with my hat in my hand and say, 'Can I come back home?' But I really believe Will means to do good.

"It's like somethin' eats on him. He sees that the years are runnin' out on him and that they ain't been too kind, and he gets depressed and goes to drinkin'.

"I read the Bible a lot when I was a girl, and I've read it a lot more since I've been married to Will. Somewhere, I think it's in Proverbs, the Good Book says, 'They that tarry long at the wine, they that see mixed wine, they have stricken me. Shalt thou say and I was not sick, they have beaten me and I have felt it not. When shall I awake? I will seek it yet again.'

"It's a terrible sickness Will's got, boy, and I don't think there's anything he or anybody else can do about it. Sometimes I'd just like to up and leave, but that's not the way I was raised. But believe me, I've thought about it a heap."

At breakfast the next morning, there was an icy feeling in the air that had nothing to do with the weather. I sat across the table from Uncle Will while Aunt Beth was at the end of the table closest to the stove. In the lamp light, Uncle Will's eyes looked like two cherries floating in a glass of buttermilk. His disposition wasn't in any better shape.

"Boy," he said near the end of the meal, "you're gonna have to be more careful and pick pimentos the company will take. I can't go to Carrollton every other day with a wagonload of pimentos and only get two dollars for 'em." I almost blurted out, "You got $3.40,

Uncle Will!" but decided I'd best keep quiet if I wanted to live to be full grown, so I just answered, "Yes, sir."

We ate in silence for a few more minutes, then Uncle Will suddenly exclaimed, "I'm gonna take that same load of pimentos back today!"

"You're crazy!" Aunt Beth replied. "They'll know it's the same pimentos, and ya won't sell a one."

Uncle Will acted like he hadn't even heard her. "The man said they just needed to be a little riper, and they're one day riper now. I'm gonna take the same load back and see if that's what's wrong. "Come on, boy," he said as he grabbed his hat. "Time's awastin'!"

I couldn't believe we were doing it, but we went out, hitched the mule to the wagon, and started back to Carrollton. When we arrived, Uncle Will backed the wagon in and started unloading the pimentos on the conveyor belt. The same fellow he'd talked to the day before came over and said, "Well, Mr. Will, you're sure here early. Ya got me a better batch today?"

"I think so," Uncle Will replied. Sure enough, they took almost half of what they'd culled a day earlier, and the man paid Uncle Will nineteen dollars. We went straight home this time, and Uncle Will gave Aunt Beth the whole nineteen dollars and told me he wasn't gonna give me my money, yet. "Ya don't need it for anything," he said, "and besides, you'll just lose it if I give it to ya right now. When we get the pimentos in and I carry ya home, I'll give ya all of it at one time."

He was right about one thing, but wrong about the other. I didn't need it because I didn't have any place to spend it. But I wouldn't have lost it.

That night as we were going to bed, it started raining. It didn't stop there, though. It rained hard all day Friday and Saturday as well. On Sunday, the one day we couldn't work (because it was the Sabbath), the sun broke through brilliantly and began drying out the fields a bit, causing Uncle Will's spirits to soar. It'd been three days since we'd been able to get into the fields, but he felt sure we could go back in Monday morning and find enough ripe pimentos to make another wagonload. I reminded him that this was the last week I could help because Daddy had said I had to go back to school the following Monday, but he assured me we could get the job done in that time. Meanwhile we walked around, looking at the sunshine and breathing the crisp, cool air that often follows a storm, and Uncle Will acted more jovial than I'd ever seen him.

As happens sometimes in those parts, however, the rain returned by the next morning. I felt terrible when I woke up and heard the drops beating on the tin roof of the old house. How can God be so mean, I wondered? Here we'd worked so hard to make a crop, and now were in danger of losing it all. I've attended a lot of wakes that were livelier than breakfast that Monday. Not a single word was spoken. I was deeply depressed, but not nearly as depressed as Uncle Will was. "They're gonna rot in the field, Beth," he finally muttered as we got up from the table. That's all he said.

The rain continued to fall nonstop through Wednesday, and Uncle Will was fit to be tied. He paced up and down and all around. He fumed. He cussed. And we must have greased the wagon wheels a dozen times. Thursday morning it turned clear again. The fields looked like rivers, with the water standing in the low spots above the contoured rows, but Uncle Will couldn't stand it any longer. "Come on, boy," he said. "Get the picksacks and let's go."

We waded out into the field, with the mud up to our knees, and started picking pimentos as fast as we could. By nightfall, we'd picked another wagonful ready to go to market. On Friday morning Uncle Will called me aside. "I know I promised ya could go with me every time I carried a load of pimentos to town, but I need ya to stay here pickin'. Put whatever ya get in the cotton house, and I'll take 'em to town in the mornin'. I'll be back as soon as I can to help ya. We've gotta get 'em in while we got clear weather." After he left, I trudged back into the field and picked sackful after sackful, then carried them to the old cotton house. In fact, I surveyed my day's work as the sun settled in the West and felt a sense of pride in what I'd accomplished.

It was after dark by the time Aunt Beth and I got the cows milked and the hogs fed, but Uncle Will still hadn't returned. We were both worried, but went on to bed anyway. Sometime during the night, I never did know when, I heard a commotion in the front yard and got up to see two men carrying Uncle Will from the wagon to the porch. It looked like he was drunk again, but I went back to bed because it was none of my concern.

At breakfast the next morning, Aunt Beth said Uncle Will had come home under the weather and wasn't up and about yet. She told me to go on and start picking, since this was the last day I could help and we didn't know how long the good weather would last, and promised that Uncle Will would be along in a bit.

I did as she said, and sure enough, Uncle Will showed up with his picksack at about noon. He looked gaunt and spent, and hardly said a word. We picked straight through until dark except to stop for dinner, then went to the house to do the evening chores.

After supper the three of us sat for a long time in front of the hearth, staring at the small fire laid there, until Uncle Will finally stood up and said, "Boy, come out on the porch. I wanna talk to ya." He had a way of saying "Boy" in different tones, depending on the situation, and I had a sinking feeling the way he said it this time that he was going to tell me he couldn't pay me any money. I decided that whatever happened, though, I was going to be brave and not cry.

We sat silently in the porch swing for a minute or two before he spoke up and said, "Boy, I ain't gonna be able to pay ya what I promised ya, at least not now. Maybe if I can save the rest of the pimentos and get a decent price for 'em I'll be able to pay ya somethin', but it's too soon to tell. It just seems like nothin' I do ever turns out quite the way I expect it to or want it to."

Neither of us said another word until I got up the courage to ask, "Do ya think your drinkin' might have anything to do with it?"

"That ain't the problem," he replied. "I'll tell ya what the problem is. I've had it all my life.

"When I was a little boy, even smaller than you are now, my grandpa sat me on his knee one night when nobody was around and said, 'William'—my grandpa always called me William, even though everybody else called me Will—'William,' he said, 'Every human on the face of this earth has a choice whether to live a good life or a bad life, but they have to make up their minds which one they want. They have to do somethin' to get the kind of life they want.'

"'Now, I've had a good life,' he says, 'and I'm gonna tell ya my secret, and if you'll take it and use it, you'll have a good life, too.'

"And this is what my grandpa told me. He said, 'William, I pray every day, and this is what I say: I say, Lord, if I must run a footrace with the Devil, please let me choose the course.'"

We sat quietly in the dark for what seemed like an hour before Uncle Will spoke again. "Boy, d'ya have any idea what Grandpa meant by that?"

"No, sir, I don't," I replied. "I'm just a kid. I don't know nothin' about prayin. You grown-up folks are supposed to know about that. I don't ever pray until I'm in a lot of trouble, and then it doesn't help, 'cause I usually get smacked anyhow."

"Well, I've had some good days, and I've had some bad days," he said, "but I believe my life would've been a lot easier if I could've ever figured out what Grandpa was tryin' to tell me." A few minutes later he stood up to go inside, but before he did, he turned to me and said, "Boy, I'm an old man, and I ain't never asked nobody the question I just asked you. I don't ever want ya to mention it again as long as I'm alive, ya hear?" I nodded. Next day, he carried me back home and dropped me off at the road. As usual, I never got a dime for my work.

Uncle Will Pays Up

One afternoon in the fall of 1942, the darkest time of World War II for the United States, Uncle Will and Aunt Beth came chugging up in the old green Model A he'd had since I'd known him. It was no longer beautiful and lux-urious, though. The canvas top was ragged and torn, the body dented and rusty, and it had no muffler. In short, it wasn't much more than a bucket of bolts.

As soon as they climbed out of the car, I noticed that Uncle Will's left arm was in a sling and his hand was in a cast. Before I could ask what happened, however, he said, "Boy, I came over to see if your Ma and Pa will let ya help me work up my winter supply of wood. I busted my arm and I just can't roll them logs over or saw 'em by myself, and Beth ain't up to it. I wondered if you'd be interested in helping me? I'll pay ya two dollars a day."

Uncle Will had burned me too many times with empty promises about money, and I was leery of falling for it again. Besides, I didn't think Mama and Daddy would let me go because they didn't like for me to miss school. While I stood there contemplating his offer, he spoke again. "I just can't do anything at all with one arm, and Beth ain't able to help in the woods. But you can take a pry bar and keep a block under the logs, and I can pull one end of the crosscut saw while you pull the other. We can get in enough firewood to last the winter with your help, but I can't do it by myself."

I looked at Aunt Beth, but she didn't say a word. She just stood staring at the ground. "I don't believe Mama and Daddy will let me go," I finally answered. "I might help ya, but I don't believe they'll let me go 'cause of school and all."

"Well, today's Thursday," Uncle Will replied. "If ya went home with us tonight, we could work tomorrow and Saturday, and I could bring ya back home Sunday. That way ya wouldn't miss but one day of school, and ya could make yourself four dollars." I glanced again at Aunt Beth, but she still didn't look up.

"Uncle Will, if you'll pay me four dollars, and if Mama and Daddy will let me, I'll come help ya cut up your firewood. But ya gotta *promise* me that this time you'll give me my money."

"Boy, did I ever beat ya outa any money?" he asked without any hint of guilt over past sins.

"Yes, sir, ya have."

"That was on things that didn't work out. I didn't have the money then, but I already got the money for this, and I'll pay ya your money for sure."

Aunt Beth still hadn't said a word, but I finally agreed to go along with them and get the firewood in if Mama and Daddy gave their okay.

We went inside, and Uncle Will told Daddy how he was injured and how there was no way he could keep that old house where he and Beth lived warm if he didn't get in some firewood. He also repeated his offer to pay me for my services.

Mama and Daddy had a conference in the other room, then called me in to join them.

"Son, I don't guess it'll kill ya to miss a day of school," Daddy said, "but you're of an age now to decide whether ya wanna work for nothin' or not."

"But Uncle Will gave his word that he'd pay me this time," I replied, "and I don't think he'd lie to me now that I'm gettin' older."

"Let me tell ya somethin' about Will," Daddy answered. "In '32 or '33 when you wasn't much more than a baby, he came by the house to make me a proposition. He said a man in town was buildin' a new home and had promised to buy the lumber for it from Will as soon as he could deliver it. He asked me to work for him for a dollar a day, six days a week, the entire month of March to help him get the lumber cut and delivered. By working straight through like that, he said we could get our money from the man as early as the first of April.

"Needless to say, I jumped at the chance. I had a wife and two children to support, and it was almost impossible to find any work at all in those days, much less work that paid a dollar a day, so for the next four weeks I started every day except Sunday by gettin' up at four in the morning to fire the boiler on the engine. It took quite a while to get a full head of steam goin' each day, too, because I had to fill the boiler by hand with water from the creek.

"By daylight, I usually had the boiler goin', and then the real work began. My job was to roll the logs up onto the carriage of the sawmill and dog 'em down to the blade. Will had the sawyer's job, which was the

77

easiest one. All he had to do was engage the carriage belt that pulled the log through the blade.

"The work was as hard as any a man can do, and I came home at night totally beat, even though I was young then and in good shape. But we finished the job and delivered the lumber by wagon at the end of March, just like we'd planned.

"After Will talked privately with the man ordering the lumber, though, he came back to the wagon and handed me two dollars. 'He says that's all he can pay us right now,' Will said without lookin' me in the eye, 'but he'll try to get the rest to us as soon as possible.'

"I never got another penny for that month of hard labor. Every time I brought up the subject, Will said he hadn't seen the money yet himself. I never knew the truth for sure, but I suspect he got paid more than he let on. One thing's for sure, though. I never let him beat me more than once.

"But that was my decision to make. The one today is yours. You can go with him or say no, it's up to you."

"I think he's bein' honest with me this time," I said. "I'm gonna go." Daddy nodded, though I don't believe I convinced him of what I felt, and I went out and crawled into the old Model A.

Early the next morning Uncle Will and I went to the woods about five hundred yards behind his house to start working up some trees for firewood. He and Aunt Beth had really fallen on hard times, from the look of things. They no longer even had a wagon, only a ground slide and an old mule that was blind in one eye. We worked until a couple of hours before sundown Friday, then loaded up what we'd cut and headed for the house. By the time we finished it was completely dark, because you can't haul a whole lot of wood on a ground slide being pulled by a eight hundred pound, half-blind mule.

That night for supper we had cornbread, buttermilk, and a potato pie Aunt Beth had cooked as a surprise. They didn't have a spare bed, so she made me a pallet in the room away from her and Uncle Will. When you've worked as long and hard as we did that day, it's not a bit of trouble to go to sleep on the floor with just one quilt under you and one over you. You have no use at all for a sleeping pill.

The next morning Uncle Will got me up well before daylight to help him with chores while Aunt Beth got breakfast ready. We fed the mule, milked the cow, slopped the hogs, then ate breakfast and were back in the woods at the crack of dawn. There was a light frost on the ground because of the chilly temperatures, but using a crosscut saw will warm you up fast, no matter how cold it is.

By the end of the second day we had a pretty good pile of firewood, enough to last a month or so if we didn't have any real cold weather. I figured Uncle Will's arm ought to be pretty near healed by then.

We didn't have to work the next morning, since it was Sunday, so Aunt Beth took a skillet, imbedded it in in the fireplace ashes, and popped popcorn. After that, they took turns telling me yarns for a while before we turned in for the night. On Sunday morning we did the chores and had breakfast as usual before Uncle Will finally said, "Well, boy, it's time I was gettin' ya home."

He didn't say anything about my money. I got my few things together as slowly as possible, hoping the subject of my wages would come up, but when it didn't, I finally asked, "What about my money, Uncle Will?"

"Boy, I had your four dollars stuffed in the cookie jar, and now I can't find it. But I got some other chores to do right now, so I'll take ya on home and bring your money over later."

I didn't see how I could go home without any money this time, not after what I'd told Mama and Daddy, and I guess my face mirrored my concern, because Aunt Beth broke in and said tersely, "That four dollars is on the mantlepiece under the old clock, Will, and you know it. You get it and give it to the lad. He's worked hard, and it's his. Now, give it to him!"

"That's all the money we've got in the house, Beth," Uncle Will replied with a mixture of anger and disbelief over Aunt Beth's command.

"It don't make no never mind," she shot back. "Ya promised the boy. I was there and I heard ya. Now give him his money. If you don't, I will, 'cause it's his!"

Uncle Will whirled on his heels, stomped over to the mantle to get the money, handed it to me and said, "Here!" all hateful-like. I didn't like the way it made me feel, but I wanted that money and I took it. After all, I'd earned it, and I couldn't hardly face Mama and Daddy without it.

"Get in the car, boy," he said in a clipped tone. "I'm takin' ya home." A little ways along, though, we turned onto an old farm road and drove about a mile to a run-down shack worse looking even than what we lived in.

"I thought you were takin' me home," I said. "Where are we?"

"I'm thirsty," Uncle Will replied. "I need a drink of liquor and I think ya oughta buy me a pint of liquor since ya got all my money."

"Oh, no!" I thought to myself. I could just see the whole four dollars going for booze, and I had no idea how I was going to resist.

About that time a large, heavy-set man in overalls walked out to the car and said gruffly, "Whatta ya want, Will?"

"A pint of liquor," Uncle Will answered.

"I ain't gonna sell ya no more liquor on credit, 'cause ya didn't pay me for the last bottle ya got."

"The boy here is gonna buy it," Uncle Will explained, motioning toward me. The heavy-set man bent over and looked in the window across at me. "He's a child. I can't sell that boy no liquor," he said.

"No, *he's* gonna buy it, but *I'm* gonna drink it," Uncle Will clarified matters. "Is it still seventy-five cents a pint?" The man nodded. "Boy, ya got seventy-five cents for your old uncle?" Uncle Will asked, turning to me.

"Yes, sir," I said, pulling one of the four dollars out of my pocket. The man went inside and came back a few minutes later carrying a brown paper sack. He handed it in the window to Uncle Will, took my dollar, and gave me twenty-five cents change. On the way home I breathed a huge sigh of relief. Thanks to Aunt Beth I was at least going to get home with something this time, and that was better than I'd ever done before.

Larnin' 'Bout Women

For nearly four years after that, Uncle Will and Aunt Beth vanished from those parts. They just up and disappeared without a trace. I thought about Uncle Will often and wondered what had happened to him. From time to time I asked my grandmother, to whom I was very close, where she thought he might be. "Lord, I've got no idea," she'd answer. "He could be dead for all I know."

Sometimes we talked about the days when they'd been children. I could never imagine Uncle Will as a boy, for some reason. In my mind he'd always been a hardened old man, but Grandmother often recalled the days when they were young and she looked up to him as an older brother. However, after the killing and the trial that followed, she said, she wondered if she'd ever really known him. One thing's for sure, though, she said. She was never close to him again after he got out of prison. Of course, I had no idea exactly what she was talking about, other than the rumors I'd heard all my life, but I nodded my head as if I understood.

Grandmother worried about Uncle Will a lot—about his soul, about him dying and burning in that eternal lake where, according to the Good Book, there's wailing and gnashing of teeth. But one day while we were peeling peaches, she looked up and said, "Will's favorite hymn was 'Pass Me Not, Oh Gentle Savior.' Now I ask ya, can anybody whose favorite hymn is

'Pass Me Not, Oh Gentle Savior' be all bad?" Then she added, "The Lord will look after him, the way He always has, the way He looks after each of us. Don't fret about your uncle, boy. Don't fret about him."

Sure enough, as unexpectedly as he disappeared, one day Uncle Will came driving up to our house in an old bus. I was so excited, I jumped up into the doorway of the vehicle to greet him, but lo and behold, I hardly knew him. His hair had turned snow white and hung clear down to his shoulders.

"It's been a while, ain't it, nephew?" he said. "Why, you've just about growed up since I saw ya. You must be a foot taller than ya was back pickin' pimentos. How've ya been?"

I was almost struck dumb. He looked so different, so pale and drawn, that I barely recognized him. Even though it'd only been four years since I last saw him, he looked like he'd aged a hundred.

"Good Lord, Uncle Will!" I exclaimed, unable to hide my shock. "What on earth happened to ya?"

"Whatta ya mean, what happened to me?"

"Ya look so old!"

"Oh, that," he answered. "I was afraid that's what ya was talkin' about." He hesitated a second as if trying to think of an answer, then said, "I don't know, boy. Somewhere along the way I think I pissed off Father Time and he wound my clock up too tight. But looks don't matter that much, 'cause there's a lot of younger folks, who took better care of themselves than I did, that's done danced their waltz with the Grim Reaper. That's how I got rid of most of my enemies. I just outlived 'em. I may not be a pretty sight, but I'm still breathin'.

"That's a hell of a greetin', though, tellin' me how old I look," he laughed. "I came by to see if ya wanted to go fishin' tonight, not to talk about how I've aged. Remember the old swimmin' hole down on Indian Creek where we watched that marsh hen hatch her chicks? I been there, and it looks like the fishin' might be good. Are ya interested? We'll drive down there in this ol' bus. I've got quilts and some air mattresses that are surplus from the Army. Ya just blow 'em up like an inner tube. We'll sleep right on the creek bank. I've got a fryin' pan and plenty of lard and bread, too, so we can cook up what we catch."

His voice grew softer as he continued. "Besides, I've been right lonesome for some kin. I ain't seen none of 'em for four years. I thought ya could fill me in on what's been happenin' around here, on who's died and who ain't."

I'd been standing in the door of that old bus as we talked, but when he mentioned the sleeping gear, I stepped up inside to take a look. Sure enough, he had a bed, a wash stand, and all the comforts of home. It was pretty tight quarters, but it looked fine for one person. "Daddy's over plowing the field, and Mama's visiting one of the neighbors," I responded to his offer. "I've got my chores done, but I'll have to ask before I take off with ya. I just hope Daddy comes home first, 'cause he's more likely to let me go than Mama is."

About that time, Daddy came riding the old mule up from the back of the barn. I ran and told him that Uncle Will was back and wanted me to go fishing with him overnight down on Indian Creek.

"What about your chores?" he asked.

"I've done finished 'em," I replied.

Daddy walked over to the bus, looked inside, and said, "Long time, Will." Will nodded his head but didn't say anything. Under other circumstances Daddy would've said no, but he knew how much I'd missed Uncle Will. "Be back by tomorrow afternoon," he said finally. With that, Uncle Will pulled the handle that shut the door and we went chugging off toward Indian Creek.

I guess it was a good hour before we reached the creek. There were a lot of sandy places where the underbrush had apparently been stomped down by people with the same idea as we had. In a little clearing, we rounded up some kindling to build a fire, then set our hooks out and got things ready for cooking the fish. As we worked together, I realized that Will was still a larger-than-life figure to me. I was fifteen years old and stood almost six feet tall, but Uncle Will, even as bent and as old as he was, still towered over me. And there was that air of mystery, that tingling sense of awe, that I'd always felt in his presence. Even now when he was an old, decrepit man with labored breath and snow-white hair, he still commanded both fear and respect in me.

After dinner we crawled in the back of the bus and got comfortable, then I filled him in on who'd married, had babies, or passed away since he'd been gone. When I finished I said, "Now it's your turn, Uncle Will."

"How's that?" he said.

"There's a lot of things about you I want to know."

"Like what?"

"Like where's Aunt Beth, and where've you been the last four years."

"Beth's gone," he answered in a soft tone. "That's all ya need to know about her. And as for the last few years, I'll tell ya about that someday, but not right now."

"Well, how about some of the stories Grandmother told me while you was away? I don't know whether to believe 'em or not."

"I've lived a lot of years, boy. You gotta be more specific than that. What particular stories are ya talkin' about?"

"Grandmother said somethin' happened between you and your Pa when you was fourteen or fifteen that mighta left its mark on ya. Why not start there, 'cause even she didn't know everything that happened."

"You don't ask much, do ya?" he chuckled. "That was only forty-some-odd years ago."

"I know it's been a while," I said, "but I'd just like ya to set the record straight for once."

"All right, boy," he answered. "If that's what ya want, that's what you'll get." And with those words, he began a tale that continued long into the night.

"I ran away from home when I was fifteen years old," he said. "Pa and me just couldn't get along. I remember one Saturday night I wanted to go over and court Miss Ila West, but Pa said no. He said that I was too young to be thinkin' about women and that I needed to get some more schoolin'.

"I didn't want to hear that, though. I thought I

needed to learn about lovin' a woman. So that Saturday night after Ma and Pa went to sleep, I snuck out in the barn and caught ol' Jack. He was a big ol' 1400-pound horse-mule that Pa had owned for two or three years. I threw a saddle on him, the only saddle Pa had, and set out to go see Miss Ila.

"She lived almost to Bowdon, about three miles away, and on the way there I got to thinkin'. 'It's near ten o'clock,' I said to myself. 'If I wake up ol' man West while I'm tryin' to court his daughter, he's liable to shoot me.' The closer I came to the house, the fainter my heart got, and when I finally reached their place I rode right on by, right through the middle of Bowdon. Every once in a while I'd put my heel in ol' Jack's flank and goose him a little bit, and he'd trot on down the road.

"Before I knew it I was in Ranburne, Alabama. 'I always wanted to go to Texas,' I thought to myself, 'and now's my chance. I've heard it's a long way, but I think I'll see for myself. Besides, I done crossed one state line. What's a couple more?' So I kept headin' west.

"Times were good then. I could stop in one place and hire out ol' Jack snakin' logs or team him up double on the turnin' plow for as high as two or three dollars a day. Pretty soon I'd worked my way clear across the state of Alabama. When I got to the other side of the state, I had my saddlepack full of things I'd always wanted. It was just me and ol' Jack, and I was feelin' pretty good. I wondered why Pa hadn't done the same thing. Instead of workin' on that hardscrabble land tryin' to dig out a livin', he oughta become a travelin' man like me.

"Of course, every once in a while I'd feel real bad about takin' the best mule Pa had, and I kept thinkin' that if I ever went back, he was gonna be real upset with me."

By this time I was growning impatient. I'd hoped maybe he'd tell me in one profound statement about some great turning point in his life. "I just wanted to know the one big thing," I butted in.

"Nephew," he shot back, "you're too impatient. You asked a question, and in due course you'll have your answer. But it's my story, and I'm tellin' it. Patience, lad, patience." Then he continued.

"In early May I rode into a town called Meridian, Mississippi. It was a thrivin' place. All the fields was planted in cotton or corn, and everybody seemed to have plenty of work to do. I stopped in at a seed and fertilizer warehouse to ask if there was any jobs a fella and his mule could do, and the owner offered to pay me four dollars a day to deliver fertilizer around the county.

"Now mind ya, nephew, that was more money than I'd ever seen back in Carroll County, Georgia. My daddy had a little bit of money from time to time, but I'd never had a dime. Now here I was fifteen years old, stout as a mule, and thinkin' I could whip the world. I felt so good my hide wouldn't hold me. I just couldn't understand how a man as stupid as Pa could have raised a boy as smart as me. I had nigh on to fifty dollars, plus a job makin' four more dollars a day, and it wouldn't cost me more than fifty cents a day to live. I'd done talked to the folks down at the livery barn and they was gonna let me sleep in the hayloft and only charge me twenty-five cents a day for feedin' my mule. I just didn't know any reason why I wouldn't get rich.

"I worked for the fertilizer dealer the whole week, and sure enough, at five o'clock Saturday he paid me twenty-four dollars. I tell ya, I felt like the richest fella in the whole world.

"From time to time, though, I'd think about Ma and Pa tryin' to eke out a livin' on that upland farm where the soil had all washed away fifty years before, while here I was makin' so much money I didn't know what to do with it. Sometimes I wished I could send 'em a little bit, but I didn't know how to do that.

"At any rate, I decided if money was that easy to come by in Meridian, Mississippi, I'd just make the town my home. I asked the fertilizer dealer where a good boardin' house was, 'cause I was tired of rakin' hay out of my hair every mornin', and he gave me the name of a place about four blocks away. I rented me a room with two meals a day furnished for six dollars a week and still had eighteen dollars pure profit for me and my mule.

"That night I ate my first meal at the boarding house, then walked out on the front porch for a breath of fresh air. It was there that I met a fella I was to see off and on for the next forty years. Wherever I'd be, whether it was Texas or Georgia or Mississippi, it seemed like I was always runnin' into him. His name was Willie Kilgore.

"Willie was a runt of a little fella. I could hold my arms straight out, and he could walk under 'em without duckin' or bendin' over. But despite our different sizes, we took a likin' to one another right away. In fact, before I knew it, he'd asked me a lot of personal questions, includin' had I ever had a woman. I must've turned every color in the rainbow. I cleared my throat three or four times, tryin' to make up my mind what to answer, until he finally said, 'I know ya ain't, kid, or you'd have done owned up to it already.' Then he added, 'How'd ya like to get ya a woman *tonight*?'

"Well, there I was, fifteen goin' on sixteen with a pocket full of money, and he's talking about gettin' a woman into bed. Was I interested?! Can a squirrel climb a tree?! Just the thought of it had my tool so hard already that a cat couldn't scratch it. I looked at Willie and said, 'Are you serious?'

"'Yeah, Will,' he said, 'there's a cathouse just across the county line. It only takes about thirty minutes to walk over there. They've got ten girls, and you can have any one ya want for two dollars.'

"'What're we waitin' for?' I said excitedly.

"'Well, I ain't got two dollars,' Willie answered.

"I told him right quick that I'd loan him the money if he'd go over and make the introductions. He allowed as how he'd do that. He also said they had the best corn liquor in the whole county at the cathouse. It was only twenty-five cents a shot, he said, and you could have anything ya wanted for a chaser. He usually bought a couple of shots, he said, to get over the embarrassment of havin' to choose one of them little girls over the others. It just made him not feel so bad about it.

"He asked if I'd loan him the extra fifty cents for two drinks of corn liquor, and I told him I'd do that, too, if he'd make the introductions. So we started walkin' to the County Line Bar and Grill. When we got there, Willie told the lady behind the bar, 'Tillie, I brought ya another customer. This here is Will. We thought we'd have a couple of drinks and sample your girls.'

"Tillie looked me over and said, 'You're a bit young, ain't ya, Will? Where'd ya come from? Your Pa and Ma don't live around here somewhere, do they?' I told her no, that I was from over in Georgia, was a full-grown man, and hadn't seen Ma and Pa now in two months.

"'Have ya ever had a woman before, Will?' she asked.

"'No,' I said.

"'Maybe ya oughta take a drink first to sorta calm your nerves.'

"'I don't wanna calm my nerves,' I replied. 'I want a woman, *now*. Who do I pay the two dollars to?'

"'Give it to me,' Tillie said, 'then go through that door there and there'll be some girls sittin' on a couch. You just pick out the one ya want, take her hand, and she'll lead ya upstairs and look after ya.'

"I walked through the door into that room, and there sat ten of the prettiest young women I'd ever laid eyes on. I just stood there with my mouth open. I couldn't make up my mind at all about which one I wanted. Meanwhile, my tool was just a throbbin'. I had to hold my hand in my pocket or it was just gonna jump out. I held my tool down with my left hand and walked over to the prettiest thing I ever saw in my life and said, 'It's you.' She got right up and led me through a door and up some stairs. I was so weak and wobbly-legged that I couldn't hardly walk. In fact, I was so giddy that I banged my head on a low door at the top of the stairs and just about brained myself.

"'Ooooh, I'm sorry,' the little lady said real sweet-like. Then she pulled me into a room with a bed and began fumblin' around with the buttons on the back of her dress. After a second or two it fell to the floor, and there she stood in front of me, bare-ass naked. My eyes just about popped outa my head. That was the first time I'd ever seen a naked woman, and the best part was, she was mine.

"The young lady reached over to put her hand on my tool and get somethin' started, but as soon as she did, I just exploded in my britches. Man, I ain't never been so embarrassed in my life. She realized what'd happened and said, 'Ooooh, Will!' Damn, I was mortified!

"An hour later I headed back downstairs. Willie was still in the bar drinkin' liquor. He hadn't seen no girl yet. I asked when he was gonna get him one, and he said, 'I think I'll just drink all my $2.50 up in liquor. I've already had four shots, so I ain't got enough left to see a woman anyhow.' Then he grinned real big and said, 'You been gone nearly an hour, Will. Sit down and tell me how it was.' I told him that if the Lord ever made anything better than that, He sure kept it for himself 'cause He didn't want none of us gettin' a hold of none of it. After sayin' that, I told Tillie to give me a drink of corn liquor.

"Now, boy, ya asked me about the turnin' point of my life. When I picked up that glass of liquor and turned it down, that was it. No sooner had it hit my belly than my head started spinnin', lights came on, and suddenly I was the smartest fella I ever knew. It was scary. I was almost God-like. It seemed that I had the power to see right through people, to read their thoughts. It was a wonderful feelin', like I was floatin' off the ground. I was smarter, luckier, and more handsome than anybody in the world. It was an instant transformation. I was the most remarkable individual I'd ever known, and I wondered why nobody had ever noticed that before. Oh, that stuff! It put ideas in my head you wouldn't believe, and I liked it.

"I don't remember walkin' home or goin' to bed at the boardin' house that night, but at eleven the next mornin' when I woke up, I felt like somebody had hit me in the head with an ax. My teeth was itchin', my hair ached, and my mouth tasted like a drove of stink-bugs had nested under my tongue. I stumbled downstairs to where the owner of the boardin' house was fixin' dinner and said, 'Good morning.'

"She put her hands on her hips and said, 'I'll thank ya, Georgia boy, to move outa here as soon as your week's up. We don't put up with such carryin' on as what went on in your room last night. I'm pretty sure that you're fired, too. Mr. Goodson over at the fertilizer warehouse ain't gonna take lightly to you showin' up in the middle of the day. As a matter of fact, son, the best thing you could do is get on your mule and ride.'

"I couldn't remember anything that happened the previous night in my room, but after her tongue-lashin' I didn't wanna ask, so I went over to the livery barn, got my mule, and left Meridian."

Will Larns
Gamblin' and Cheatin'

Sometimes when Uncle Will got to talking, he'd hold to one subject for hours like he was replaying a tape of certain portions of his life, something that was indelibly inscribed moment-by-moment in his brain. When he told about leaving Meridian, I wanted very much to ask more questions, but I decided to wait and see if he'd continue the story or quit for the day. You never knew the outcome until he stood up and said, "Well, that's enough for today." Then you knew he was ready to go about his daily business and save the reminiscences for another time.

As we sat there, I could almost see him going word-by-word over the story he'd just recounted, making sure he had told it right and proper so I could understand it. When he was satisfied that everything was clear to that point, he took out his old corncob pipe, stuffed it, lit it, and then continued talking.

"For a big part of that summer, I wandered on west through the state of Mississippi. I knew there was only one other state between me and Texas, whether I choosed it to be Arkansas or Louisiana, but I didn't know exactly how to get to either one so I asked around. Folks said if I continued headin' due west I'd go through Jackson and Vicksburg, then hit Louisiana.

"By the time I got to Vicksburg, I'd spent the better part of summer workin' and savin' up money. Sometimes at night I'd get lonesome for Ma and Pa, and think maybe I'd done 'em wrong. Sometimes my conscience would bother me about stealin' Pa's best mule.

I told myself the first week or two that I only borrowed the mule, but I really stole it.

"I went to the post office when I got to Vicksburg and asked how I could send some money home. They told me I'd have to buy a money order 'cause it wasn't safe to send cash through the mail. But there was a charge for the money order, and I decided it just wasn't worth the trouble. So I never did send 'em anything.

"At Vicksburg I saw the mighty Mississippi for the first time. To my notion, that was the dividin' line between the east and the west. I hungered mightily to get across that river and seek my fortune. I think I'd done made up my mind I was never goin' back to Georgia. I watched the paddle-wheel steamers go up and down the river for several days, then hired me and ol' Jack out to drag freight around the waterfront. I even got on a barge and rode back and forth across the river.

"I liked the people that lived and worked the 'Big Muddy', as they called it. In fact, I got to thinkin' again about tryin' to take root somewhere and make somethin' of myself. Pa used to tell me, 'Will, you ain't never gonna amount to nothin' 'til ya learn to listen to somebody that's got more sense than you got, and I don't think you're ever gonna do that.' I'd get real mad when he said that, but now I realize he was right. I always thought I had more sense than anybody else did.

"After a week or two I decided Vicksburg was a good place to settle down. I got me a room at a boardin' house on a little bluff overlookin' the Mississippi so I could watch the sun go down across that big, wide river. It was awful hot late in the evenin', since my room faced west, but after sundown a coolin' breeze would pick up. All in all, it was a nice place to stay a piece.

"One evenin' as I sat down to supper at the boardin' house, I looked down at the other end of the table, and who should be sittin' there but Willie Kilgore! It was like runnin' into somebody from Indian Creek. I hadn't seen a soul I knew since I left home, and even though I only spent a few hours with Willie in Meridian, it was almost a family reunion. As soon as we finished supper we went out on the porch and fell to talkin' about where we'd been that summer and where we was goin'. Finally Willie said, 'Will, I'm plumb dry from talkin'. Let's go have a drink.' I thought back to my first encounter with liquor and how I felt afterward. I hadn't had no liquor since and didn't want none now, so I said, 'I don't want a drink, Willie. I just wanna get reacquainted.' It wasn't five minutes, though, before he prevailed on me to go to one of the night spots close to where we lived.

"When we got there, it was a dive. That's all I can think to call it. There was three or four card games goin' on, and an ol' player piano goin' for all it was worth over in the corner. Willie sat down and ordered straight whiskey with a glass of water. I told him I was just gonna watch him drink.

"Willie tossed down the first drink and started in about wantin' me to have one with him. I told him how bad it made me feel in Meridian, how I lost my job and got kicked out of the boardin' house, and how I didn't want to fool with liquor no more. He said, 'The trouble with you is ya don't know your limit,' he said. 'Just don't drink more than two drinks, and everything will be all right. Ya won't feel all that awful, and ya won't get into trouble.' I tried to tell him about the landlady in Meridian gettin' mad over somethin' I couldn't even remember happenin', but he didn't wanna hear it.

"We sat there while he had a couple more drinks, then he got up and walked around the room to watch the card games that was goin' on. In a few minutes he came back to where I was sittin' and whispered, 'Will, do you know how to play poker?' I told him I didn't know how to play any card game except Rook, which we played from time to time when I was a little boy. 'I want ya to come over here and watch this,' he whispered again, pointin' to a table nearby. 'They've got a bunch of dummies that have no idea how to play poker.'

"I went over with him and watched. Somebody would bet two dollars and somebody else would raise two dollars, then everybody would throw in their cards. The game didn't make a whole lot of sense to me, and I got bored rather quickly, but when we went back to our table, Willie was all flushed with excitement. 'Will,' he said, 'if you'll loan me some money, I can make a fortune at that game. I tell ya, they're a bunch of dummies.'

"I was pretty skeptical about why he was so broke if he was so smart, but he was such a persuasive little fella I gave him twenty dollars. When I handed him the money, he saw I had a lots more, but didn't ask for it.

"He sat down at the game the first chance he got, and I pulled a chair up behind him to watch. He drank a couple of more drinks, which worried me a bit, but before long he'd made seventy or eighty dollars. He had close to a hundred dollars in front of him, and I was beginnin' to think maybe he knew what he was doin'.

"There was a whole lot of money on the table, more than I'd ever saw at one time in my life. Around midnight, one of the players that didn't appear to be the smartest fella in the world suggested that they raise the stakes to a no-limit game. Up till then they'd had a five dollar limit, which was the most you could bet at one time. But they voted on it and decided they'd have no limit. Then they got in an argu-ment over whether it was gonna be table stakes only or whether they'd be allowed to use money out of their pockets. They finally agreed that you could bet anything ya had on the table or in your pocket. Now the game got real serious.

"They was playin' five-card stud. In that game ya get one card face-down—what ya call your hole card—and four cards face-up. The player with the best hand wins. I began to catch on to the game, what would win and what wouldn't, and it became right fascinatin'. I got to where I could look over Willie's shoulder and usually tell what he had in the hole. He'd made a whole lot of money in a pretty short time, and he must've had three hundred dollars on the table in front of him. He'd slipped me back my twenty dollars early in the game.

"Willie was gettin' a little drunker, but so was everybody at the table. I had just one drink and decided I wasn't gonna drink anymore. The game got so in-triguin', though, that I finally ordered another one.

"A new hand started with five men sittin' in, and

Willie let me see his hole card. It was an ace, and the first card face-up was an ace, too. The fella straight across from Willie was dealin'. He got a king up. There was several dollars bet—I don't remember how much on that first card. Everybody stayed in the hand, so the dealer dealt a third card around the table.

"Willie got another ace. Three cards, and Willie had three aces. Nobody else even had a pair showin' on the board. Willie bet twenty dollars, and everybody else threw in twenty, too. I was amazed, because any fool could see that the next highest card on the table was a king, and there wasn't but one of them. I didn't under-stand the finer points of the game, but I knew that the best anybody could have would've been a pair. Meanwhile, Willie already had three aces. By now I was really excited. I could just see Willie rakin' in all that money.

"The dealer dealt a fourth card around the table, and as he went, everybody made a pair of some kind— a pair of fours, tens, or what have ya. Willie only got a deuce, but his pair of aces still entitled him to bet first, and like a crazy man he up and said too loudly, 'One hundred dollars.'

"There was two people between him and the dealer, and both put in a hundred dollars. I was so taken by that big pile of money and how casually people it on the table that I didn't know what to do. Why, there was banks back in Georgia didn't have that much money.

"When the bet got to the dealer, he called Willie's hundred and raised him a hundred. The fella to the left called both bets and laid two hundred dollars on the table. Now it was Willie's turn to bet again.

"He counted his money, which was an even two hundred dollars, then called the dealer's raise and raised him a hundred. That left Willie without a dime. The two fellas next to him got outa the game. Now it was the dealer's turn. He counted out a hundred dollars and put it in the pot, then looked over at the bare table in front of Willie and said, 'I raise ya two hundred.' With that, he dropped two hundred more dollars in the pot.

"By now the other folks in the room had all gathered around the table. It was so smoky you could hardly see. There was little conversations goin' on here and there as they watched, but when the dealer raised Willie two hundred dollars you coulda heard a pin drop in the place. It was plain to see that Willie didn't have any money on the table. The fella on the dealer's left called the two hundred, and now it was back to Willie.

"I was new to this thing and didn't know what was goin' to happen next. Suddenly Willie turned around to me and said, 'Will, how much money ya got?'

"'I've got $120. That's all,' I told him.

"'Will ya loan it to me on my hand?' he asked.

"Well, I'd worked the whole summer and that's all I had in the world, that and ol' Jack, my saddle, and my gun. I knew the dealer must've had three kings. The other fella that stayed in had a pair of tens showin', and probably one in the hole, but he wouldn't draw the fourth one 'cause one of the fellas that folded earlier had had it. There was another king and another ace in the deck, I figured, though I didn't know for sure. None of those cards had showed up durin' the deal. But mainly, I knew that Willie didn't have anything to pay me back with if I let him have the money I'd worked so hard for. That put me in a terrible sweat.

"About that time the dealer spoke up and said, 'He ain't got but $120. I bet two hundred. Where's the other eighty comin' from?' Willie looked at me again and said, 'Will, you've got a 1400-pound mule. You'll put him up on this hand, won't ya?'

"Now I was really in a sweat. Here was the only fella I know this side of Georgia askin' me to put up the mule I stole from Pa, not to mention my whole life's savings, against some pasteboards in a poker game. I looked Willie in the eye and said, 'What if ya lose?'

"'I ain't gonna lose,' he answered.

"'Yeah, but what if ya do?'

"'I'll pay ya back,' he promised.

"I guess the liquor was takin' it's effect by then, because I said, 'All right, Willie. Ol' Jack is worth $250. That plus $120 is $370. But if ya lose, you're gonna owe me, and I'm gonna collect. Is that clear?'

"'Yeah, Will,' he replied, 'but don't worry, 'cause I ain't gonna lose.'

"About that time the dealer spoke up again, 'I don't know if I wanna play against a supposed 1400-pound, $250 mule belonging to somebody who ain't even in the game. That's a pretty dumb proposition as far as I'm concerned.' By now I was feelin' my oats pretty good, and said, 'Listen, son-of-a-bitch. The mule is worth $250, and Willie here just called your bet of two hundred. That leaves $150 change.' I stood up, and I guess me bein' young, strong, and six-feet-six tall made an impression on the man, 'cause he said, 'Okay, that means between the two of ya you've got $150 credit left in this game.' I sat back down when I heard that.

"The dealer dealt a ten to the man on his left, and a deuce to Willie, givin' him three aces and two deuces. He dealt himself another king, givin' him three showin'. When he finished, he laid the deck down in the middle of the money and said, 'Three kings is high, and you ain't got but $150 credit, little man, so I'm gonna bet $150 right into you and right into the three tens.' Then he said, 'It's your call or raise, three tens. All the little man can do is call with the mule that ain't here.'

"The man with the tens said, 'All I've got is $160, so I'm just gonna call.'

"'That's all I can do, too,' Willie said, and with that he pulled his hole card out and showed the dealer aces full of deuces.

"The dealer shot a crooked little grin across the table at Willie, then turned up the fourth king. As he reached over and drug all that money to his side of the table, he looked at me and said, 'Georgia boy, I'll pick up my mule first thing in the morning if ya don't mind.' I looked at him, and I wanted to kill him. I looked at Willie, and I wanted to ring his neck.

"Just then Willie stood up and stared at the dealer. 'You cheated me,' he said in a tense voice. 'That king was on the bottom of the deck earlier. I saw it.' When he said that, I jumped up too, but about that time we heard a shotgun breechin'. I looked over, and there stood the owner of the bar with a double-barrel shotgun pointed at us."

Bottom Dealin'
and Sinkin' Lower

"A murmur ran through the crowd as the owner stood there. Then he spoke.

"'I run a peaceful place, and that's the way it's gonna stay,' he said. 'This establishment is closed as of now. If you got a problem with anybody, you take it off this property. You can do anything ya want to, as long as ya do it somewhere else. Now, I want everybody to file outa here in an orderly fashion, and I want ya to do it now.'

"I grabbed Willie and dragged him out the front door. When we got outside, I asked him what did he mean, the guy had cheated him. 'I swear to ya, Will, that last card he got—the king of clubs—was on the bottom of the deck when he started dealin', he said. 'He flashed it once accidentally durin' the hand. He pulled that king off the bottom of the deck, and that means he's been dealin' bottoms all night long.'

"Well, I'd never heard that kind of talk before," Uncle Will said, "but I knew about cheatin', and I sure didn't like somebody doin' it to me. So when the dealer man walked by, I reached over, grabbed him by the collar, and walked him across the road, away from the owner's shotgun. I had the dealer in one hand and Willie in the other. When I turned to confront him, though, the dealer stuck a .45 right up under my nose. I could see the muzzle shinin' in the moonlight. I tell ya, nephew, that gun looked as big as a cannon.

"'Big boy,' he said, 'I let ya drag me across the road so I wouldn't have to kill ya in front of witnesses, but there ain't no witnesses now.' I froze, fully expectin' a bullet to come roarin' out of that barrel at any moment. The last thought that ran through my mind was, 'Dear Lord, I'm too young to go now.'

"He didn't pull the trigger, though. Instead, he said, 'Probably the smartest thing I could do right now is blow your brains out, but I'm not gonna do that unless ya make me. But I'll tell ya what I am gonna do. I'm gonna walk you and your half-pint friend down to the ferry landin', and you're gonna get on that ferry and cross Big Muddy. And if I ever, *ever*, catch ya back in Vicksburg, I'll do what I oughta do right now while I got the chance. Now, start walkin'.'

"We marched down to the ferry and waited 'til it was about ready to pull out. Then the dealer said, 'Boys, it's time you was on your way to Louisiana. It's best ya don't ever come back to Vicksburg. But here ya go,' he continued, handin' me a piece of paper. 'I believe in givin' every man a fair chance.' It was so dark that I couldn't see what it was, but I took it anyway.

"As the barge shoved off with us aboard, he called out a final piece of advice. 'Big boy,' he yelled, 'ya better watch that half-pint friend of yours. He's gonna get ya killed one day. You're lucky it wasn't in Vicksburg.'

"When we got to the Louisiana side of the Mississippi, we walked into the ferry office, and by the light of a kerosene lamp I looked at what the dealer had stuck in my hand. It was a ten dollar bill. I showed it to Willie and said, 'Now ya only owe me $360.'

"'You'll get your money,' he replied defensively. I wanted to know when and how.

"'Back in the '90's,' he said, 'I helped build a railroad through a place called Monroe, Louisiana. The best I recollect, it's about fifty miles west of here. We can walk there in two days. I remember somethin' peculiar about that railroad that'll help us get your money back.'

"It was four in the mornin' when we left the ferry station. Around noon we came to a little town called Waverly and looked for a place to eat right away, 'cause I was powerful hungry by then. There was a neat little house with a sign hangin' outside that read, 'Sally's Boarding House. Dinner Plates, 25 cents,' so we went in and sat down to one of the better meals that I'd had since I left home. It cost me fifty cents, of course, because Willie didn't have any money. When we got through eatin', we headed on up the road toward Monroe. I told Willie I only had enough money to buy nineteen more meals like that, so he better be thinkin' hard about how he was gonna get my money back.

"He stopped in the middle of the road and said, 'I'll tell ya how we're gonna get your money back, Will. We're gonna rob a bank.' I couldn't believe my ears! 'Willie, you crazy fool!' I screamed. 'That dealer was right last night when he said you was gonna get me killed. I didn't think much about it then, but I believe it now.'

"'No, Will,' he said calmly, 'he was wrong. How old are you? Fifteen or sixteen? Well, I'm thirty-three—more'n twice your age. I've already robbed three banks, and I ain't never spent a day in the penitentiary. Ya see, it's all in how ya plan the job. That's the reason I told ya I helped build the railroad track through Monroe. Now I'm gonna explain why that's important.

"'Monroe's a good-sized town with a good-sized bank. There's a big bluff back up behind the town that kind of skirts the edge of the Piney Wood Mountains, and the railroad runs along the edge of that bluff. When the freight train comes through there it has to slow down to a crawl because the grade is so steep. In fact, a man walkin' alongside that train can climb aboard real easy and go right on to Shreveport.'

"'What does a train slowin' down where ya can walk alongside it got to do with robbin' a bank?' I asked.

"'If ya rob a bank, ya gotta have a sure-fire way to get away. Otherwise you'll end up servin' time. We're gonna use the train to get away after we rob the bank.'

"Well, I couldn't believe it, but I found myself taken by this little squirt's idea. I tried to tell myself to get away from him before what the dealer said came true, but I just couldn't. My conscience was wrestlin' with Ol' Ebo. Ol' Ebo was Uncle Will's name for the Devil. I never did know the origin of it, whether it came from the word "ebony" or something similar. But to Uncle Will, Ol' Ebo was a real being who haunted his every step.

I knew what this little runt was proposin' was preposterous, wrong, and illegal, but I loved the thought of walkin' into that bank with a gun and takin' money from folks. It just sent a shiver up my spine. I'd read stories about Jesse James doing that sort of thing, and it always downright appealed to me, even if I knew it was wrong.

"Somewhere on that dusty road in Louisiana I made a decision I'm not sure a fella can ever turn away from. I don't know if I ever really *wanted* to turn away from it. Certainly not while I was young and felt good, that's for sure. But somewhere between Waverly and Monroe, I made a pact with Ol' Ebo, and even at this late day I'm still payin' for it.

"It took us two and a half days to make it to Monroe. When we got there, we sat around in the shade and watched the bank 'til closin' time to get an idea of how things worked. After that we headed up to the woods behind town and watched the freight train come chuggin' up the bluff. Sure enough, it almost came to a stop, just the way Willie said it would, before it got on over the hill and took off.

"We bought soda crackers, pork and beans, and sardines to stretch our money, then went back up to the woods and laid there all night. Three trains passed while we was there. One came by just after good dark. That's the one we was gonna catch after we pulled the robbery. We only had five dollars left, which wouldn't even buy a good gun, much less any mules or horses to get away on after we did the job, but once again Willie had the ready answer.

"He said ya couldn't be a good highwayman and be lazy. Ya had to be willin' to work. His plan was to get a good ways from Monroe before we did any meanness, so we walked about ten miles north of Monroe until we found a prosperous lookin' farm. We climbed up into the woods above the house so we could look down on all the comin' and the goin'. There was people in the fields plowin' and smoke risin' out of the stove flue where they was cookin' dinner.

"About midday they stopped plowin' and brought their mules to the house. Willie said, 'You stay here while I go down and meet these folks and get a look around the place. Maybe we can get our mules and guns right here.'

"He cut across a little hill, got back in the road, and walked up to the house just as the menfolk was puttin' the mules in the barn to feed. As I watched, he walked up and started talkin' to 'em, then went in the house with 'em. Once they was inside, I took a nap, knowin' that Willie would fill me in on the details when he got back.

"Around mid-afternoon Willie kicked me on the bottom of the foot and woke me up. 'I think we hit the jackpot!' he said excitedly . 'I asked those folks if they had a job for a fella with no family and no place to stay, and they said they did. I told 'em I'm from the Piney Wood country in Arkansas, so's when we steal their things, they'll go lookin' for us up north, not south towards Monroe. I'm gonna spend the night with 'em tonight and start work tomorrow. You just stay here. Tomorrow night I'll get our guns and horses.'"

Robbin'

Uncle Will must have noticed how engrossed I was in his story, because he suddenly stopped and asked, "Nephew, why is all this so important to ya?"

"Uncle Will," I said, "ya know in all my growin' up, half the family feared ya and the other half hated ya. You beat me out of enough money when I was younger that I shoulda hated ya, too, but I never did. When I was a kid, the old folks would be talking about you when I came in the room, and they would stop. You were such a mystery, Nobody would tell me what I wanted to know about you, and I'd just like to understand ya better.

"Besides, right now I'm fifteen goin' on sixteen, the same age as you when you were doin' all this. I've never been out of Carroll County, and there you were already nearly to Texas. That's excitin'! And you talk about makin' a pact with Ol' Ebo. I can't figure why anybody would wanna do that."

"Let me explain about making a pact with Ol' Ebo, how that's done," he answered. "Ya see, it ain't like ya sit down face-to-face with him and sign a contract. That ain't the way it works at all. Ol' Ebo just nibbles around the edge of your conscience. In fact, ya hardly know he's there. Then when the proposition comes along to do somethin' ya shouldn't do, it don't seem like any big deal.

109

He hesitated a moment as if trying to think of something to help explain his point, and his eye came to rest on an old sticky tape hanging overhead that he used to catch flies. "Ya see that fly that just landed on the edge of the paper?" he said. "Watch him. He's gonna put one foot down on that sticky stuff, and it ain't gonna seem like no big thing. Then he's gonna put another foot down to pull the first one out, and neither foot's gonna come out. The poor dumb bug is then gonna put all his feet down, and he's gonna be stuck for good.

"Now he's frantically wavin' his wings, tryin' to get loose, but it won't help. He's gonna die right there. Now he knows it's a big deal, but to him the first foot and the second foot wasn't anything to worry about. That's the way it is with Ol' Ebo, nephew. Ya have to constantly watch your step, 'cause one foot at a time is how ya make your deal with him.

"As soon as Willie told me we was gonna stick up that bank, I got tingly all over. That was the first foot. It was a thrill, and I felt sorta giddy right away. Then we started makin' plans, and I jumped right in.

"There's somethin' about me that's just made that way. I always jump into things with both feet. But I do think there's somethin' I didn't know, and that's how hard it'd be to stop makin' bad choices once I got started. I don't think I knew that. As a matter of fact, I don't guess I even thought about it."

"Go on, Uncle Will. Tell me how it came out."

"Well, let's see. Where was I?"

"You were waitin' up in the woods above the farmhouse while Willie went down to work with those folks."

"Oh yeah. Well, it was a lazy summer afternoon, and I got mighty bored with nothin' to do. My mind drifted back to Ma and Pa diggin' in that red Georgia dirt, half starvin' to death, while here I was fixin' to rob a bank and beat honest folks outa their money. Instead of it botherin' me, though, I got a euphoric rush just thinkin' about bustin' into the lobby of that bank with a shotgun. I shoulda been scared, but I wasn't. I wanted to do it. That, I don't understand to this day.

"A while after dark, Willie snuck back up the hill to bring me a blanket and do some more plannin'. 'I was thinkin' this afternoon that I'd have ya steal the horses and guns one night after everybody went to bed,' he said. 'I'd stay around a couple of days to avoid suspicion, then join ya later. But if I do that, they're liable to go to Monroe or any place lookin' for ya.

"'If I disappear the same time the horses do, though, they're gonna head north toward Arkansas first 'cause I told 'em that's where I'm from, and that'll give us more time to take care of business in Monroe. So, you keep on watch. Tomorrow night sometime, I'll be up here with horses and whatever else we need. You stay outa sight 'til then.'

"With that, Willie left, and I was on my own again. About twenty-four hours later I heard him makin' his way back up the bluff and went out to meet him. He had a couple of horses with good-lookin' saddles and saddlebags, plus a shotgun and a pistol for each of us. Standin' there leaned up against the horses, smellin' the fine leather of the saddles, I felt like I had the whole world in the palm of my hand. I had no reason to feel so wonderful 'cause I was about to commit a terrible crime, but I did.

"'Let's go,' Willie said, and we climbed in the saddles and headed for Monroe. When we got there, we climbed up the bluff above the railroad track and settled in for the night.

"Willie's plan was simple. We'd ride into town just as the bank opened at ten o'clock and be the first ones there. Then we'd clean out the safe, tie up the workers, and ride outa town before the robbery was discovered. Once we was outa town, we'd hide the saddles under an old bridge, whip the horses so they'd look like runaways to anybody who saw 'em, then circle back and spend the rest of the day in the woods just above where we planned to catch the train.

"Nephew," Uncle Will said, "I could hardly sleep that night because of the thrill of what we was fixin' to do. Why, even to this day the feelin' of anticipation I experienced still sends a shiver up my mine. Of course, I wish I'd never gone through with it, but I also wish I could just once get that same feelin' about doin' somethin' honest.

"There's one thing special I remember about that night," he continued. "When I did fall asleep, I dreamed I was a huge eagle, flyin' over the countryside. I could see for miles. I'd dive and swoop down, and people would look up at me and point. It was a wonderful dream that I've never forgotten. A lot of my dreams nowadays I dream over and over, but I never had that one again. I think it was all a part of that heady feelin' I got from decidin' to become a bank robber.

"Anyway, the next morning went pretty much the way Willie planned it. We walked the horses down Main Street without anybody payin' attention to us and got to the bank just as they was raisin' the shades on the door. I slipped the shotgun out of the rifle-sling on the saddle and held it down to my side like it was a walkin' stick 'til we got through the door. Inside, there was two old men. One of 'em had a little cap with the green plastic bill that tellers always wore. The other one was dressed in a pin-striped suit. I figured he was the president.

"We was in so fast and so smooth that neither of 'em even noticed. Willie turned around and pulled the shades back down while I drew the shotgun up and told the two men to empty everything in the safe into a couple of sacks that would fit in our saddlebags. I thought I'd probably tremble and not be able to talk, but it wasn't that way. With that double-barrel shotgun in my hand, I felt powerful. Nothin' or nobody could stop me.

"We wasn't in that bank more than two minutes. We cleaned it out, tied up the men, left the shade down, and locked the bolt as we went out. Then we climbed on our horses and started walkin' 'em outa town. I think I held my breath near to the whole way. Willie didn't look at me even once and I didn't look at Willie. We just looked straight ahead.

"We was well outa town before we heard church bells ringin' back in Monroe. They was goin' for all they was worth, and we knew then that the robbery had been discovered.

"Five minutes later we reached the bridge we was lookin' for, unsaddled the horses, then whacked 'em across the rump and watched as they galloped outa sight. Next, we climbed down under the bridge and started countin' our money. There was just over $5000. Willie handed me my half and said, 'There, Will, you've been paid back. Now let's head back to the train.'

"I picked up the shotgun, but he said, 'No, leave it. We don't need any guns.'

"'I'm gonna at least take the pistol,' I replied.

"'No, don't take any guns. You take a gun, and somebody's gonna get killed — and it could be you. Leave the guns. We got the money. That's what we wanted.' I did as he said, though I wasn't convinced he was right.

"It was probably a little after eleven o'clock when we got settled down to wait for the train. That left us a good ten hours before the freight we wanted came through that night. It was one of the longest ten hours I ever spent in my life. Here I was with all that money, and I couldn't do anything with it. I couldn't even move. I just had to sit and wait for that ol' train."

Slow Motion Getaway

"About thirty minutes after dark, we began to hear voices in the distance and see a light flashin' through the trees," Uncle Will went on. "We stood very quiet and listened, and pretty soon it became obvious there was a bunch of men with kerosene lanterns and dogs workin' their way through the woods. For the first time that day, I felt fear. I started wishin' I'd brought that gun Willie didn't want me to have.

"As the men got nearer to us, I could hear 'em talkin' to the dogs, encouragin' 'em on, and I could just picture in my mind's eye a pack of bloodhounds runnin' us to ground.

"'We gotta do somethin'!' I whispered to Willie. 'That's a posse comin' for us!'

"'I don't think so,' he answered. 'I think it must be a bunch of coon hunters. They're north of the railroad like we are. Let's give 'em five more minutes, and if they keep comin' towards us we'll cross over to the other side. I don't want those dogs pickin' up our scent, 'cause even if those men are coon hunters, they'll have guns, and how are we gonna explain bein' up here?'

"Suddenly the hounds started barkin' like they was hot on the trail of somethin'. We could tell from the sound of things that they was headin' away from us, though, so we stayed put as the lanterns grew dim and faded outa sight.

"A few minutes later we heard the train comin' that was gonna get us outa Monroe. As it chugged up that steep grade it went slower and slower, just like it'd done two nights earlier when we first checked it out. We hung back in the woods 'til it was even with us, then slipped down the embankment and climbed aboard a boxcar through a side door that somebody had been kind enough to leave open. Soon as we sat down inside, Willie grabbed my arm and said excitedly, 'We pulled it off, Will—we're home free!'

"'Not yet ya ain't!' came a voice from the corner of the boxcar. It made both of us nearly jump out of our skins.

"I sat there for what seemed like an eternity wondering who said that and what it meant. It was as if whoever was hidin' there in the corner had been expectin' us. Finally Willie said, 'Who's there?'

"'You wouldn't be the boys that robbed our little bank today, would ya?' the voice replied. 'That was a right nice piece of work. My congratulations. But before ya get any more bright ideas, I want ya to know I can see your outline in the light of the door. That's why I left it open. I want both of ya to stay right where ya are, 'cause if ya make a move toward me, I'll have to shoot, and this twelve-gage shotgun is gonna make a terrible hole in ya.

"'But like I say,' the voice went on, 'I wanna congratulate you boys on a pretty piece of work. And if I do say so myself, I have to congratulate myself for figurin' out your plan. In fact, that's why I'm here. I'm cuttin' myself in on the job, sorta like a partner, so to speak.

"'Ya see, after we found the guns and the saddles under the bridge, we also found the horses. So I asked myself why two bank robbers would abandon their mounts only a few miles outa town. They musta had a better way of gettin' away, that's why. But what on earth could it be?

"'Then it came to me. Ya see, a few years back I helped lay this railroad track. I remember thinkin' at the time that this bluff was awful steep. Today when I studied the evidence, I told myself, "I betcha those fellas plan to catch that freight tonight when it slows down and be in Shreveport by mornin'."'

"As the voice continued talkin', Willie raised up just enough to get in my ear and whispered, 'This train ain't movin' fast enough to hurt us, so when I punch ya with my elbow, just roll outa here like a rubber ball and hit the ground runnin' away from the train. We'll find us another way outa this town.'

"And that's what we did. When he elbowed me, we both tumbled out backwards. Just as I cleared the edge of the boxcar, I heard a shotgun blast and felt one buckshot catch my right ear. If ya look, nephew, you'll see there's a little nick in it even now." I leaned over for a closer look, and sure enough, there was a piece missin' from his ear. "That put wings on my feet, I guarantee," he said.

"We left the car from the right side just as the train started around a curve to the left, so our mystery man lost sight of us for a few seconds. It was a long train and really hadn't got to rollin' yet, so I grabbed Willie and said, 'Let's jump in another car,' and we did just that.

But this time we made sure it was good and empty before we started congratulatin' ourselves.

"Willie said, 'Will, if that fella was smart enough to figure out what we did, there's bound to be other folks that can do the same.

That means we better get off this train the first time it slows down again. I don't think we oughta go all the way to Shreveport. We can't risk it. There's a town up ahead fifty miles or so named Minden, as I recall. It should be the first town we come to of any size. As soon as we pull in there, we best get off and head north.'

"He stopped talkin' a minute as if he was catchin' his breath for the first time, then said, 'I'd sure like to know who that smart-ass was that was hidin' in that boxcar. He was one gutsy son-of-a-bitch.'

"'I'd like to know how that dealer man in Vicksburg figured you out so well,' I replied. 'I'd like to know how he knew you was gonna get me killed.'

"'I've been a runt all my life,' Willie answered. 'When you're a little man, ya gotta do things to make up for it. Ya gotta have more courage, more guts, and more nerve than any big fella. People just natural-born pay attention to somebody like you, Will, but nobody pays attention to a little man unless he forces 'em to. So that's why I take chances sometimes. That's why I spit in people's eye now and then.

"'Anyway, what are you complainin' about?' he asked. 'Ya got $2500 in your pocket, more than ya ever saw in your whole life, and only a little nick outa your ear to show for it. You stick with me, Will, and I'll make somethin' out of ya, I promise. That dealer man didn't know nothin'. He was just tryin' to make sure ya stayed outa Vicksburg, that's all.'

"We sat and talked a while longer as that ol' freight train rumbled on through the night. Now and then we saw a house with the lamps still burnin' in the window, but otherwise it was dark as pitch. Willie finally fell asleep, but I was too fired up. I laid there countin' the bumps as the wheels crossed the joints in the track, tryin' to figure out how many bumps made a mile. I didn't have any idea how to judge that, but it did help pass the time a bit. Every once in a while I'd feel of that little nick in my ear and think about how close that shot came to splatterin' my brains on the side of the boxcar. No sir, there wasn't no sleep for me that night.

"Around four or five in the mornin', it started gettin' light, so I woke Willie up and told him we better bail out the first chance we got. I felt sure that everybody in the whole state of Louisiana must 'a had a description of a fifteen-year-old giant and his midget of a sidekick by that time.

"About that time the train pulled off on a side track and slowed to about ten miles an hour. Up ahead I could make out what I guessed to be the town of Minden. A minute or two later we curved around to the left, which meant if the mystery man still happened to be in that front boxcar, he couldn't see us if we bailed out now. So I grabbed Willie and said, 'Let's go!'

"We hit the ground runnin' and ducked into a patch of woods alongside the tracks. When we was pretty sure nobody was followin' us, I said, 'Willie,

119

we're gonna have to split up. We just make too visible a pair, especially when I know they must be lookin' for us all over the southwest.'

"'No, no, Will,' he responded in a reassurin' tone, 'we don't need to split up. You need me and I need you. We just don't need to be seen together, that's all, at least not in any town that's got a police department. What we'll do is, you'll go into a store alone and buy somethin' to eat, or I'll go in alone and buy somethin'. They probably have a description of us at the telegraph office and the police station in most of the towns around here, but outside of that we should be safe.'

"What he said made sense, so we headed out as near north as we could through the woods, stayin' to high ground. I knew that somewhere to the north of us was Arkansas, and I was beginnin' to realize that Willie was familiar with the territory, too.

"A little before noon we came to a dusty little town called Homer. There was a blacksmith's shop, a general store, and a bank of all things. We stopped under a shade tree about fifty feet from the blacksmith's shop, and Willie said, 'Will, we need to find some way to get around. If we get caught walkin' and they arrest us for vagrancy or search us or anything, we're gonna have a lot of explainin' to do. But if we've got a horse and some suitcases and clothes, it's gonna make us more respectable. Besides, we need to get as far away from Monroe as we can, and the quicker the better.

"'I'm gonna go up to this smithy and tell him you're my simple-minded son,' he continued. All I want you to say is, "Duh." No matter what I say, you just look stupid, grin, and say, "Duh." Okay?' I argued for a minute or two 'cause I didn't particularly like the idea of playin' the village idiot, but he was a good deal older than me and we sure couldn't play like *he* was *my* son. So I told him okay, but to get us some transportation and do it quick 'cause I didn't intend to play a simpleton for long.

"We walked over to the blacksmith and Willie said, 'Howdy. Say, me and my boy here was travelin' west to Texas when our horses dropped on us a few miles back. I figure they musta gotten hold of some poison water. Anyway, we're plumb wore out walkin', and I'm lookin' to buy a horse and buggy if I can find one at the right price. That beats sittin' in the saddle any day. Do ya know where I might find a good horse and buggy at a reasonable price?'

"The blacksmith looked me and Willie both over real good from head to toe, then asked suspiciously, 'He's your boy?'

"'Yeah, he's my boy,' Willie replied. 'He's an idiot, but he's the only son I got.' When he said 'idiot', I said, 'Duh.'

"'Yeah,' Willie went on, 'I've studied the history of my family back almost two hundred years, and he's the only idiot in the bunch. But in every life a little rain must fall.'

"'That's a damn shame,' the blacksmith said, shakin' his head from side to side. 'He's big enough to go bear-huntin' with a switch. Too bad he ain't got sense enough to do nothin', ain't it?'

"'Yeah, I really think he took after his ma's side of the family, bless her soul, may she rest in peace,' Willie answered real sad-like. 'Weren't none of her people too bright. But he's all I got left, and I try to make the best of it. We're both tuckered out from ridin' them horses all the way from South Carolina, though. That's why I'd be interested in a rig.'

"I thought Willie was enjoying my stupidity a bit too much, but once again I said, 'Duh.'

"The blacksmith seemed to take pity on us, 'cause he said, 'I just happen to have a fine horse and buggy I took in on a deal with a fella last week. The horse is out there in the feedlot behind the barn, and the buggy's in the shed. I'll take five hundred dollars for the horse, buggy, and harness. You look it over, and if ya like it, I'll be happy to sell it to ya.'

"We walked out in the lot and both examined the horse real close, then Willie took the bridle from a nail on the side of the barn and led her around a bit. She appeared to be sound in every way. He put the gear on, hitched her up to the buggy, and drove around in the yard, then pulled up alongside the blacksmith and said, 'I can buy this same rig in South Carolina for three hundred dollars.'

"'Damn shame you ain't in South Carolina, ain't it?' the smithy replied matter-of-factly. 'Here in Homer, Louisiana, it's gonna cost ya five hundred.'

"'I'll go three-fifty, and that's my last offer,' Willie shot back.

"'Go put my horse back where you got her,' came the answer.

"Willie thought for a moment, then said in a self-righteous tone, 'My kind sir, there's one thing I failed to tell ya. I'm a minister of the gospel, and it would help me spread the word of the Lord a good deal faster if I owned this horse and buggy.'

"The fella looked at Willie for a long time before he spoke again. 'Preacher man,' he finally said, 'you're gonna have to come up with five hundred dollars for that horse and buggy, or else you're gonna have to be satisfied with your present pace of spreadin' the word of the Lord. Now pardon me, but I've got work to do.'

"'Write me a receipt,' Willie answered with a snort.

"After we left the blacksmith's shop, I asked Willie about the wisdom of travelin' in a horse and buggy. Wouldn't it be a lot faster for us to get away from the scene of the crime if we took a train, I wondered? Willie argued —and I guess it made sense—that we needed to be at least a hundred miles from Monroe before we boarded a train, 'cause news naturally traveled faster up and down the railroad tracks. So we decided to go north for three or four days in the rig, then sell it and get our money back. I gave him $250, which was half the purchase price, and we became formal partners in a horse and buggy.

"We spent that night in Haynesville, Louisiana. Willie liked bein' a preacher so well, he started takin' on a pious attitude and convinced me to keep actin' like I was his idiot son, at least 'til we could get well away from where we'd robbed the bank.

"Late the next afternoon, we pulled into Magnolia, Arkansas, about a hundred to a hundred-and-fifty miles from Monroe. It was Wednesday, and after dinner the lady who ran the boardin' house where we took a room announced that any of the people there was welcome to walk with her to the church for Wednesday night prayer meetin'.

"I don't know if it was a measure of thanksgivin' or just another way to play his little game, but Willie told the lady he'd be glad to go with her. As a matter of fact, he said, he was a minister of the gospel and would be willin' to say a few words durin' the service if they'd like. She was delighted. I guess more or less to make conversation, she turned to Willie along the way and said, 'Isn't it strange, Brother Kilgore, for the father to be called Willie and the son to be called Will? It seems it ought to be the other way around.'

"As usual, Willie was ready with an explanation. 'As a matter of fact, madam,' he replied, 'I'm William Andrew Kilgore, Jr. My father was William Andrew Kilgore, Sr., and Will here is William Andrew Kilgore, III.'"

"'Ya see, ma'am,' Willie told the lady, 'When I was growin' up, my *daddy* was Will and *I* was Willie, which is certainly the way you'd reckon it to be. When Will here came along I gave him the family name to carry on after me. Of course, I had no way of knowin' he was gonna grow up to be an idiot and put an end to the great name of Kilgore. But it's the will of the Lord, and who am I to question the will of the Lord?'

"I wanted to grab him and shake his eye teeth out," Uncle Will said, half-laughing and half-growling, "but that woulda given us away, so I didn't really have any choice except to stand there and say, 'Duh.' My day would come, though. I promised myself that.

"When we got to the little church, I sat and listened to Willie preach. I guess I listened to it better than any sermon I'd ever heard in my life. I was right fascinated. I believe I'd have been as taken with 'Brother Kilgore' as those folks were if I hadn't known that he'd robbed a bank just the week before. The people there who *didn't* know he was a bank robber were mightily moved, however. In fact, the little congregation gathered together in a corner and had a serious discussion after the meetin' ended, then approached Willie with the proposition of him becomin' the minister of their church. They'd just lost their former minister, they explained, and thought Willie would make a wonderful replacement.

"Willie told 'em he'd have to decline. He said he had business further on east, but if he could ever find a place where he felt good about somebody takin' care of his idiot son—which, he said real dramatic-like, was his greatest cross to bear—they might look up someday and see him come ridin' back. For now, he told 'em, he needed to get to the nearest railroad station; he had business back east.

"Of course, Willie just said that. We both knew we was goin' west. But if there was a train goin' east, more than likely there'd be one goin' west, too. They told Willie we needed to go on to Camden, Arkansas, 'cause we could get a train goin' from there to almost anywhere, so we got up before sunrise the next day, hitched up the horse, and headed for Camden.

"Along the way, I asked Willie where he learned to preach like that, what with all the time he'd spent robbin' banks and workin' on the railroad. He told me that up until he was fourteen years old he had to go to church every Sunday, and a Baptist church at that. He said it looked like the preacher man managed to live pretty well without ever doin' any real work, so he practiced alone out in the fields until he'd developed the gift for himself. 'You need to learn how to preach the Word, too, Will,' he concluded. 'Ya just never know when it might come in handy.'

"For the next few hours I practiced my preachin'. Willie would tell me I needed to put more emphasis here or less there, and by the time we got to Camden I think I coulda passed for a minister of the gospel. One thing's for sure, I told Willie in no uncertain terms that I didn't intend to play his idiot son any longer.

"We pulled into Camden around nightfall and found a mule barn to put up our horse. Willie told the owner that we'd be wantin' to sell the rig come mornin', and to pass the word along to anyone he thought might be interested. We needed to catch a train to Memphis 'cause he'd been called to serve a church there, Willie explained, and the buggy would never get us there on time.

"The next mornin' we asked the fella if he'd been able to find anybody interested in the rig. He said he had an offer of three hundred dollars. Willie immediately began weepin' and wailin' and askin' how anyone could take advantage of a poor minister of the gospel that way. 'Why, that rig's worth at least five hundred dollars,' he cried.

"'Well, Reverend, ya don't have to sell it,' the barn owner replied. 'You can drive on in to Memphis. Of course, you'll be about a week late, but you'll still get there. Besides, you're probably gonna need a horse and buggy when you get to town.'

"As I stood there and watched Willie tryin' to get rid of that horse and buggy, one thought came to me: He might be a good preacher and a fine actor, but he was sure a lousy horse trader.

"Finally in desperation Willie said, 'Go ahead and pay me the three hundred. I told 'em I'd be there next Sunday if not providentially hindered, and I'm a man of my word.'

"'I'll need your signature on the bill of sale, plus some identification,' replied the barn owner. The request for identification made me real nervous, but Willie calmly reached into his hatband and pulled out a tattered business card that read, 'W. A Kilgore, Ordained Minister of the Gospel. Licensed to perform weddings, funerals, and baptisms in the state of South Carolina. Ordained in the Year of Our Lord 1899, Charleston, South Carolina.' He signed the receipt as Reverend Kilgore, counted his money twice, then turned to me and said, 'Let's go.'

"We got to the railroad station just as they was announcin' the train to Texarkana, Texas, so we purchased two tickets and climbed aboard. As the train started movin', I felt a great sense of relief that we was finally on our way.

"Late that afternoon when we pulled into Texarkana, we immediately walked into the depot and looked at the timetable. Accordin' to it, the next train left for Dallas, Texas, at 6:30 PM. That gave us about an hour and a half to take care of some business.

"During the trip from Texarkana, we'd made several decisions. For one thing, we decided to take a sleeper to Dallas so we could rest up. We also agreed to continue the father and son act, since it had worked so well. Besides, it was a lot easier to explain than two strangers of such different ages travelin' together. So, he was to be William A. Kilgore Jr., nicknamed Willie, and I was William A. Kilgore III, nicknamed Will.

"We bought us some luggage, clothes, and had some business cards and luggage tags printed for Willie showin' that he was a minister of the gospel from Charleston, South Carolina. By the time we got back to the railroad station, it was time to board the Pullman to Dallas.

"Since we was feelin' rather rich, we got us a com—partment of our own. We also decided to have supper there in order to be seen by as few people as possible 'til we got further away from Monroe. When the porter came in to change over the seats into beds, a copy of the Shreveport Gazette newspaper dated five days earlier fell out onto the floor of the compartment. It musta been stuck down in the bed. There on the front page was a story that nearly made my eyes pop right out.

"'Bandits rob Monroe bank of $10,000,' screamed the headline. The article went somethin' like this:

"'Mr. Steven Young, vice-president of Monroe's largest bank, The Farmer's and Merchant's Bank, said that two bandits stole $10,189 from the bank today. Mr. Young further stated that the bandits rushed in with double-barrel shotguns at the instant the bank opened, cleaned out the safe, and tied up the cashier and the head teller. The whole operation took less than three minutes, according to Mr. Young, then the bandits just up and vanished into thin air.

"'However, later in the day a posse organized for the purpose of catching the bandits found two saddles and some guns hidden under the Stinking Creek Bridge outside of town, which suggested that the thieves had some method of escape other than horseback. Mr. Young was at a loss to suggest what other means they might have expected to use or did use.

"'Mr. Young described the bandits as a midget and a giant. The giant was a fellow that looked to be only fifteen or sixteen years old but stood well over seven feet tall. The midget appeared to be in his late 30s or early 40s and was well under five feet. If they are still traveling together, they should be easily spotted. Monroe's police department telegraphed ahead to Shreveport authorities and asked them to be on the lookout for such a pair. A lookout for them has also been posted state-wide, as well as over most of Arkansas and eastern Texas.'

"When I finished reading the story, I passed it to Willie without a word. After a few minutes he said angrily, 'I can't believe it! $10,189? Well, we got some embezzler off the hook, that's for sure, and whoever it is must be hopin' we never get caught. I'll lay ya odds it's that vice-president they interviewed, 'cause you sure ain't over seven feet tall, and I ain't under five feet,' he continued. 'He just said that to make sure nobody identified us.'

"We both sat there thinkin' about the situation for a while before Willie said, 'Will, maybe we oughta split up. There's no use in temptin' the Gods.'

"By now I'd grown rather fond of the man, however, and really didn't want us to go our separate ways, so I started tryin' to figure out how we could stay together without it bein' dangerous for us.

"'Willie,' I replied eventually, 'I stole my Pa's best mule when I left Georgia. It was a spur-of-the-moment kinda thing, but I feel bad every time I think about how rotten I treated my own folks.

"'Now, we've got plenty of money, you and I. We could take half of it and buy a section of land in Georgia, put mules and horses on it, and become gentleman farmers. I'd feel a whole lot better if I could make it up to Ma and Pa for the way I done 'em, and I've got a good-lookin' red-headed sister that just might make you a good wife. Whatta ya say? When we get to Dallas, let's buy us a ticket to Kansas City and head back east.'

"I think Willie wanted to stay with me just as bad as I wanted to stay with him, 'cause it didn't take him long to agree to go back to Indian Creek with me. When we got to Dallas, he bought two tickets to Kansas City. I stayed outa sight 'til we boarded the train, 'cause that newspaper story had put the fear of God in me.

"On that long ride, I asked Willie about his family. I'd known him off and on for six months and knew nothin' about his upbringin'. He said he didn't have any family, that he was raised in a Baptist orphanage in New Orleans. He ran away from the orphanage when he was twelve, but they caught him and brought him back. He ran away again when he was fourteen and they never found him.

"He went on to say he'd worked every job known to man—ranchin', railroads, farmin', even pickin' fruit in the citrus orchards of south Texas. He'd also robbed three grocery stores and three banks besides the one we just robbed. He'd been married to three women but left them all after only a few months 'cause they started tryin' to tell him what to do. He'd never divorced any of 'em. He'd told me on the road to Monroe that he was thirty-three, but now he admitted to bein' thirty-eight.

"He also said he'd been in almost every state in the Union except Georgia and that he sorta liked the idea of settlin' down on a farm on Indian Creek and becomin' a gentleman farmer. That pleased me to no end.

"Most of the time Willie was talkin', he had his eyes shut and his head down, but he finally looked me in the eye and said, 'I can do that, Will. I can settle down. You remember what that dealer man told ya about me gettin' you killed, though? Well, you're gonna get *yourself* killed. I noticed how much you loved throwin' that gun on those folks in the bank. It was a big thrill for ya. When ya throw a shotgun on somebody, you've gotta be ready to pull the trigger, and you were. That's what's gonna get ya killed. The difference between you and me, besides the fact that you're big and I'm little, is that you *like* to rob folks, and I never did. If you've got any sense at all you'll never rob anybody else or pick up another gun, 'cause chances are you're gonna get yourself killed. Why? Because ya enjoy it too much.

"'Anyway, like ya said, between the two of us we've

got enough money to buy a good section of land in Georgia. Let's go back, settle down, get married, and raise a family. You say you've got a good-lookin' red-headed sister? I'm ready to go see.'

"Ten days later we got off the train in Tallapoosa, Georgia. I looked over the mules in Barr's Mule Barn, picked out the biggest one they had, and asked how much he cost.

"'I'll take $160,' Barr answered.

"'Sold!' I said. 'How much ya want for that good-lookin' saddle there?' pointin' to a right special beauty in the corner.

"'Sixty.'

"'Sold!' I said again.

"Willie bought himself a big bay mare and saddle, then we both climbed aboard our mounts and headed toward Pa's house so I could make my amends.

"By now it was gettin' on close to Christmas time. There was a cold, east wind blowin', so we stopped, opened up our suitcases, and got out our overcoats. 'I'm not sure I want a farm in Georgia if it's gonna be like this,' he said disgustedly.

"Ma and Pa lived just southwest of Tallapoosa at the time, and we got to their house right about dinner time. Pa had been doin' some fall plowin' and was just takin' the gear off his mule when we rode up.

"He stood lookin' up at me for what seemed like forever, then said, 'Will, it was a bad thing ya did to your Ma and me. A terrible bad thing.' He stopped for a few seconds, then proceeded. 'Now come on in and let's eat some dinner.'"

Prodigal Will

"Nephew," Uncle Will said, interrupting his story, "sometimes I think you're too damn nosy for your own good, and sometimes I wanna tell ya to get lost and get outa my hair. But you're a damn good listener, which is more than I can say for most folks I know.

"Now, as ya may have heard whispered from time to time over the years, I spent a good part of my life in one penitentiary or another. What most people don't know, and what I'm gonna tell you, is what got me there. Ya see, back when these things happened, there was a mess of people who'd have given their right arm to know what went on and who did what.

"Of course, I ain't got much longer on this earth. Most of the people I did harm to are dead and gone; as for the ones that ain't, I done paid my price. When ol' Gabriel toots his horn and calls my name, I figure I'll be dang lucky if there's enough people show up for the funeral to tote me to the grave. I suppose if anybody does show up, it'll be mostly to make sure I'm really dead.

"But I got no reason to lie to you or anybody else any more. So when I'm gone and ya hear somebody talkin' about somethin' I did or didn't do, you can tell 'em that ya know the truth of the matter, 'cause there's one thing that I pledge to you right now: I'm either gonna tell ya the truth, or I ain't gonna tell ya nothin' at all.

"Now, where was I?" he said, coming to the end of his speech. "I get to thinkin' about one thing or another and forget where I am in the story."

"You and Willie had just rode up to your Pa's house. That's where ya stopped."

"So it was, nephew, so it was. Well, I remember that afternoon very, very well. I introduced Willie to Ma, Sis, and Jim, and we sat down to a dinner of collard greens, cornbread, and buttermilk. All the while we was eatin', Pa talked about farmin' and stuff as if I'd never left, even though I'd been gone from home for seven months. He asked Willie what his plans were, and Willie said he was thinkin' about buyin' some land. He told Pa that me and him had worked in the loggin' business out in Arkansas and made quite a bit of money.

"'The ol' mule Will stole from ya got killed,' Willie lied. 'We cut a big tree down on him and killed the sucker. But Will had enough money to buy ya another mule, and that's what he did in Tallapoosa. I'm right proud of the boy for doin' what's right. He said ya got a better mule and saddle now than what he stole from ya. Is that so?'

"'Well, he *looks* as good as ol' Jack,' Pa said, 'but Will took the best saddle I ever owned. It set so comfortable.' That was his only comment on the matter.

"When we finished eatin', Pa shoved his chair back from the table and said, 'Will, take that mule and go plow the back ten acres. I wanna get it listed up and ready for the winter rains. Time's a-wastin' so ya need to get over there now.'

"I was flabbergasted. 'Pa,' I said, not hidin' the shock I felt, 'I just come back from a thousand-mile trip and you're tellin' me to go plow this afternoon in that cold wind?'

"Pa raised his hackles and said, 'Will, when ya put your feet under my table, ya do what I tell ya to do, and I'm tellin' ya to go plow the back ten acres with the one-horse turnin' plow.'

"'You ain't changed a damn bit,' I replied angrily. Then I turned to Willie and asked, 'Can we ride double back to Tallapoosa so I can buy me a horse?'

"'You and your daddy are speakin' some hard words,' he answered cautiously. 'I think ya oughta sit down with him and talk things over.'

"'I done talked all I'm gonna talk,' I snapped. 'Let's go.' Ma and Sis started cryin' and pleadin' with me not to leave. Sis was even hangin' onto my neck. But I wouldn't change my mind. 'No, I'm goin',' I said. 'I know when I ain't wanted, and I ain't wanted here, so I'm leavin'.' I walked out the door and left the mule tied, then Willie and I climbed on his horse and headed back to town.

"By the time we got there it was nigh onto evenin', so we decided to spend the night in town and move on the next day. I'd heard that down in Florida it stayed warm the whole winter, and here at Christmas time that sounded like an awful nice place to be. After a little discussion, we decided we'd go to Miami. That looked on the map about as far south as you could get.

"After supper we went to the depot and checked the timetable. The train we wanted left at eleven the next

morning and arrived two days later. While I bought
two tickets for a Pullman berth, Willie went to sell his
horse back to the mule barn. He got about two-thirds
of what he gave for it the day before, which was about
what I'd come to expect of his horse-tradin'.

"The next mornin' on the way to the depot, I
stopped and bought a deck of cards at a drug store. I
wanted Willie to show me how that dealer man had
managed to cheat us back in Vicksburg. Even though
I had a lot more money now than I'd loaned Willie in
that poker game, I didn't ever want to get cheated out
of it again.

"For nearly two whole days and nights on the trip
to Miami, Willie taught me how to play poker. I was
fas-cinated by the game. But even though Willie knew
all the rules, he wasn't any good at teachin' fancy
dealin'.

"When we finally pulled into Miami, we found a
boardin' house close to the waterfront. I'd always been
interested in the sea, and for the first few weeks after
we got there I just sat and watched the waves roll in
and out. But pretty soon that got borin' and we decided
to inquire about the ships we saw comin' and goin'
every day. Most of them was takin' people back and
forth to Cuba, we found out. Folks said they had all
sorts of gamblin' down there, and nearly all of it legal.
Since passage to Cuba was only twenty-eight dollars,
Willie and I decided to go down, do a little gamblin', and
see how the rest of the world lived.

"Durin' the trip, I played poker night after night
with the same dealer until I got right friendly with

him. In fact, sometimes it'd only be me and him playin'. Now and then when the boss wasn't lookin', he'd show me some amazin' card tricks. One night he told me that if his hands was as big as mine, he could deal a card from anywhere in the deck he wanted. From that moment on I worked at usin' my God-given gifts to beat people outa their money.

"I turned twenty-one in Havana, Cuba. As a matter of fact, we stayed there nearly ten years. Durin' that time, I learned how to make a deck of cards talk. I could deal the bottom, middle, or second card down and drink a quart of liquor at one sittin' without lookin' drunk. When I wasn't playin' in a game, I'd sit in our hotel room and practice. Willie didn't much like the idea of me becomin' a cardshark, though. 'You're learnin' more than ya oughta know,' he'd scold. 'When someone learns how to cheat with as much determination as you have, they're plannin' to use what they know. But just remember that no matter how smart ya are, there's always somebody else who's just as smart. Remember that, Will.'

"One night we was sittin' in the hotel room after a very successful evenin' at the poker table. We'd both won over five hundred dollars. I was layin' on the bed, practicin' my dealin', when I suddenly became aware that Willie was watchin' me intently. He didn't say a word, but the way he was eyein' me I knew he was thinkin' somethin' bad. Finally I couldn't stand it any longer, threw the cards down, and shouted, 'What?'

"'My daddy used to tell me about folks like you,' he said, 'but I never did believe him. I thought he was just tryin' to keep me outa trouble. I didn't really think people like you existed.'

"'Man, what on earth are you talkin' about?' I replied. 'I'm not a whole lot different than anybody else I know.'

"'Yes, you are. You're one of those folks that Daddy said has sold their soul to the Devil. There *are* such people, ya know, and some of 'em do it when they're so young they don't even remember it. The way you can spot 'em is that they don't care about nobody but themselves. Everything's gotta be just the way they want it. If it's not, they're gonna make it that way. I've been runnin' with you the better part of ten years now, Will, and sooner or later you've had your way about everything. Why, I watched ya walk outa the house with your own sister hangin' around your neck, beggin' ya not to go, and ya went on away anyway.'

"'Yeah, but Pa wanted me right back under his thumb like I was before I left. I'd done been to Texas and back by then, though. I'd even brought him his mule and saddle, or one better, so I wasn't under any obligation to him. I didn't owe him nothin'.'

"'He raised ya. Ya owe him for that.'

"'I had no say in the matter.'

"'That's what I'm talkin' about, Will. You've always got to have the last word. Ya ain't willin' to listen to nobody. Take cheatin' at cards, for instance. No matter what I say, you're gonna learn to do it and you're gonna use it, and one of these days it's gonna get somebody killed. It might even be me. But you don't care. Instead of you gettin' away from me like the dealer man said, I oughta be gettin' away from you, and I would if I had any sense. But I like ya, and that fact alone scares me to death.'

"'You're a pretty somebody to talk,' I shot back at him. 'You done robbed three grocery stores and four banks, and you're accusin' *me* of sellin' my soul to the Devil? Hell, you taught me most of the mean things I know.'

"'There's one difference,' he said, lookin' me straight in the eye. 'You like it and I don't. I'm scared and you ain't.'

"'Oh, yeah, I'm scared. When that fella blasted his shotgun and the buckshot caught my ear, I was scared. Believe me.'

"That was the last we ever said about who was gonna get who killed. We never talked about it again.

"We stayed in Cuba until April of 1913, and both of us made a lot of money at the gamblin' tables durin' that time. I never did know whether my dealer friend was dealin' me cards to let me win, but when we boarded the boat for Miami that spring, Willie and I each had a pocketful of money.

"We was tired of hot, sticky weather, so as soon as we got back to the States we took a Pullman compartment and headed up north to New England where it was cool. Along the way a fella told us about a place called Bar Harbor, located off the coast of Maine on a place called Mt. Desert Island, and that's where we decided to stop first. It took several days to get there, as best I can recollect, most of which I spent practicin' my fancy dealin' with Willie.

"Not long after we arrived in Bar Harbor, it became obvious we was gonna have to get gainful employment, 'cause our money was runnin' out fast. There was some awful rich people that lived in that area, and the prices was higher than I'd ever seen. Even though we had a lot of money by Georgia standards, we saw right away that we'd have to find a way to make more if we wanted to rub elbows with that crowd. We did find a right reasonable boardin' house with meals furnished, though. That's where I ate my first lobster, and I loved it.

"One day as me and Willie was sittin' out across from the lighthouse watchin' the ships go up and down the channel, a thought came to me. 'We ain't got a lotta money,' I told him, 'but I bet these rich folks play poker just like everybody else. What we need to do is find out where they play and get in on the action. With my skill and your brains, I bet we could make a livin' gamblin' with these big shots. We could go in at separate times like we was strangers, and I could make you the winner when I deal. Why, over the course of an evenin' we oughta do right well. We wouldn't cheat 'em much, just a little bit. It looks like as rich as they are, they oughta be able to afford it. Whatta ya say?'

"He didn't hesitate a second. 'I'll scout around and see what I can find out. Nobody's gonna tell you nothin', 'cause you're too young-lookin'.'"

Pot Luck

"Willie made friends with the maitre d' at one of the restaurants in town and asked about the habits of the well-to-do in Bar Harbor. The fella told him the real big-shots did their gamblin' at the Yacht Club and said Willie didn't have a chance of gettin' in there. The initiation fee was somethin' like five thousand dollars, with five-hundred-a-month dues. But he said there was a less exclusive yacht club over at Sand Point on the eastern bay. They had a five hundred dollar initiation fee and small dues, he thought, and some of the very wealthy went there to gamble when they were slummin' or out sailin' and had to pull into the Sand Point harbor for any reason.

"Accordin' to the maitre d', most of the people that belonged to the Yacht Club at Sand Point were either over-the-hill people who'd never quite made it big, or else young folks who were still on their way up. But if ya really wanted to be accepted, ya had to have a yacht. The best way to handle it if ya didn't have one, he said, was to tell 'em that ya came up to wait on delivery, that your yacht was bein' finished on Long Island and would be delivered in a month or two. That would give ya plenty of time to make up your mind whether ya fit in with the rich crowd or not.

"Unfortunately, the maitre d' got a little bit nosy. He said he figured if Willie was willin' to spend that kind of money to get into a poker game, he must know somethin' about gamblin' the maitre d' didn't. Without revealin' our plan, Willie told him that if he'd keep their conversation confidential, Willie'd make a small wager for him from time to time. That seemed to satisfy the fella fairly well.

"The next day, Willie headed over to the Sand Point Yacht Club and inquired about how to become a member, what it cost, and all that sort of thing. It turned out the maitre d' was right. The initiation fee was five hundred dollars and the dues was fifty dollars a month—which was a very reasonable price if we could get into the kind of poker game that we figured went on. So Willie joined on the spot.

"I stayed at the boardin' house that night and read a book while Willie went to play cards. Just as I was about fallin' asleep around three o'clock, Willie came bustin' in all flushed and excited. He'd won back his whole initiation fee in the poker game without even havin' to cheat, which made him mighty proud. 'There's more money floatin' around in that poker game than I ever seen in my life!' he exclaimed. 'With your magic hands and my know-how, we oughta get filthy rich!' He'd learned that there was a game every night, but an especially big game on Fridays and Saturdays. Tons of money changed hands in weekend games, he was told.

"Needless to say, I went over and joined the club the next day. I told Willie that after joinin' I was gonna stay on, chat with the people, and get acquainted. He was to show up later and act like he didn't know me. If we got in the game together, he was to make a big show of askin' my name two or three times to be sure everybody caught on to the fact that we'd never met. We also agreed we'd hold our winnings down to a modest level on any given night.

"The Yacht Club itself was a big, ramblin' buildin' just a wee bit to the east of Sand Point. It went right down to the wharf. There was a restaurant inside that served the general public, plus a private dinin' room and bar for members only. The poker room—or game room, as they called it—was one of several rooms and offices that ran down either side of a long, narrow hallway. Besides the door to the hallway, there was an outside entrance to the poker room so that you could enter or leave without bein' seen in the rest of the buildin'. The outside door was kept locked, though, and ya had to identify yourself properly before anyone would admit ya, because gamblin' was illegal in the state of Maine.

"When ya sat in on the poker game for the first time, whoever was dealin' the hand at the moment went through the rigmarole that this was a gentlemen's game, that ya shouldn't put any money on the table ya couldn't afford to lose, that the things said in the room were to be left in the room, and that no markers were offered or accepted. The only money that ya could bet was United States currency in the amount ya brought to the game. No checks or drafts were allowed, and the club cut every fifth pot one dollar in order to provide services like a waiter to bring drinks, sandwiches, and cigars.

"To keep a gentleman-like atmosphere, the dealer would continue, you could bet any amount of money that ya could produce the cash to cover. However, you could announce on one occasion durin' one game that you'd played all the money ya had and call whatever portion of the bet that had been made to that point. If ya lost, ya had to leave the game until the next night. Ya couldn't go somewhere and get funds and get back into the game the same night.

"All of this was told to me by a dealer named Mobley as soon as I sat down for my first game. Then he said, 'You're pretty young to be sittin' in a man's game, aren't ya?' That stung a little bit. I wanted more than anything at that moment to demonstrate my skills in handlin' the cards. I coulda made his eyes pop right outa his head. But I resisted the temptation. Instead, I just said, 'We age slowly where I come from.'

"Willie came in about 9:30 that night and was introduced to everyone. Like we'd planned, he asked me to repeat my name several times so it'd be obvious we didn't know each other. We'd also agreed beforehand that he'd only win every fourth time I dealt. I'd only run the cards up every fourth time. That way nobody would suspect we was workin' together."

"Uncle Will, what does 'running the cards up' mean?" I interrupted.

"Boy, I don't know whether ya need to know what that is or not," he chuckled. "Ya certainly don't need to know how to do it. But runnin' the cards up is settin' 'em up in the deck in such a way that ya deal people around the table the hand you want 'em to have. In a high-stakes poker game, it's necessary to set the deck for at least two or three good hands, 'cause if ya deal your partner four aces or a straight flush, ya certainly want the other people in the game to have a hand they'll bet on, too. Ya don't want 'em to have a hand that'll beat him, but ya want 'em to have a good enough hand that they'll bet a lot of money and not be tempted to get outa the game.

"That's what's known as runnin' the deck up, and that's what I'd grown very good at. I could set the cards up so that three or four players got good hands. Of course, the person I wanted to win would get the best hand of all. Some cardsharks use a cold deck, but I always ran up the deck we was playin' with."

"Wait a minute. What's a cold deck?" I interrupted again.

"Boy, ain't you never played cards?"

"Yes, sir, cousin Hal and I always play when I stay the night with him. He taught me all the hands, what beats what and all that, but he ain't never said nothin' about cold decks and runnin' the cards up."

"Well, I hope you'll take a lesson from my life and realize there are some things ya just don't need to know," Uncle Will answered, "but a cold deck is one ya run up some place else and bring with ya to the game. Then when it comes your deal after the cut, ya slip the fixed deck into the game. By sleight-of-hand ya just switch decks, but that's not very smart 'cause it's hard to do without gettin' caught. In fact, there's a couple of requirements before ya try that. Ya need a lot of money in the game to make it worth the risk, and ya need for most everybody in the game to be drunk. Like I say, it's an awful hard thing to do and not get caught. It helps if most people sittin' around the table are good an' liquored up.

"I don't know why I'm goin' to such pains to tell ya these things. I'd be a lot better off if I'd never known 'em," he observed. Then he went on with the story.

"Willie and I played very modest, conservative poker and agreed we'd take no more than five hundred dollars in a single night. When we reached that figure, he was to get up and leave. Since I was the card mechanic and could better protect myself against losses, I'd stay a while longer before callin' it a night. We also agreed in the beginnin' that we'd play at least a month with very little winnings so we could learn the routine, get to know all the different people that played, and find out what we could about the powers-that-be in the area. Still, after playin' for only a week or two we both felt like there was enough money to be won in the game that we could retire for life. And ya know, to be considerin' retirement at the age of twenty-five when only ten short years earlier I'd been plowin' a mule, that was heavy stuff.

"As long as I live, which ain't gonna be long, I'll never forget that summer. After livin' in Havana all those years and every day bringin' the same hot, endless, sticky weather, the cool mornin' air in Bar Harbor made me feel like a million dollars. Sometimes I'd get up early in the mornin', hire me a horse and buggy, and ride around the island. Now and then I'd drive up on Cadillac Mountain, the highest point on the island, and the fog would be so thick there I could hardly see my hand in front of my face. Then suddenly the sunshine would break through and I'd see layer after layer of fog all the way to the horizon. As the sun climbed higher in the sky, they'd bubble and boil and disappear before my very eyes until I could see the rocky shore of that beautiful island as clear as day.

"Sometimes I'd tie the horse and scramble all the way to the very top of the mountain. On clear days it seemed like you could see a million miles. The sky was so deep and so blue that it almost looked black at the edges. I'd sit there and think about Ma and Pa still grabblin' out their meager livin', about how it'd been ten whole years since I'd seen either one of 'em, and I'd wonder how it came to be that I just abandoned my kin without hardly any remorse —just an occasional moment of loneliness.

"I remember hearin' the preacher's sermon about strong drink, about how wine is a mocker and all that, and I'd think about the fact that I usually got drunk every night before I left the club. I'd sit there with my head achin', wonderin' what made me do it and swearin' I wouldn't do it again. But when the night came and I felt better, I usually wound up doin' it anyway.

"Sometimes I'd even think about goin' back home and findin' me a girl to settle down with, but it just wasn't in me to be a sharecropper and raise a house full of young'uns. I could sit at the Yacht Club and see more money cross the table in one night than was in all of Carroll and Haralson County, Georgia, put together. It was excitin'! Besides, Willie had found himself a girl-friend, so he wanted to stay around as long as he could. And since he was the only true friend I ever knew, the only one who'd listen to my troubles and problems, I couldn't stand the thought of leavin' without him. By now, he was nearly fifty years old. To me, he was an old man with one foot in the grave, but of course when you're twenty-five, anybody over thirty seems ancient.

"Actually I didn't see Willie much that summer because we'd taken rooms at separate boardin' houses in Sand Point. We'd meet at the card game most every night, but otherwise we didn't spend time together except to rendezvous now and then at Cadillac Mountain to talk strategy.

"Anyway, we decided to wait 'til the season was almost over before making our big killin'. By that time we knew who the big-money boys were and how free they were with it when they got in the game. We'd also made ourselves into regulars that people trusted and respected. They didn't know that we cheated 'em a little bit every once in a while. Most of the time it wasn't even necessary, they were such bad players.

"In early September, the skies began to turn gray and hide the sunshine more and more. People were beginnin' to make preparations to go back down the coast to their businesses, so Willie and I got together and agreed we was gonna clean out our poker friends the followin' Friday and Saturday. Then we'd head south to warmer weather. Besides, there was already talk of a big storm—maybe even a hurricane—headin' our way. Word comin' over the wire said it was off the coast of Florida and movin' slowly toward us. Willie and I'd gone through two of those suckers in Cuba and they'd nearly blowed us away. We didn't intend to do it again.

"Over the summer, we'd both managed to save a little over fifteen thousand dollars apiece, which was more money than I woulda believed existed in the whole world just a few short years before. I thought once about openin' up a bank account, but I never did do it. I remembered how back in the 90's, people lost everything they owned when the banks went bust, so I just bought me a good money belt and wore it everywhere I went. Willie did the same thing.

"On Friday night, the thirteenth of September in 1913, I walked into the poker room of the Yacht Club about seven o'clock. There was already five people playin', and they didn't allow but seven. I sat down and made six. If Willie didn't hurry up, I thought to myself, we was in trouble 'cause he wouldn't get a seat. But he walked in about fifteen minutes later, before the last seat was taken.

"Nephew," Uncle Will interjected, "one of the funniest things in the world about me is my memory. It just occurred to me that I can see the people sittin' around that poker table as if it was yesterday, even though it's been nearly thirty-five years. I can't remember half the women I ever went out with. Willie used to say, 'Remember that little red-headed gal in Baton Rouge?' or 'Remember that little dark-haired girl in Miami?' and I couldn't recall a thing about 'em, but I never forgot who was sittin' where durin' a card game in my life. It's almost as if when I do recall a certain thing, I remember every detail about it.

"It wasn't the things that happened that night in Bar Harbor that makes me able to do so, either. I can do it for nearly every game I ever played. But then, poker players are a strange breed. A lot of 'em, if they get in a game that goes on from night to night, always sit in the same seat. Maybe it's just superstition, but they have to have the same seat every night. I've seen a fair share of 'em that wouldn't play unless they got the seat they wanted. I was one of those fellas.

"The poker table at Bar Harbor was backed into a bit of a corner. It was far enough away from the wall that ya could get in and out to the toilet, and there was room for people to stand around and watch, but still, there wasn't a whole lot of space around the table.

"I always sat with my back to the corner of the room where there wasn't no doors. That way I could see both the other doors. I just *would not* sit with my back to a door. It may have been from readin' about Jesse James gettin' shot from behind, I don't know, but I always liked to have a solid wall to my back when I was playin' poker. I just felt a whole lot safer."

"That night, Willie sat down on my left. He'd been to see his girlfriend and was dressed up real sporty-like. To Willie's left was a fella named Carlton Mobley. He was a regular who worked for the Carnegies somewhere. I don't remember what his job was, but it obviously provided him with plenty of money.

"Next to Mobley sat a man named Phillip Beard. He claimed to have a lot of stock in some company, I think it was Studebaker Wagon Company. He was a big fella with a red, puffy face that was covered with freckles. And what a mouth! He had a huge mouth. Beard was one of those people that sets your teeth on edge the moment ya meet him. It was nothin' you could put your finger on, but just talkin' to him made the hair

stand up on the back of your neck. I never did understand why some people did that to me and others didn't,
but he was one of those that did. Have ya ever known
anybody like that, nephew?"

"No sir, I don't guess I ever have," I replied after
giving it some thought.

"Well, consider yourself lucky if that's the case.
But back to Beard: he was a lousy poker player. A
couple of times late at night when I was pretty drunk,
I thought I saw him dealin' off the bottom of the deck,
but I never was sure. He was such a lousy player that
I couldn't imagine him tryin' to get away with cheatin'.

"On his left was Andrew Beldon. I'd seen him the
whole summer, off and on. He was a reserved kind of
fella and a conservative bettor, but when he got a good
hand, he'd bet more money than you could tote.

"The next player, Ben Moore, was a playboy who
drank lots of liquor. His family ran some sorta chem-
ical business and always kept him in money. In fact, I
bet he'd never done an honest day's work in his life.

"On his left and my right was Matt Kellam, a short,
beady-eyed little man who lived in Bar Harbor year-
round. I think he looked after the property of some of
the big shots from down south who needed a caretaker
durin' the winter. Kellam was a disagreeable, quarrel-
some type and maybe just a bit crazy, especially after
he'd had a few drinks. Trouble was, he usually had
more than a few every time he played.

"Willie and I had already made up our minds that
that night and the next was gonna be the end of our stay
in Bar Harbor. We was goin' back to Miami and maybe

back to Cuba for the winter. Come Sunday we planned to leave Bar Harbor a good deal richer than when we arrived.

"These games sometimes took on a different complexion from one night to the other, though. Some nights it seemed like everybody would bet very conservative, with ten or fifteen dollars bein' the highest bet that was made all night. On other nights when the cards was runnin' hot, there'd be a lot of good hands and the players would bet a thousand dollars a card. You could never tell what was gonna happen. Each game seemed to have an ornery life of its own.

"That night Beard stacked up what looked like eight to ten thousand dollars in front of him in hundred-dollar bills. He'd already had quite a bit to drink, and he even ordered and paid for a round of drinks for everybody at the table, which was a little unusual. As a matter of fact, it was very unusual. I'd never seen that happen but once before, and that was *after* the game was over and one of the winners was feelin' generous. This came *before* the game, so it was sorta strange.

"By eleven o'clock that evenin', there was probably thirty people in the room. A lot of money had changed hands, but it was one of those games where nobody was really winnin' it all. It seemed to flow back and forth. I was playin' conservative and was about even. However, I'd dealt Willie a couple of hands that I knew put him ten or eleven thousand dollars ahead. Everybody was talkin' about havin' to go back home and leave this wonderful summer pastime, which was probably why everybody also seemed to be drinkin' a mite more'n usual.

"About 11:45, while Beard was dealin', somethin'

big started to happen. He dealt everybody a hole card, then went on around the table again. I got a two up and had a two in the hole. Willie got a king up. I found out later he had a king in the hole.

"Beldon, the man to the left of the dealer, got an ace and bet a hundred dollars. Everybody around the table called. I started once to raise with a pair of deuces but decided to let everybody play and see what the next card was. Nobody raised, so Beard dealt around again.

"Kellam, on my right, got a pair of tens. Nobody else around the table paired. 'A pair of tens bets,' said Beard.

"'A pair of tens bets five hundred,' Kellam replied. I had a pair of deuces and saw another two elsewhere on the table. The odds of me makin' trips was not all that great, so I folded.

"Willie called, and so did Mobley. Now it was back to Beard. He had a queen and a jack showin', and raised the bet by five hundred more. More or less out of idle curiosity, I sat and looked over the hands. There was not another queen or jack on the table, so the chance of Beard havin' a pair that beat the tens was pretty good. I thought he was playin' a good game, even if it was a little bit reckless.

"Beldon, who had an ace and a nine showin', looked at his hand a long time before he finally called. Moore, with a three and four of diamonds, called, too. When it got back to Kellam, he called Beard's raise and raised him a thousand. Willie and Mobley threw in their hands before Beard, Beldon, and Moore called the thousand dollars. This was suddenly gettin' to be a very interestin' poker hand. The pot was right, and Beard dealt another card.

153

He gave an ace to Beldon, which made a pair showin'. Moore got a two to go with his three and four. Kellam drew a third ten, and Beard dealt himself a second queen.

"With three tens, it was Kellam's bet again. He very carefully counted a thousand dollars in hundred-dollar bills, laid them down in front of his stack of money and counted them again, then threw them in the pot and said, 'I bet one thousand dollars.' Beard very deliberately counted out ten hundred-dollar bills and laid them off to the side of the pot. Then he slowly counted out fifty more, placed them next to the other stack, and said, 'The dealer calls your thousand and raises five thousand.'

"Once again, Beldon looked at his hole card like he was hopin' to change its spots. He drummed his fingers on the table top, picked up the corner of the hole card and stared at it again, then drummed his fingers some more before finally countin' out sixty hundred-dollar bills and sayin', 'I call.'"

At that moment, Uncle Will stopped and said, "Nephew, I've gotta take a leak. I'm about to pop." I couldn't believe it! Here I was, hanging on to his every word, and he's gotta go take a leak. But I knew there was no use in arguing.

"Besides that," he said, "it's about bedtime." He could see I didn't like *that* idea a bit. I think he knew I wasn't gonna let him rest until he finished the story, and he was playing it for all it was worth.

I followed him as he crawled out of the bus and walked over to the edge of the woods to water the bark on an old oak tree. It was clear and crisp outside. The stars were so brilliant and seemed so close that you could just about reach out and touch them.

"Nephew, did I ever tell ya about the constellation Orion?" Uncle Will asked. "That's Orion, the mighty hunter. See it right up there?"

"Uncle Will, you're funnin' me," I replied. "Let's go back and finish the story."

"It ain't a pretty endin'," he warned.

"I don't care. I wanna hear it anyway."

Once again he looked up at the sky. "I tell ya what I'll do. I'll tell ya about Orion, the mighty hunter. Look over there. In front of Orion are the Pleiades, the seven sisters, the daughters of Atlas. Orion is chasin' 'em. That's Sirius, the dog star, trailin' right along behind him."

"I don't wanna hear about the stars," I pleaded. "I wanna hear about the card game."

"Well, come on, then," he replied. Once we were back in the bus, he stuffed his old corncob pipe full of tobacco, then hunted around for some matches. As he took his time lighting up, I realized more than ever he was teasing me. He knew he was a spellbinding story-teller, and he also knew I was hooked. In fact, he was enjoying himself immensely. Finally he took a couple of drags off his old pipe and said, "Now, where was I?"

"Beldon just called a six thousand dollar bet, and now it's Moore's turn. He's got a two, three, and four. The three and four are diamonds. You didn't say whether the two was a diamond or not."

"You listen good, don't ya, nephew?" he said. "And you're right, I didn't tell ya what suit the two was. But do ya remember somethin' else about the two?"

155

"Yes, it was the last two in the deck. You said you had a pair and folded them, and you saw another one on the table but didn't say what suit it was."

"You are payin' attention, nephew, indeed you are. Well, now I'll tell ya. Beldon did have the two of diamonds and I suddenly realized that this was the biggest card game I'd seen all summer in Bar Harbor, so I started watchin' Beard a little closer. He was nervously fiddlin' with the cards, and I caught a glimpse of the one on the bottom of the deck. It was a queen.

"I glanced at Kellam, who was starin' at his stack of money. It didn't look like he had more than five or six thousand dollars in his pile, but he picked it up and counted out five thousand, which only left him four one-hundred dollar bills. He said, 'I call the five thousand raise. Now, I know the rules of this game as well as anybody. But this is all the money I've got on me. I wanna write a check for twenty thousand, put it in the pot, and let it play for money because I ain't done bettin' this hand. Everybody here knows that I live here the year-round. This check is on the Bank of Bar Harbor. You all know it's as good as gold. There's only four of us left in the hand, and if we agree to let the check play as money, the other three who already folded don't have nothin' to say about it. The rest of the night we'll count that check as money between us four. Will you gentlemen permit that?'

"The dealer man, Beard, was the first one to speak. 'I won't agree to let it play as money for the rest of the night,' he said, 'but I'll agree for ya to cash it out of this pot. Leave the check in the pot, and whoever wins this pot puts that check in his pocket and doesn't let it get back into the game tonight. That's the way I'll let it play. How about you, Mr. Beldon?'

"'I have no objections to that arrangement,' Beldon replied. 'How about you, Mr. Moore?' Moore also said he had no objections to the arrangement as long as the winner of the pot put the check in his pocket. 'Very well, Mr. Kellam,' Beard said, 'put your check in, make whatever bet ya want, and take out the change.'"

"Kellam wrote out the check, laid it in the pot, then said, 'I already called your five thousand dollar raise. Now I'm gonna raise ya ten thousand and take ten thousand out for my change.' He counted out a hundred one-hundred dollar bills and stacked them back in front of himself.

"Beard counted ten thousand out of a money belt he was wearin', threw it in the pot, and said, 'I call.' Once again he nervously picked up the deck of cards, and once again I saw a corner of a queen on the bottom. There's no doubt in my mind that's what it was.

"Beldon didn't make us wait this time like he did before. 'Gentlemen,' he said, 'it's only money. I've gotta see that last card.'

"Now it was Moore's turn to fidgit. He glanced at his hole card and his up cards, then looked at all the cards on the table. As he sat there strugglin' over whether to bet or fold, he went through nearly the same ritual Beldon had done the card before. He drummed his fingers on the table, stared at his hole card some more, and mentally counted the money that was already in the pot. Finally he said, 'Pa's gonna be madder than hell if I drop a bundle tonight, but I think he can stand it. I call.'

"'Cards,' announced Beard. He nervously picked up the deck and proceeded to deal Beldon one that gave him two pair showin'. He had a pair of aces and a pair of nines. Moore got a seven of diamonds, meanin' no straight flush, and Kellam drew a six to go with his three tens. Beard dealt himself a third queen.

"As he set the deck down, he flashed the bottom card again. Now it was a five. Beard looked down at his three queens and said, 'Three queens is high. Dealer bets—'

"In a single motion so quick that I hardly saw him move, Kellam had a Colt .44 pointed straight at Phillip Beard's head. 'You son-of-a-bitch,' he growled through clinched teeth, 'that queen was on the bottom of the deck before you dealt the last four cards.'

"As I said before, Beard was a big man. As soon as he heard Kellam's challenge, he laid both his massive hands on the table and started to rise. He never made it, though, because at that instant the loudest explosion I ever heard came out of Kellam's .44. At the same instant, a little red spot appeared in Beard's forehead, and the back of his head jumped off. The impact of the bullet, combined with Beard's dyin' convulsion, made him look like a rag doll bein' thrown across the room. He landed dead, crumpled in the corner of the room in a bloody heap.

"For a full minute, the room was silent as a tomb. I looked at Beard and I looked at the table. There musta been close to a hundred thousand dollars in cash. Then chaos struck as everybody realized that a man had just been murdered over an illegal card game. Suddenly everybody began pushin' and shovin', tryin' to get out of the room. Everybody, that is, except Kellam. He just stood there, frozen in his tracks like a zombie. He didn't make a move.

"I did, though. I reached in my pocket, pulled out my pocket knife, and shattered the light hangin' above the table. That left the room darker than pitch. Then with a few quick strokes I reached down and cut the velvet cloth loose from the table, gathered it up with all the money inside, and headed out the door with Willie in tow behind me.

"It was a ten minute walk to where I lived. When we got there, we took the back stairs to my room so nobody would see us. As soon as we was inside with the door locked, I spread out the velvet tablecloth on the floor. There was a king's ransom inside! 'It's all ours, Willie,' I said excitedly. 'Every bit of it.'

"Willie stared down at it for a minute, then looked at me and said, 'Will, I knew you'd sold your soul to the Devil, and this proves it. There that man got his head blowed off, and you didn't even think about him. You only thought about the money.'

"'Kellam was right. That queen was on the bottom of the deck when Beard started to deal the last four cards. He got what he deserved.'

"'How can you say that?' Willie shrieked. 'That's what you've done the whole summer! But the rules that apply to other folks just don't apply to you, do they?'

"'Let's talk about this some other time, okay?' I answered. 'The question is, what are we gonna do now?

What's gonna happen? Are the people who was there gonna put us in the room with that dead man when they tell their stories? Do we stand a chance of gettin' outa Bar Harbor with all this money? That's what I wanna talk about.'

"I sat there lookin' at that pile of money and ponderin' what all it would buy in Georgia. Here in the playground of the rich, it was a toy of the wealthy. I doubted if anybody in the whole state of Georgia had that much money, though, and I wanted to be the first.

"'We've gotta figure a way to get all this money off the island,' I said. 'While I pack it in my suitcases, you go back down to the Yacht Club and see what's goin' on there. See if anybody knows who got the loot.'

"Willie looked at the money, then at me, then at the money, then at me again. Finally he said, 'Will, you *did* make peace with the Devil, just as sure as the world.'

"'Okay, we may as well have this out now,' I snapped. 'Do you want that money, too, or is it just me? Do you wanna get outa Bar Harbor with it as bad and as fast as I do?'

"Willie hung his head. 'Yeah, I want it, too. I'm gettin' old, and it'd sure make life easier for me.'

"'Then go find out what's happenin' back at the Yacht Club. See if they know we got the money. If they don't know who got it, then they won't know where to look for it. And somethin' else, Willie—pick up a tidetable for at least the next day or so. Remember that pivot bridge connectin' the island to the mainland? If we drive there in a horse and buggy and the bridge happens to be turned wrong, we're gonna be in trouble, but if the tide's

down we might can wade across just below the bridge.
So we need to get to the bridge at low tide, just in case.'

"Willie slipped back to the Yacht Club and made
his way into the smokin' lounge. There were four or
five people there that he remembered bein' in the poker
room at the time of the shootin'. Some of them raised
their heads with a flicker of recognition across their
face as he walked in, but then quickly looked away.
Other than that, there was nothin' but quiet conversation goin' on, which was certainly unusual considerin'
what had just happened.

"Willie walked over and sat on the couch next to a
fella he knew was in the poker room when Kellam shot
Beard. 'What's goin' on about the killin'?' he asked the
man in a hushed tone. 'It seems awful quiet.'

"'They're out lookin' for the guy that did the shootin'. 'Nobody seems to know where he lives.'

"'Who, Kellam?' Willie said in disbelief. 'Hell, he's
a year-round resident. Shouldn't be hard to locate 'im.'

"'It wasn't Kellam that killed him,' the man replied
matter-of-factly. 'It was that big, young fellow named
Will somethin'-or-another. Nobody even seems to know
his last name.'

"'You're crazy as hell!' Willie exclaimed. 'You were
there, I saw ya. That little beady-eyed bastard Kellam
shot him point-blank!'

"'Mister, let me give ya a friendly piece of advice,'
the stranger said coldly. 'If ya think that Kellam killed
Beard rather than that young giant called Will, ya best
keep it to yourself, 'cause everybody the police have
talked to so far has told 'em that Will did it.'

161

"'Why would they say that, when everybody who was there knows it was Kellam?'

"'Because the giant is an outsider, and down-east folks stick together to protect their own.

"'Let me give ya one other piece of advice, friend,' the man continued. 'You talk funny yourself, like you're not from around these parts. It might just turn out that you're an accessory to the murder. So if I was you and was approached by any of the authorities, I'd either say I didn't see what happened, or that Big Will killed Beard. Of course, you can do whatever ya wanna do. It's up to you. But I'd think it over a mite if I were you, 'cause you talk funny, too, and there's already fifteen or more of us that's said Big Will did it.'

"'Where are all of 'em now?' Willie asked. 'It sure seems quiet after such a bloody murder just an hour ago.'

"'They've all gone home or back to their boats. But Big Will'll never get off the island. The police will see to that.'

"'Well,' Willie said as he stood to leave, 'I guess if that's the case, I'll be goin', too. I was just curious and came back to see what was happenin'.'

"The fella looked up at Willie. 'Who ya gonna say did it if they ask?'

"'I'm gonna make it unanimous,' he answered as he walked away.

"When Willie came back to the boardin' house and told me what he'd heard, I was mad as hell! 'We've got a $100,000 besides what's in our money belts, and now I may not have a chance to spend it 'cause there's a murder warrant out for me,' I cried. 'I can't believe it!'

"'Believe it, Will, believe it,' replied Willie."

162

Ol' Ebo
and the Pinkerton

"I've never been so stunned in all my life. I just sat there starin' at the piles of money I'd packed into my suitcases. Finally, Willie broke the silence. 'We need to get off this island *tonight,*' he said. 'If we don't, half the Maine State Police will be lookin' for us by tomorrow. They'll go house-to-house if they have to, and they'll search 'til they find us. If we don't get off this island before daylight, you're as good as dead.'

"'But I ain't done nothin' wrong,' I pleaded, conveniently forgettin' the money I'd stolen.

"'Will, I don't think ya understand. For once in your young, stubborn life, listen to somebody who's been around. I'm forty-eight years old, and I ain't never spent a day in jail. If we don't get outa here tonight, you're gonna end up goin' to the penitentiary—or worse. If the police ask for volunteer help, somebody's gonna "accidentally" shoot ya on sight, 'cause a trial would raise too many questions.'

"'But you're willin' to testify I didn't shoot that fella Beard, ain't ya?' I continued to protest.

"Willie looked at me like I'd never seen him look before. 'Am I?' he said in a tone that made my blood run cold.

"'Whatta ya mean, Willie?'

"'Remember what that fella said about me talkin' funny, too? About how it'd be the two of us against all the locals?' he replied. 'No, Will. It won't work. If ya listen to me, you'll get off this island tonight, go somewhere to a railroad station in the boonies, and buy a ticket away from here. We've gotta get out of Maine. These are big, rich, powerful folks. They ain't gonna let some stranger come in here and kill one of their own. They'll turn heaven and earth to catch ya, I guarantee.

"'Besides, anywhere we see a policeman on this island we're liable to be questioned and searched, 'cause like the man said, we talk funny. And havin' two belts and a suitcase full of money ain't gonna look too good for us.'

"What Willie said made all the sense in the world, but I just couldn't get over being accused of a murder I didn't commit. Apparently, they was gonna make it stick if they caught me, though. I didn't believe they could really do that, but I was afraid to take the chance, so I said, 'Okay Willie, how do we get off this island?'

"We'd spent the whole summer there, so I knew somethin' about the geography of the island. The closest way to the mainland was across a very narrow channel on the road to Ellsworth, where the only bridge off the island was located. Any other method of escape would have to be by boat. We didn't know anybody with a boat, however, because we'd kept to ourselves durin' the time at Sand Point.

"'Before I start helpin' ya off this island, there's a matter that we need to discuss,' Willie said cautiously.

"'What's that?'

"'The ownership of that hundred thousand dollars ya stole out of the poker game. I want half of it.'

164

"Nephew, at that moment I coulda killed him. I'd figured all along that we was partners in whatever we did, and I thought he knew that. The idea of that little squirt suddenly *demandin'* half the money set my teeth on edge, especially since he knew I was at his mercy. He was the only one who could get out on the streets and see what was happenin'. But from then on, even though I showed no outward change as far as Willie could tell, there was a difference in our relationship. I can't put my finger on it. I just never felt quite the same toward him after that.

"But I knew I couldn't afford to alienate him at this point, so I said, 'Sure, Willie. I considered it half yours from the moment I took it. I have no problem with that. Now, have ya got any idea how we're gonna get away?'

"'Yeah,' he answered, 'I got the tide table when I went back to the club, and I also picked up a map of the island. Here it is. You can see we're here at Sand Point. As the crow flies, it looks like the farthest we can go away from here without leavin' the island is Bass Harbor, which is on the very southern tip.'

"Even though I'd been on Mt. Desert Island for close to six months, this was the first time I'd seen a map. The island itself looked like two fat bananas lyin' side-by-side with their curved parts away from each other and a body of water runnin' between 'em.

"'I think they're gonna concentrate most of their effort around the bridge to Ellsworth,' Willie continued, 'so if we avoid that part of the island, we stand a lot better chance. But we gotta get ya out by daylight, 'cause they're gonna check every hotel and boardin'

165

house on the island tomorrow to see if anybody knows where ya live. I know from time to time you rent a buggy and ride to Cadillac Mountain for sightseein' in the mornin'. I need to know where ya rent it and what time they open for business.'

"About that time I saw lightnin' in the distance, followed by a roll of thunder, and for the first time that night I remembered the hurricane that was due any time now. I'd forgotten about it because of all the trouble I was in. Havin' to travel in stormy weather made things even worse.

"By now it was nearly seven o'clock. We'd spent that much time talkin' over the situation. I told him how to get to the livery barn and suggested he go on up and see about gettin' what we needed. 'Don't rent it, buy it,' I told him. 'Do ya know how much a good horse and buggy is likely to cost? I don't.' He thought a thousand dollars would get us a good rig with isinglass curtains and all the extras.

"The barn was about a fifteen-minute walk in the direction of Cadillac Mountain, and the guy who ran the place was named Fred Apple. I started into this long rigamarole about how I'd gotten on downright friendly terms with him durin' our time in Sand Point, when suddenly I remembered I was a fugitive from the law. 'Get outa here and find us a horse and buggy before I talk my way into the penitentiary!' I told Willie in a nervous voice.

"The following is what he told me when he returned. Of course, I wasn't there, but Willie swore it was true, and I have no reason to doubt it.

166

"When he walked into the office of the livery barn, a well-dressed fella was standin' there talkin' to Mr. Apple. There was somethin' awful familiar about the man, Willie said, so he walked around to the opposite side of the horseshoe-shaped counter in order to get a look at him. The man glanced over at Willie, but then turned back to the livery owner and continued his conversation.

"'And you don't know anything more about last night's shooting?' the man asked.

"'No, all I know is that the guy who shot Phillip Beard was a young giant with a southern accent,' Apple replied. 'Everybody says he came from Georgia, South Carolina, Alabama, or somewhere down there. You know how funny those people talk. Somebody who lived down there might could tell exactly which state was his home, but it all sounds alike to people who live around here.'

"'You say he was a giant?'

"'That's what everyone says. From time to time durin' the summer, I've rented a horse and buggy to a tall fella. I wouldn't say he was a giant, though— probably six-four or six-five. I'd guess he was twenty-five to thirty years old, but then I'm fifty-five, and anybody under forty looks young to me.'

"The man continued to probe. 'Did he have a midget with him durin' any of the times he came in to rent a rig?'

"'No, he was always alone. To tell ya the truth, I thought he was probably tryin' to impress some girl. He always wanted a nice horse and buggy and never argued about the price. He acted like he had plenty of money, but yet he didn't have plenty of money, if ya know what I mean.

It's like maybe he worked hard and saved his money, and then was spendin' it to impress somebody. Of course, that's just a feelin' I had about him. He may have been a wealthy man for all I know.'

"'But ya never saw a little half-pint with him, a man just over five feet tall?'

"'I just told ya, mister. I never saw anybody with him.'

"'What was this big fella's name?'

"'I don't remember.'

"'Surely you didn't rent a horse and buggy to somebody that had no name?' the stranger said accusingly.

"For the first time, the owner began to show annoyance with the stranger's questions. As a way of puttin' him off a bit, he turned to Willie and said, 'Can I help ya, friend? I'll be through with this gentleman in just a minute.'

"'No, no. Take your time,' Willie responded. 'I'm in no hurry.' Willie was real interested in what the gentleman wanted to know. There was somethin' familiar about him, but he couldn't quite place it. He shut his eyes, tryin' to recall where he'd seen this fella before. As he stood there, the fellow spoke again, and the truth suddenly struck Willie like a thunderbolt. That was the voice, the exact same voice, from the darkness of the boxcar the night we robbed the bank in Monroe!

"Willie's knees started knockin' so hard, he just knew the fella could hear 'em. They sounded like two castanets rappin' against each other. He looked around the room for a place to hide, but then it hit him: the man had never seen his face! There was no reason to be afraid, 'cause the fella didn't have any idea what he looked like.

Still, even knowin' that was the case, he couldn't get rid of his jitters completely. "Finally the livery man walked around the counter to where Willie was standin' and said, 'Now, what can I do for ya?'

"'I'd like to buy a horse and buggy,' Willie said, his voice breakin' a little as he noticed the stranger starin' at him. Every time he cut his eyes back in the man's direction, the fella was studyin' him, and it made Willie squirm."

"Keepin' his voice as calm as he could, Willie asked what price range the man had for a horse and buggy. He said he had horses anywhere from two hundred to eight hundred dollars and buggies from three hundred to a thousand. He even had a fancy surrey with front and back seats and springs on each wheel that rode like a feather pillow, he said. It cost twenty-two hundred dollars. He swore it was so light and well-built that a horse would hardly notice the weight of it.

"'Where can I see this wonderful machine?' Willie asked.

"'Right this way,' the livery man said, showin' him to the yard. As they reached the door, Apple turned back to the stranger. 'Is there anything else I can do for ya, mister?' he asked.

"'No, never mind,' was the reply, 'You've been very helpful.'

"They walked outside to look at the surrey, which was just what Willie had in mind. It was plenty big, with a box beneath the undercarriage that I might could crawl into and hide from the police. At least it was worth looking into.

"As he stood there considerin' the possibilities, the thunder and lightnin' began to move closer. The livery man eyed the horizon nervously and told Willie that the only other time he'd ever seen it thunder there in September was when they had a hurricane years ago. It was the most horrifyin' experience he'd ever had in his life, he said.

"But Willie's mind was elsewhere. Where was the man with all the questions, the fella who was so curious about a certain giant and his half-pint sidekick? Even though Willie knew the man had no idea what he looked like, he couldn't help but feel a bit uneasy. He kept glancin' around from side to side as he talked to the livery manager, until finally the man said, 'Sir, you seem awful jittery. Are you afraid of storms?' That gave Willie a perfect out. 'Yeah, I didn't realize it was so obvious,' he nodded. 'I've always been dreadful scared of 'em, but I thought I had it under pretty good control.'

"He used the opportunity to get out of the place as fast as he could. 'You appear to me to be a honest, straightforward man. The best horse you've got, whatta ya want for it?'

"'I've got a beautiful bay mare that weighs about twelve hundred pounds. I'll sell her for eight hundred dollars. She's got a blaze in her face that looks like a thunder bolt, and three white socks. You talk about a high-spirited, high-steppin' animal—that's her. But she's gentle as a lamb.'

"'I'll take her and that big black surrey,' Willie replied quickly. 'I want the best set of harness ya got, too. How much for the whole thing?'

"'Well, the surrey is twenty-two hundred and the horse is eight. That makes an even three thousand. I tell ya what I'll do. If you're willin' to spend that kinda money, I'll throw in the nicest set of harness I have at no charge.'

"'Deal!' Willie shot back. 'Now I need one other thing. While we go in and take care of business, can ya have your man hitch up the rig and deliver it around to the front of the buildin'?' The manager allowed as how he could do that.

"When they went back inside, the stranger was nowhere to be seen. Willie felt a bit relieved, but still apprehensive. The fella had set Willie's teeth on edge, and when he stared at Willie he seemed to look right through him. It had given the little man a queasy feelin' in his stomach, sorta like he'd had cockleburrs for breakfast and one mouthful of cockleburrs was waltzin' around another one inside his stomach.

"As the manager of the livery wrote the bill of sale, Willie felt himself relaxin' a little bit more. Maybe things was gonna work out after all, he thought. He raised his shirt up slightly, opened the lid of his money belt, and took out what he guessed to be thirty one-hundred dollar bills. When he counted them, it turned out to be exactly that. The manager allowed as how he certainly had a sensitive touch to pick out thirty bills on the first try. Willie gave him a half-hearted smile and said it was 'the luck of the Irish' or some such nonsense, though he knew it came from years of bettin' on cards. He took the bill of sale, thanked the man, and hurried back to the boardin' house in the new rig to pick me up.

"When I saw him pull up, I ran downstairs with the bags, tossed 'em behind the front seat, and said, 'Let's get off this God-forsaken island!'

"By now the thunderstorm was on top of us. The wind was strong and gustin' hard enough to rattle the isinglass curtains. Soon huge rain drops started peltin' the carriage, and a big bolt of lightnin' flashed not far from us, sendin' thunder crashin' in all directions. The horse startled at that and began racin' down the road at breakneck speed, though we could barely see because the sky was so dark.

"Then a storm that was gonna make Noah's flood look like a morning dew struck. The wind howled, rain came in torrents, and the lightnin' was almost a steady flash. Durin' one of those flashes, I saw a barn with a shed alongside the road up ahead. 'We better pull into that shed and wait 'til this passes or we could get completely lost!' I yelled at Willie. Though the storm would make a good cover during the ride to Bass Harbor, I was afraid we'd be blown off the road. I'd seen such things happen in Havana many times.

"Willie pulled the horse into the shed beside the barn, and we was just settlin' down to wait out the storm when I happened to glance over into the back seat of the surrey. I tell ya, nephew, my heart almost jumped outa my chest, 'cause sittin' there was a fella wearin' a bowler hat and pointin' a .44 straight at me! He grinned and said in a voice that I'd heard somewhere before, 'Hello, Big Will. Long time.'

"As the lightning flashed outside again, I got a good look at his face. I knew I'd never seen the man before. It was only his voice I recognized. About that time Willie turned to me and said, 'I shoulda known he didn't just up and leave the livery. Will, if I ain't mistaken, this here is the fella that plugged your ear in the boxcar in Monroe.' The man extended his left hand forward to shake hands while he held the gun in his right. 'Steve Young, Pinkerton Detective Agency,' he introduced himself. 'Nice to meet ya finally, big man. Ya mean I really hit ya that night on the train?' I showed him the nick outa my ear. 'Well, I'll be damned!' he exclaimed. 'I came powerful close to your livin', didn't I?'

"'I've never had the pleasure of meetin' ya 'til now, Big Will,' he continued, 'but our paths have nearly crossed a time or two since that night on the freight train. I was never more than one day behind ya all the way up through Arkansas and back west to Dallas. Ya almost lost me there when ya turned north, though. Willie here musta bought your tickets alone, 'cause the agent swore he couldn't remember sellin' tickets to a giant and a midget. It cost me fifty dollars to jog his memory. He finally recalled that a little half-pint bought two berths on a Pullman to Kansas City, and that there was some big fella lurkin' nearby just as everyone was about to board. I followed ya all the way to Tallapoosa, Georgia, always just a day or two behind. Then I lost ya. I tell ya, I've never seen anyone as tight-lipped as those folks in Tallapoosa, and I didn't figure out 'til later that it was probably 'cause you was one of their own.

"'Anyway, I decided I'd never see ya again. Then last spring I was on a case in Havana, Cuba, and talked to a dealer in a casino. I mentioned that I'd run down every crook I ever chased except for a giant and a midget that robbed a bank together nearly ten years before. He said two men fittin' that description had shown up in Havana about that time and had just left for the States a few weeks earlier. He'd made friends with the tall one, he said, and had taught him how to handle a deck of cards until the boy became a real magician with 'em. That's you, Big Will,' Young said, motionin' at me with the barrel of his .44.

"'I decided if I was that close again—and if you boys hadn't been caught in that length of time—that I'd just get back on a ten-year-old trail. Besides, I figured by then that you oughta be rich. So I went to the boat dock and found a ticket agent who remembered ya leavin' Havana and, by sheer luck, a railroad agent in Miami who recalled ya buyin' a ticket to Maine. You asked for Bar Harbor, he said, and he didn't tell ya there was no train to Bar Harbor, he just sold ya a ticket to Ellsworth, the nearest town.

"'I'd have been up here back in May,' Young continued, 'but I had to take the fella I caught in Cuba all the way back to Arizona to face charges. That's the reason I was so late. But I'd just walked into the police station in Ellsworth last night when the telegraph came alive, askin' the authorities to monitor all traffic leavin' Mt. Desert Island and to be on the lookout for a young giant who'd murdered a man in a poker game.

"'When I heard that, Big Will, I knew it had to be you,' he finished with a tone of satisfaction in his voice.

"'Well, Mr. Detective, you've got me,' I replied. 'That .44 speaks louder than words. But as I sit here starin' down the barrel of that thing, I wonder if I decided to take my chance in this storm and leave ya here and now, would ya really pull the trigger?'

"'You won't ever know that until ya try, will ya?' the detective answered calmly. 'But just remember: one night I did pull the trigger.' And that I did. I remembered that night very, very well."

Suddenly Uncle Will stood up, stretched deeply, and said, "Nephew, I'm an old man and it's way past my bedtime. That's all the story you're gonna hear tonight. I'll think about finishin' it in the mornin', but right now I'm goin' to bed."

•

I was awake long before Uncle Will the next morning. As I studied him there in his Army surplus sleeping bag, I realized just how ancient he now seemed. His shaggy white mane was spread over the pillow and his drawn, wrinkled face bore little resemblance to the man he once was. Even in his sleep his breathing was labored as a result of what I now know to be emphysema, probably caused by that ever-present corn cob pipe he smoked. I didn't understand how anybody could be afraid of him, nor could I imagine him doing the terrible things that he himself described to me.

Around ten o'clock, Uncle Will finally stirred and opened his eyes. Once he was fully awake, he looked over at me and asked how I'd slept. I told him that except for being awakened once or twice by thoughts about the story he was into, I'd slept well.

"If you'll behave yourself, you'll always be able to sleep well," he said. It seemed like the last years of his life, Uncle Will was obsessed with giving me advice on the right way to live so I'd be able to get a good night's sleep. "A clear conscience is the softest pillow in the world," he'd say, "and I ain't had one since I was fifteen years old. But boy, it's somethin' to be desired above all things."

After breakfast we walked down and sat on the bank of the creek for a while. He kept talking about a million other things, as if he were trying to avoid finishing the story, and it was nearly noon before I got the courage to call him on it.

"Uncle Will, you promised that you'd finish the story of your escape from Mt. Desert Island. When are you gonna do that?" He thought for a moment as if trying to decide whether or not he *wanted* to finish the story, then answered, "Let's go find us a nice shady spot under a tree where the chiggers won't get us, and I'll finish tellin' ya all about it."

When we found a place we liked, he backed up against a big beech tree, and I plopped down against one directly across from him. He shut his eyes and lowered his head for a minute, then looked up at me and said, "Now, where was I?"

"You were in the shed alongside the barn, the hurricane was blowing something fierce, and the man had a gun pointed at your head."

"Oh, yeah. Well, the Pinkerton—Steve Young— was tellin' me how our paths kept crossin' through the years, when suddenly he stopped and changed the subject a bit. 'Big Will,' he said, 'there's a strange thing about this killin'. I spent most of the night tryin' to find out what happened, and everybody I talked to told me that you shot the man. But nobody told the same story about *why* ya shot him. Some of 'em said you'd been feudin' with him all summer. Some said ya cheated him and he started to draw on ya, but you shot him first. Some said *he* cheated *you*, and you up and shot him dead. None of the stories were alike.

"'Ya know, I've been with Pinkerton somethin' over ten years, and I ain't never seen or heard as many different stories from people who was in the same room. There's just somethin' strange about what went on at that card game last night. I'm not exactly sure what it was. Would you care to tell me your side of the story?'

"'Would ya believe me?' I asked.

"'It depends on what ya say. I'm sure it's gonna be different from anything I've heard. Maybe I can piece all the stories together and figure out what took place.' Before I could reply, however, he blurted out a question I'm sure had been on his mind from the moment we first met face-to-face: 'What happened to the money, Big Will?'

"Sittin' there with that gun pointed at my head and the lightnin' flashin' all around and a Pinkerton man grillin' me with questions, I shoulda felt like a trapped animal. But somehow I got a sense that this was a fella I could bargain with. I didn't say anything for a minute or so, and neither did he. It was like we was both waitin' for the other one to make the next move.

"Finally he said, 'Maybe I need to tell ya somethin' about myself. I was vice-president of the bank you two robbed in Monroe. I was late to work that mornin' or you'd have had to tie up an extra man. I'd embezzled five thousand dollars and was probably about to be caught when you boys had the good graces to come in and rob the place. Ya got me totally off the hook. I just told 'em that ya got ten thousand, which made the books balance and cleared me of suspicion.

"'I also convinced the sheriff that you two was plannin' on catchin' the train on that bluff up behind town,' he continued. 'I told him that since it was my money, it was my responsibility and I oughta be the one waitin' in the boxcar if and when ya showed up. And believe me, the sheriff was such a coward, he didn't argue for one minute. He just deputized me and let me take charge.

"'Now, the interestin' part is what happened next. If you'll remember, the door to the third car behind the engine was wide open. That was my idea, too—sort of an invitation for you to come pilin' in, which ya did. I intended to blow both of ya half in two, 'cause a trial woulda been too risky. Folks mighta believed ya really did get only five thousand dollars. But this way, I could convince 'em that ya hid the rest of it and was comin' back later for it. So ya see, you're lucky ya got away with only a nick in one ear, 'cause I was sure shootin' to kill.

"'The only part I didn't figure on in the whole deal was you boys jumpin' back on board the same train. That was a brilliant maneuver. Why, we stumbled around in those woods all night with guns and dogs and never did strike your trail. It didn't dawn on me until nearly daylight that ya both had hopped right back on that freight. When it come to me that that's what you'd done, I had great admiration for ya. And it's the only thing that saved your lives, 'cause I was gonna find a reason one way or another to shoot ya. I just couldn't let ya tell your side of the story.'

"'But because I had figured out your plan and even got a shot off at ya, I became somethin' of a hero in those parts. And when Pinkerton heard about it, they offered me a job as a detective. I've never stolen anything since. Of course,' he finished with a wry smile, 'I've never been this close to a hundred thousand dollars, either.'

"Suddenly I realized where all this was leadin'," said Uncle Will. "He was a thief just like me, and he was tryin' to strike a bargain. He'd figured out—or at least was pretty sure—that I had the money from the poker game, but he didn't know where it was. So I was right. Here was a man I could do business with. I didn't wanna show my hand too soon, though, so I said,

'You've obviously got somethin' on your mind, Mr. Young. You got a proposal to make?'

"'Yeah, Big Will, I'll just lay my cards on the table,' he answered. 'I wanna become your partner. From what I found out about the game last night, the pot was over a hundred thousand dollars. That split three ways is more money than I've made in the last five years, and that's what I want: a third of the pot. I would ask for half, but I don't figure you're gonna cut out your half-pint friend here. In return, I'll help ya get off this island, which I can do. The simplest plan is for us to drive this surrey right over the bridge into Ellsworth, then catch a train goin' south. If we go ahead in this storm, there won't be anybody there to stop us, but my Pinkerton credentials should get us through if there is. Now, whatta ya say?'

"I knew he had me where the hair is short," Uncle Will said, "so I decided for the moment that I was gonna let him help me. But I also decided without a shadow of a doubt that I was gonna kill him the first chance I got, 'cause no one backed me into a corner like that. And not once durin' the next several days did I consider anything other than my decision about the fate of Mr. Steve Young. For the time bein', though, I played along with him.

"'Let's do it,' I said.

"'Just one other thing,' he said. 'I'm gonna get mean if ya try to cheat me, Big Will. To be on the safe side, I'm gonna put handcuffs on ya and manacle ya to the surrey. That'll look more official if anyone stops us, too.' He handcuffed me to a brass ring that was welded between the right and left seats of the buggy, and in the drivin' rain we headed for freedom.

"It was probably 10:30 in the morning when we reached the pivot bridge that connected Mt. Desert Island to the mainland. Apparently we was the only ones smart enough or stupid enough to be out in the middle of a storm, 'cause there was nobody else in sight. We drove the surrey across into Ellsworth and right up to the railroad station without once bein' stopped. Young sent Willie in to buy three tickets to Buffalo, New York, and to find out which platform the train would leave from. When Willie returned, he said it was less than thirty minutes 'til the train was to depart. Young looked so cocksure of himself at that moment that I coulda killed him on the spot if I hadn't needed him.

"'You haven't said anything to the contrary, so I assume the money is in your baggage somewhere,' he said. 'Now, I'm just gonna give ya a brief little talk about what can happen. We're still in Maine. I want ya to remember that. I'm an officer of the law. I want ya to remember that, too. Your life is in my hands. But it's not gonna do us any good for ya to board that train in handcuffs. Somebody might get suspicious, and we're too close to makin' it outa here. So I'm just gonna help with the baggage and be sure ya get on that train. We have two compartments, and I want ya to bring my share to my compartment before we get outa state. After that, you're off the hook. Just make certain ya deliver the money before we get out of Maine. Then maybe we can talk about a partnership in other ventures. I think we could do well together.'

181

"I thought to myself, 'If you think you're gonna stick a .44 under my nose and order me around the way ya have for the past few hours, then talk me into becomin' partners with ya, ya don't know Big Will as well as ya think ya do.' But of course I didn't say that. I just sorta grunted, grabbed my bags, and headed for the train. Not one lawman did we see. If they was watchin' the ticket booth at the railroad station, they apparently didn't expect Willie to buy our tickets.

"After we boarded the train and settled in, I asked the conductor how long it'd be before we crossed the state line into New Hampshire. He said we was scheduled to cross it about 4:30 that afternoon. He said we'd reach Vermont about an hour and a half after that, and then get into New York State around 7:30 or 8:00 that evenin'.

"The hurricane must not have gone very deep into the mainland yet, 'cause by 3:30 that afternoon the sun was beginnin' to break through the clouds. We was less than an hour away from the New Hampshire border when I walked back to Young's compartment with a paper sack in my hand. The poker pot had come to just over one hundred and twelve thousand dollars, and I brought him exactly one third—thirty-seven thousand dollars and change. After he counted it two or three times, he asked what I thought about a partnership. With my nerve and his knowledge of bankin' and the law, he said we'd never want for anything. And he was right when ya think about it. But all I could think of was how good it was gonna feel to kill that son-of-a-bitch.

"I told him I wanted to be out of Maine before I considered any business proposals, so we sat there chattin' in his compartment for nearly an hour and a half. All that time I had the strangest sensation. It was like I was talkin' to a dead man, like the fella across from me no longer even existed.

"After a while the train started windin' up and down through mountains like I'd never seen before. I guess now it was the White Mountains of New Hampshire, but I don't know for sure. I never went back to that part of the world to find out. We was goin' through tunnels, over trestles and across deep ravines. It was almost scary. Some of the ravines looked like they was a mile deep.

"'Mr. Pinkerton man,' I finally said, 'if ya wanna form a partnership, let's head back to the observation car and talk about it there. I get an eerie feelin' whenever I'm boxed in that somebody is on the other side of the wall listenin' to everythin' I say. We can stand out on the observation deck and nobody but the birds will hear us.'

"He had no quarrel with that, so we left the compartment and strolled back through the train to the last car. There, outside to the rear, was an open-air platform. Not a soul was anywhere around, I guess because the weather had been so foul all day.

"As we stepped out onto the platform, I leaned back real casual-like against the rail of the car and took a look up ahead. The train was just startin' a sharp turn and headin' across a tremendous gorge. I stood there fascinated, 'cause I'd never seen anything that high or deep. Lookin' down into it was like starin' into a bottomless pit.

"'Okay, I'm ready to listen to your idea now,' I said.

"'Well, like I said earlier, Big Will,' Young said as he joined me against the rail, 'with my brains and your balls, neither of us should ever want for anything again...'

"Nephew, when I heard him braggin' about how smart he was, a fury took hold of me that I can't believe to this day. In one split second I reached down and grabbed the back of his pants legs, gave a hard jerk with both hands, and flipped him off the train. His head caught the track with a loud thud as he tumbled over and slammed against the trestle. That probably killed him right there, but if that wasn't enough, he dropped to the first row of cross timbers and each one caught him and flipped him like a rag doll over and down against the next one. It was as if those cross timbers was alive. Each one grabbed him, bent him double, and spun him on until the last one finally flung him violently down toward the bottom of that tremendous gorge.

"I stood and watched as he faded from view. A second later we entered a tunnel, and my rage slowly turned to remorse as I closed my eyes and again saw Steve Young's body bein' thrown from one cross timber to the other, down, down, down, with arms and legs flailin'. The Pinkerton man was no more, but it didn't feel good like I thought it would." Uncle Will stopped and stared off into the distance for several minutes before he cleared his throat and went on.

"I walked back through the train to my compartment, then went on to his compartment and gathered up the money I'd left there earlier. After stuffin' it in my money belt, I made my way to the dinin' car and joined Willie for supper. He kept lookin' around for Young, but of course Young didn't show up. When we finished supper and got back to our compartment, Willie said, 'Will, now that we're outa Maine, we're probably outa trouble. Whatta ya say ya give me my split now, just in case we accidently get separated?'

"I got the suitcase and counted him out 370 one-hundred dollar bills. The wad was so thick it made a big bulge around his middle when he stuck them in his money belt. In late 1913, the thirty-seven thousand dollars I gave him, and the fifteen thousand he already had, made quite a sum of money, to say the least.

"It was probably 10 or 10:30 that evenin' when I crawled into my Pullman berth to go to sleep. As usual, my mind began to drift, and I began to float on that foggy, feathery pillow that lowers us into slumber, when suddenly I was racked by a sickenin' vision of Steve Young tumblin' down into that gorge. In a second I was snatched back to bein' fully awake. My palms were sweaty, my brow was wet, and my mouth was dry as cotton.

"I jumped outa bed and hurried to the dinin' car, but it was already closed. Finally I found a porter sittin' in the other end of the car and told him I needed a bottle of whiskey.

"'It's against the law to sell whiskey at this time of night,' he said.

"I stuck a hundred dollar bill under his nose. 'Would this possibly ease your conscience about breakin' the law?'

"'Yes sir, it would soothe it a bit,' he answered. 'You stay here and I'll be right back.' A few minutes later he brought me a quart of liquor, and I carried it back to my compartment and downed it.

"Nephew, that was thirty-five years ago, and since then Ol' Ebo has made every night a livin' hell. Sometimes I shut my eyes and nearly drift off to sleep before he knows it, but then I'm jolted awake by the vision of Young's body crashin' toward that bottomless pit. And what's worse, the trestle gets higher and the ravine deeper every time. No sir, don't never let Ol' Ebo into your life, 'cause he'll stay forever.

"But anyway, the next mornin' when Willie and I went to the dinin' car, he again asked about the Pinkerton. I didn't say a word, though. I couldn't think *what* to say. We pulled into Buffalo not long after that and went to a little diner next door to the depot to discuss what we was gonna do with the rest of our lives. After some discussion we decided we'd get us a ticket to Miami and maybe go back to Havana, at least for the winter.

"Late that afternoon we boarded another train headed south. My sleepin' pattern was the same that night as it was the night before, and I must say that some of the zest I had for livin' just went out of me, nephew. I couldn't shut my eyes without seein' that Pinkerton man fallin' into the canyon again.

"There was about an hour's layover between trains in Richmond, Virginia, so Willie and I sat down on a bench in the station. After a long period of silence, Willie said, 'Will, it's been over ten years since I've been home. Course, I've never really had a home or any kin, but somehow I need to go back to Mississippi and Louisiana. I'm lonesome for that country. You're a big boy now, and you can sure as hell take care of yourself, so I'm gonna go my own way. Maybe we'll meet up again some time, but for now I'm gonna leave ya. I think maybe I'll settle down in New Orleans with a good Cajun woman, open a little eatin' joint, and try to live out my last days in peace.'

"Nothin' much else was said after that. He changed his ticket from Miami to New Orleans, we shook hands, and I caught the train south as he headed west.

"Nephew," Uncle Will said soberly, "I hope what I've told ya holds some lessons that'll keep ya from some of the grief I've known over the years. You asked me about a turnin' point in my life. Well, if ya remember, this whole story started with me stealin' my Daddy's mule to go see my girl on Saturday night. Ten years later I've got more money than I ever knew existed, but I've also murdered a man in cold blood and got Ol' Ebo as a constant companion. And it all happened so easy, just like a snowstorm. It starts with one snowflake, and before ya know it, you've got a blizzard.

"Now when I sit and ponder my past, I wonder if there was any point durin' that time when I coulda turned back, but I don't know, I just don't know. Nephew, you was at Ma's funeral. I didn't cry, not a drop. I couldn't cry at my own Ma's funeral. Ya know why? 'Cause I'd shed all my tears for *me.* I didn't have any left for her."

187

Runnin'

During the last two years of Uncle Will's life, he frequently came by the house and wanted me to go hunting or fishing with him, though I don't think he ever really had any serious intentions of doing either. He just used the outings as an excuse for us to be together so he could talk about his troubled life and try to set the record straight.

One day a few weeks after he told me about killing the Pinkerton agent, he picked me up in his old bus to take me still-hunting for squirrels. To still-hunt squirrels, you didn't need anything except a .22 rifle. The idea was to just sit as still as possible in the woods and wait for the squirrels to come out and start feeding. Usually you didn't have to wait long before you spotted a squirrel. Then if you were of a mind to, you could shoot it out of the tree.

But mostly we just talked. I think more than anything, Uncle Will wanted somebody to know that he wasn't all bad. He was born with an impulsive, uncontrollable temper that ultimately was his undoing. But when those fits of temper had passed and the deed was done, he was truly remorseful. Somehow I think he hoped that would stand him in good stead with the Almighty as his day of reckoning rapidly approached.

Most times on our outings, Uncle Will chose the subject of discussion, but on this particular day I had other ideas. No sooner were we in the old bus, rattling down the road toward the hunting spot, than I started pumping him with a thousand questions.

"Ho, ho, hold it!" he said. "Nephew, you ask more questions in two minutes than I can answer in a month. Now, one question at a time. What is it that ya really wanna know?"

"What happened after you and Willie split up in Richmond? That's where ya stopped before. He headed west, and you headed south for Miami." He didn't answer until we pulled to a stop at the edge of the woods where we always hunted. Then he shut off the motor of the bus and turned to me.

"Well," he said, pausing briefly to get his thoughts in order, "I never made it to Miami. When I got to Atlanta I began to feel a bit homesick myself. It made me sad to think about Willie havin' no kin, while I had more family than I knew what to do with. I guess ya could say nostalgia got the best of me. Anyway, when I got to Atlanta I had a pocketful of money as ya know, so I went over on Whitehall Street to the Harley Davidson motorcycle people and bought me a brand new motorcycle with a side car, then headed for home.

"That's the sweetest ride in the world, a motorcycle is. I loved to ride one more than anything in the world, to get out with the breeze in my face in the summertime. It was just like sittin' on a cushion of air.

"It didn't take long for my sentimental feelings to wear off once I was home, though. Pretty soon I got antsy to see Willie again, so I buried all but four or five hundred dollars in a spot along the Big Tallapoosa River and took off for New Orleans.

"Of course, ya know how I always got to drinkin' and gamblin' when I was out on the road. I'd always find some place to win or lose money, 'cause no matter how bad the times is, somebody's always willin' to make ya a bet. As a matter of fact, nephew, one of my favorite songs is 'The Roving Gambler.'" And with that introduction he began to sing in a coarse voice:

Oh, I am a roving gambler,
I've gambled all around.
Wherever I meet with a deck of cards,
I lay my money down.

I gambled down in Texas,
I've gambled up in Maine,
I'm on my way to Georgia
To knock down my last game.

I had not been in Georgia
For many more weeks than three,
When I fell in love with a pretty little girl
And she fell in love with me.

"I don't remember the rest right off hand," he said as the words faded. "It goes on and on. But that was always one of my favorite songs.

"At any rate, I spent more time and money than I meant to spend on the road to find Willie, mainly 'cause I had a terrible run of luck. The cards was against me, and pretty soon I was broke. I mean stone, flat broke.

"I still remember the afternoon I lost my last dollar. It was in Bogalusa, Louisiana. As best I recollect, there wasn't a whole lot of money in the game. I was down to nickels and dimes, and so was the fella across from me. He was a two-bit gambler and a two-bit hood, but he was pretty slick with a deck of cards and bold as a bank robber.

"We was playin' Five Card Stud. I had a pair of eights showin', and he had a pair of deuces, but that sucker bet me two dollars, the last two dollars he had in the world, and I couldn't even call him. He won 'cause I ran out of money first. Afterward, I sat around 'til everybody else had gone home, and then asked to have a word with him.

"I never will forget that fella. His name was Zeb Kinlow. He was a tall, raw-boned man, probably twenty-six or twenty-seven years old, with nerves of steel. You could tell that from the way he played cards. And that's just what I liked about him. He wasn't one of those fellas who was gonna run out on ya in a tight spot. He'd stay with ya until the bitter end—at least that's the way he impressed me.

"After everybody else left, I told him I was a man of means but that my funds was back in Georgia, six or seven hundred miles away, and I was broke. I also told him he didn't appear to have a whole lot of money himself, or else he wouldn't have been in that penny-ante poker game. He wasn't the most talkative person I'd ever met, but he did admit that I'd made a pretty astute observation.

"'Well, this penny-ante stuff ain't becomin' to a fellow with your talents,' I continued on. 'Now, I'm temporarily, financially embarrassed, and there's no way I'm gonna get back to Georgia without funds. You ain't never seen me before, though. I know that. And I ain't gonna ask ya to loan me no money. You can rest easy about that, 'cause I don't think you've got enough to get me back home anyway. I ain't bashful about askin' to borrow, I just don't think it'd help, so let's get that outa the way right now.'

"He didn't respond one way or the other, which is pretty much what I expected. He just sat there with a stone-cold look on his face, just like the one he'd used durin' the poker game. He didn't stop me, though, so I went on.

"'I've been fairly successful in a couple of armed robberies over the years, and I wonder if you'd be interested in helpin' me pull a little job that'll get you a stake and help me get back to Georgia. I'm not talkin' about nothin' as risky as robbin' a bank, but do ya know where there's a country store we could knock over without any trouble? Since you're from around these parts, ya probably know a place like that where we could both make a hundred dollars or so for a few minutes' work. Whatta ya say? Are ya interested?'

"Zeb lowered his head into his hands, both elbows restin' on his knees, and didn't say a word for a long, long time. I'd about decided my proposal to stick up a store had totally overwhelmed him, when he looked up at me and said, 'What's your name, friend? I don't rightly remember hearin' anybody call ya by your name.'

"'Maybe you're not as sharp as I gave ya credit for,' I thought to myself. 'Surely it didn't take ya that long to put together one question.' But I went ahead and answered, 'Most people call me Will.'

"'Well, Will, I can't think of a grocery store within fifty miles of here that you'd get more than thirty or forty dollars out of, but there is one place where we could get a whole lot more,' he said, showin' the brains I figured he had. 'I was just tryin' to remember if I ever saw a gun there. It's an auction barn between here and Poplarville, Mississippi. This is pretty fair cattle country, and folks raise some good breedin' stock. They have a cattle auction every Wednesday at the barn, and I suspect there'd be seven or eight thousand dollars in the cash register, especially late in the afternoon between the time the buyers pay for their cattle and the sellers collect. In fact, on a real good day it might even get up to ten thousand. Would half of that be enough to carry ya home?'

"I'd guessed he was a nervy bastard, but I hadn't counted on this. 'Really, Zeb, I didn't have anything that big in mind,' I sorta stuttered. 'Besides, they must protect that kinda money pretty well.'

"'There may be a gun or somethin' hidden under the counter, but I ain't never seen it,' he replied. That sounded good to my ears.

"'If it ain't too far, let's go take a look.'

"'Let's go,' he answered.

"It was Thursday and a full week before we could actually do this thing—if we decided to do it at all—but I had to have some operatin' money in the meantime, so I asked him whether he was gonna be able to feed me, buy gas for my cycle, and find me a place to stay 'til the big day. He said he could. With that, he climbed into the side car of my Harley and we took off.

"The auction barn was just a big ol' barn with stalls down each side of a double-wide hallway. As the cattle was brought in, a worker stuck a numbered tag through the thin part of each cow's ear, then wrote the owner's name and the number they'd assigned the animal on a talley sheet for later. Next, he tore off the sheet and gave it to a boy who ran it up to the office. That way the office would know the owner of a given-numbered cow. When the cow sold, they'd send another sheet to the office showin' who'd bought it, so as soon as a man's cows was sold, he could go into the office and pick up his money, less some little commission the barn charged for handlin' the sale.

"When the cows came in, they ambled down one side and filled up all the right-hand stalls. Then they was slowly led past a platform at the far end of the buildin' where the farmers sat and bid on 'em. When an animal was sold, it was driven on around the platform, which was in the shape of a half-moon, and placed in a stall on the other side of the hallway. That way they could keep the sold and unsold cattle separate.

"I'd never seen anything like the system they had set up, but it seemed to work pretty well. The business office sat just behind the platform where the farmers did their biddin', and, like the barn, it wasn't guarded or locked durin' the day. We looked the place over as casual as possible, with Zeb showin' me where this person and that person stood and how they paid money out and took money in.

"There was a few things I didn't like about the set-up. For one thing, the office had too many doors leadin' into it. There was two in back near the platform where the farmers sat, and one in front that opened to the outside. Of course, I realized that the buildin' wasn't built to please robbers. It was designed for the convenience of the cattle-buyers. But I didn't like the prospect of somebody screamin' while we was robbin' the office, and people pourin' in through three doors to block our way out. If Willie had taught me one thing when I was runnin' with him, it was to make damn sure ya got away after ya got what ya came for.

"I told Zeb I needed to go somewhere and just think about the whole job, so he carried me to the home of a friend named Billy Simpson. Billy had a pretty red-headed wife and two darlin' little kids, but he had somethin' more: a spare bedroom. Billy thought Zeb was a genius. He acted like he'd follow Zeb to the end of the earth. Billy also had a good-lookin' Ford automobile, which I thought might play a big part in our escape plans.

"Zeb told Billy that I'd only stay a few days and be no bother, which was fine with him. I think he'd have let Ol' Ebo Himself stay there if Zeb asked him to.

"After that, I dropped Zeb off at his pa's place and said I'd be back the next day to tell him if I thought we could pull it off. 'Ya may need this,' he said, handin' me ten dollars, 'in case ya decide to look around some more. Just remember, it's a loan, not a handout.'

"The next mornin' I drove back over and told Zeb that after due consideration, I didn't believe it was possible for two men to rob the auction barn. We needed at least two more men that would listen and follow orders without any questions.   We also needed to go somewhere far away and steal a car, 'cause with no more cars than there was around those parts, the authorities would come lookin' for us before the dust settled if we used a local vehicle.

"'What about Billy?' Zeb asked. 'He follows orders right well.'

"'No, he's got a wife and kids to think about. We need somebody who ain't got no ties.'

"Zeb said he had a couple of cousins over in Poplarville that wasn't afraid of nothin', so we headed out to see if they wanted in on the deal. When we got there, he introduced me to Frank and Paul Mellon. They wasn't twins, but I swear they coulda passed for ones. Both was in their early twenties, stood about five-foot-five, and had strawberry-colored hair. And freckles? Why, I ain't never seen so many freckles on two human beings in my life. They was just one solid freckle. No, I guess they wasn't a solid freckle. There musta been a fleck of white on 'em here and there or I wouldn't have knowed they had freckles. But they had enough for any ten people, I guarantee.

"When we was out of hearin' from the other folks at the house, Zeb told 'em what we had in mind and asked if they'd be interested in joinin' us. They thought it over, looked at each other, grinned, and decided it sure as hell beat farmin'.

"Lookin' back on it, nephew, it seems a bit crazy. There we was, schemin' to pull off a tricky robbery that was as likely to get us killed as it was to make us rich, while I had more money than I knew what to do with back in Haralson County, Georgia, but no way to get back to it. It was one of those kind of things that I didn't really wanna do but couldn't see any good way out of. And it's another of those moments that I look back on and wonder how my life woulda been different if I'd turned and walked away. Sometimes there's a thin line between right and wrong, and it's amazin' how easy it is to cross over it.

"As it turned out, Frank and Paul had forty dollars between 'em, and after listenin' to us talk about how much we was gonna get from the sale barn, they was perfectly willin' to use it any way Zeb and I felt was necessary. Before we went any further, though, we had a little vote and named me the head of the gang. They'd do exactly what I said, when I said it, 'cause I had more experience in this sorta thing than any of them. I was to be the absolute boss of our little band of thieves.

"It was now Friday, and we had gotten a little money together. Frank and Paul and I decided to go to Wiggins, Mississippi, which was about forty miles from Bogalusa, and take a room in a boardin' house until the followin' Wednesday. I took one room and Paul and Frank shared another one, which they'd done most of their lives anyway. We got us some nice-lookin' clothes, had a good meal, and then cruised around town on my motorbike to get an idea what the village of Wiggins was like."

"There was a big white church in Wiggins," Uncle Will went on. "I don't remember what denomination it was, I just remember that an almost new, black, 12-cylinder Packard was parked in front of it. You've probably never seen a car like that, nephew. It didn't have a top on it, just a fold-down canvas cover. That was long before they made hard-top automobiles.

"The Mellon brothers was good drivers, or so they said, and I figured that Packard would run about seventy-five miles an hour, so there was no way a horse was gonna catch us. Once we got the money and got rollin', we was home free.

"Accordin' to Zeb, the sale usually started around noon and ended about four o'clock, but most of the farmers liked to sit around the first few hours and talk, chew tobacco, gossip, and do all the things that farmers do when they get together. Then there was a rush on the office around 3:30. From what he said, it looked like three o'clock would be an ideal time to make our move.

"Still, people came and went from the office of the barn all afternoon, and that presented a problem I didn't like at all. In fact, I didn't sleep much Saturday or Sunday night for thinkin' about it. I could just see three or four people walkin' in the doors as we was holdin' up the place, and us havin' to kill some of 'em for one reason or another. After the incident with Steve Young, I didn't wanna get involved in that sorta thing again, and I was beginnin' to get cold feet about the whole operation.

"Then I got an inspiration. The two doors that came from the barn itself into the back of the office opened right behind the counter where the office workers handled all the transactions. It occurred to me that we could take a wood auger one night when no one was around and bore a hole through the jam of each door and the slats of the doors themselves. Then when we started the holdup, two of us could walk over and stick an iron pin through those holes. That would keep anybody from openin' them from the outside, which would mean we only had to worry about bein' confronted from one side.

"Suddenly, things were beginnin' to look better.

"While Frank and I went over Monday night to fix the doors on the sale barn so we could lock 'em, Paul checked around to see if he could find out where the big V-12 Packard stayed when it wasn't parked in front of the church. We suspected it belonged to the preacher, and sure enough, when Paul walked the mile from the church to where the preacher lived, the Packard was sittin' in his yard.

"The preacher lived on top of a little knoll and had a horseshoe-shaped driveway in front. From the looks of things, he entered on one end and drove around until the driveway started slopin' back down to the road at the other end, then stopped the car in that position. I figured he did that because electric starters were new at the time and the batteries were notoriously bad. Even though the preacher was a God-fearin', God-trustin' man, he still parked his car so he could let it roll off and crank in the event the battery died.

"The Packard looked almost new, so we didn't expect to have any mechanical difficulties with it, but the V-12 engine bothered me. It was supposed to run seventy-five miles an hour, but there wasn't any roads in the immediate area that would support that kind of speed for very long. I was afraid if our driver got too excited, he'd wreck us with all that power. Besides, I only wanted enough speed to outrun the folks that might be chasin' us once we left the sale barn.

"Frank and I fixed the doors of the barn real careful-like so's no one would notice unless they looked real close, then headed back to the boardin' house. Zeb joined us there Tuesday afternoon, and we fell to talkin' about the project. After a while we decided to go over and make sure we had a good place to hide the Packard in the woods above the sale barn, 'cause if anyone found it there, they'd suspect somethin' since it was such a high-class automobile. In fact, I think even if I hadn't been wantin' to rob the barn, I'd have stolen the car anyway, it was so beautiful. But that's neither here nor there.

"Although I'd decided earlier not to let my motor-cycle be seen in the vicinity of the sale barn, I changed my mind and risked it because we was short on time. The barn sat on the north side of the road that ran east and west from Bogalusa to Poplarville. A small road from the north ran down beside the barn and dead-ended into the Bogalusa-Poplarville road. We found a good place well off the side road where the ground was firm enough that we could turn the car around and back it into the woods. It looked safe because there wasn't no farm land for better than a mile on either side of it. The only problem left to solve was where to hide my motorcycle. I intended to high-tail it back to Georgia the minute the deed was done and get as far away from that place as I could between three o'clock and sundown Wednesday.

"Zeb and I finally decided the best thing to do was to just keep the car and motorcycle at the same place. In the Packard, we certainly could outrun anybody that was chasin' us, whether they was on horses or in automobiles. When we reached the hidin' place, I would take my share of the money and bail out while they continued on north up the road. Then I'd crawl on my motorcycle and head south. Of course, I knew I'd meet the posse goin' after the robbers, but they wouldn't know I was one of 'em. I mean, nobody would be stupid enough to double back and meet 'em, would they? After I got to the sale barn, I'd swing left and go through Poplarville and on past Wiggins. Meanwhile, the other three could do whatever they wanted to with themselves and the car. I never expected to see any of them again, and they understood that.

"This plannin' and hustlin' around gave me a headache, and it was all because I didn't have enough money to get back to my *own* money. That's awful, ain't it, nephew? It was dumb of me to get in that predicament. Here I was runnin' some scam where I could get my head blown off, and me with all sorts of money at home. I'd probably have been better off to start walkin' and bum my way back to Georgia, but I never did anything the easy way.

"Anyway, when Zeb and I got back from decidin' where to hide the vehicles, we went to Paul and Frank's room for a conference. Paul borrowed the Grier's Almanac from the landlady and found that a full moon was due to rise at eleven that night. Since the sky was clear, that meant we'd probably have enough light to

201

drive all the way back to Bogalusa in the Packard without ever turnin' on the headlights. We'd have to go slow, of course, but most likely we'd be the only people on the road that night, least-wise I hoped so.

"Zeb made a pallet out of a quilt, and we all decided to get a good nap before it was time to steal the car, but I hadn't no more than closed my eyes when I had that dream again about Steve Young. In a split second I was wide awake. I laid there in the dark thinkin' about how innocently my life of crime had started. It just seemed to snowball until I couldn't stay outa this sorta thing anymore.

"Even though it was a hot evenin', several times I felt my hands and feet grow cold and clammy as I went over our plans for our holdup. The thought crossed my mind that maybe the nightmare was a warnin' that this time I wasn't gonna pull it off. Maybe I was gonna get somebody killed. Maybe it was gonna be *me*.

"I thought seriously about sneakin' out, gettin' on my motorcycle, and goin' as far toward Georgia as that tank of gas would carry me. I still had a couple of dollars Zeb had given me to pay expenses. That would get me part of the way to Tallapoosa. As a matter of fact, I did walk around Zeb's pallet and pull the window shade up to take a look out. I'd slept longer than I realized, 'cause the moon was just beginnin' to rise over the horizon. It was a beautiful sight, and as I stood there watchin' Ol' Ebo, I swear he winked at me. I winked back at him and immediately felt better about the whole thing. Maybe I'd pull this off after all.

"A few minutes later I woke the other three up, and we started walkin' over to the preacher's house. Nowa-

days when ya go out at night, the cars are whizzin' up
and down the road so fast ya can hardly hear yourself
think, but back then everything was so still that we
could hear ourselves breathin' as we walked along the
road. Nothin' and nobody was stirrin'. Everybody was
home in bed where they shoulda been. Meanwhile here
we was, four princes of the Devil, out to do mischief to
the good folks of the community. I felt a pang of guilt,
so I glanced at the moon to see if Ol' Ebo would wink at
me again, but this time he looked like Pa waggin' his
finger at me. I looked back down at the ground real
quick as we walked on.

"Just as I expected, it was gonna be plenty light for
us to drive down the road without any headlights. All
we had to do was slip that car away from the preacher's
house and get it cranked up. There wasn't any lights
on in the house when we went sneakin' up the driveway, but I still felt awful exposed. As tall as I am, I felt
like an elephant tryin' to be the size of a mouse. We had
a couple of spark-plug wires to hot-wire the car, but as
it turned out, the preacher had left the key in the car.
He was obviously a trustin' soul, but this time it was
gonna cost him.

"I slid in the front seat, took the hand brakes off,
knocked it outa gear, and whispered, "Push!" The
others gave a little shove, then jumped in, too. I didn't
try to crank it until we were five hundred yards from
the house, but when I did finally fire that big engine up,
I swear ya could hardly hear it, even in the dead of
night. Oh, it was one beautiful machine! Sittin' on
those soft-leather seats was like restin' on a pile of

goose down. Yes sir, that was some automobile, and it was all mine—for a few hours."

"About three miles outa town, we got to where Zeb and I'd stashed the motorcycle that afternoon. I tell ya, I sure did hate to give up the wheel of that car. I even seriously thought about tryin' to drive it back to Georgia right then and there, 'cause that preacher was gonna be awful mad when he woke up Wednesday mornin' and found his beautiful Packard had been stolen. And anybody with that much money in a car was gonna come lookin' for the people that took it.

"After we picked up the motorcycle, it took us another hour to get to our hidin' place north of the sale barn, but we did finally manage to get the car hidden at about 2:30 that morning. Once we was finished, I pulled my old bedroll outa the Harley, spread it out on the ground, and promptly fell asleep, Ol' Ebo or not.

"It was well past sun-up when I woke up. The boys had discovered my stash of sardines, pork and beans, and crackers in the side car and was havin' themselves some breakfast. We had five or six hours to kill before it was time to descend on the sale barn, but we didn't waste it. No, sir. We sat there drawin' diagrams of our plan in the sand, talkin' about anything that could go wrong or cause a problem. A lot of it was probably nervous energy, 'cause I was the only one who'd ever been involved in such an endeavor.

"I tried to reassure them that everything would go smoothly if we just didn't get excited when we walked in the front door of the place. We all was gonna have shotguns. Frank was gonna drive the car, Paul and Zeb was supposed to lock the doors after we got inside, and I was to get all the cash behind the counter. The way I figured it, we shouldn't be in the place more than a minute at the most. One reason we didn't wanna be there any longer than that was that the Packard would draw a crowd of admirers real fast, and we didn't wanna have to wade through a bunch of people gettin' back to the car.

"As three o'clock approached, we climbed in the car and rode by the sale barn. There wasn't many people out front, though there was lots of horses and wagons around. A truck or two was parked here and there, but none of them looked like they would give us any problem in a chase. We made a couple of slow passes, then turned in. Frank drove right up to the front door and kept the car runnin' while the rest of us walked inside. I kept real quiet until Zeb and Paul had shoved the metal pins through the holes we'd bored in the doors, then I said just loud enough to be heard, 'Folks, I came to get your money!'

"The three workers had been busy totalin' their figures, but suddenly they stopped and stared at us like we was the most outrageous thing they'd ever seen. When they saw those sawed-off shotguns lookin' them straight in the eye, they backed away just like they was supposed to. We was outa the place in good time, and we had a bundle of money.

"Outside, there was three or four farmers with their feet propped up on the runnin' board of that beautiful car, lookin' it over and tryin' to make conversation with Frank, who looked awful nervous. We waved the guns and scattered them outa the way, then jumped in and took off. Frank turned left into the road to Poplarville. I yelled at him to take it easy and not show any outward signs of haste, but before we could drive the three hundred yards to the road that turned north to where the motorcycle was hidden, we was showered with buckshot. I don't know where those farmers kept their guns, but I think everybody in that sale barn was shootin' at us.

"Frank got so excited, he didn't make the left turn, he just kept on toward Poplarville. Meanwhile, the farmers came after us like a swarm of mad hornets. Frank put the gas pedal to the floorboard, and pretty soon we was roarin' along at nearly seventy miles an hour. I knew we couldn't maintain that for long 'cause that ol' dirt wash-board road was not designed for that kind of speed, but nobody chasin' us could keep it up, either.

"Now, nephew, you're not gonna believe this, but we'd been drivin' less than five minutes when that damn car ran outa gas! Here we'd had it for twelve hours, and nobody had bothered to check and see how much gas it had in it. We just assumed the preacher kept it full, I guess, but it died no more than three miles from the sale barn. 'Boys, we best get the hell outa here!' I yelled as we slowed to a stop. Nobody argued with me, either. I grabbed the pillow case with all the money in it and we hit the woods in a dead run.

"It was a dismal patch of woods, which is about what you'd expect, considerin' how our luck was goin' that day. No sooner was we into it than we ran into canes, saw briers, and blackberry and dewberry vines. I've never been in such dense undergrowth in my life, not even down on Indian Creek. The thorns was tearin' at the pillow case and rakin' at my flesh so bad that pretty soon I had to slow down. We was workin' our way single-file through there, though, makin' some headway, when suddenly we heard the hounds bayin'. That put the fear of God in us.

"A few minutes later we finally got through the worst of it and into regular underbrush. I started out in a long lopin' gait, the other three dead in my tracks, and ran until I was totally out of breath. From the sound of things, we was slowly losin' the dogs, but if they was bloodhounds—and I had no doubt they'd get bloodhounds sooner or later—we was gonna need to find some water to throw 'em off the scent.

"When I thought we was far enough ahead of the chase, we sat down to rest for a minute and count the money. There was eight thousand dollars, which worked out to two thousand each. I handed each one of them their share and put mine in the money belt I'd carried with me since Bar Harbor. Then I made a little speech. 'Boys, it's been good to know ya,' I said, 'but it's every man for himself now. We need to split up, at least into two groups. If we get back to my motorcycle, I can take one of ya along for a while. Make up your mind what ya wanna do, though, 'cause we need to be coverin' all the ground we can. If one of ya wants to come with me, fine. If ya don't, good-bye.'

"'I'll go with ya, Will,' Zeb answered. 'The way I've been actin' lately, Pa is bound to figure I had somethin' to do with the hold-up, so I may as well clear out. It wouldn't surprise me a damn bit if Pa *told* 'em I was one of the robbers. So let me go with ya. I need to get as far away from Bogalusa as I can. Besides, the brothers oughta stick together.'

"By now I was pretty much rested. Me and Zeb took off in a dead run in one direction, and Frank and Paul went the opposite way. I tried to steer a path a little bit west of north, hopin' to intersect the northerly road that led to my Harley, but the road was so new to me that I wasn't sure I'd know it if I came across it. That's why it was some comfort to have Zeb along with me. If we hit a road, at least he'd know if it was the right one.

"Meanwhile, either the men was holdin' the hounds back, or they was havin' trouble making it through the cane break, 'cause the dogs seemed further away with each passin' moment. In fact, I was beginnin' to feel a little bit safer as we loped along through the woods. As we ran, however, I kept askin' myself, if I was those farmers, what would I do? I'd keep after my money, that's what. Since we'd had the misfortune to run outa gas, it was actually better that we missed the north turn after the robbery, 'cause now those farmers was gonna think that our escape route was east toward Poplarville. They'd be searchin' that road—both sides of it—while we headed north on the motorcycle.

"Before long our path began slopin' downhill until we reached a swift runnin' stream. Keepin' in mind that we needed to go in a northwesterly direction, we found a place to cross and waded out into it. After walkin' along in the middle for a good little piece, we came to an old fallen tree and walked up it so's not to leave any tracks for the dogs to follow.

"As we was makin' our way up the steep bank on the other side of the creek, we heard a couple of distant gunshots. It sounded like they came from near where we split up with Frank and Paul. Of course, we couldn't tell for sure, but that was our guess. We stopped a few minutes to listen, and pretty soon we heard more. Zeb started chatterin' nervously about what mighta happened. Did I think Frank and Paul had been run to ground? he asked. Did I think they'd been shot? I told him I had no way of knowin', but it seemed very likely.

"'You mean they're gonna shoot us if they catch us?' he said, his eyes wide with fear.

"'That's a very definite possibility.'

"'My God, this is serious!' he moaned.

"'Zeb, ya knew this was no Sunday school outin' when we started,' I answered.

"'Yeah, Will, you're right. But I guess this is the first time I've really thought about how bad it might get.'

"'Well, that's the way it happens,' I said matter-of-factly. 'Ya do somethin' like this, and then ya realize how serious it is. But if we're gonna avoid the same fate as Frank and Paul, we'd better move on and find the Harley.'

"By now the sun was hangin' just above the horizon. We hurried on and finally came to what looked like a clearin' up ahead. I thought maybe it was the road, so I put my hand on Zeb's shoulder and signaled him to be quiet as we approached the open area. Sure enough, it was a road. I asked him if it was the one we was lookin' for, but he couldn't make up his mind. 'I don't know, I just don't know,' he whispered. 'I ain't never been on the side lookin' toward it. Let me get out in the middle and look.'

"There was nothin' comin' from either direction, but I told him to find a big tree first that he could jump behind in case we heard anybody or anything. I didn't think there'd be a posse on the road, but we couldn't be sure. The only thing I was sure of at the moment was that we'd made a bunch of farmers awful mad.

"A minute after Zeb stepped out in the road to study the situation, we heard a car comin' from the north. He dived back into the bushes just in time to avoid bein' seen by four men with shotguns ridin' on the back of a Model T truck. 'What in the world are those bastards doin' way over here when we abandoned the car on the other road?' I said to myself. 'They just couldn't be that smart!' Then it came to me. Frank and Paul had been captured and had spilled the beans about our plan. That was the only possible explanation for those men to be patrollin' this far away from where we'd left the car. That meant that Frank and Paul had more than likely told 'em, as best they could, where we hid the Harley. If that was so, we was takin' a big risk tryin' to get to it. But it appeared to be the only chance we had of gettin' away.

"Zeb stepped out again but didn't recognize any landmarks, so we decided to keep headin' north and hope for the best.

It wasn't long 'til it began to turn dark. Since neither of us knew the territory we was coverin', we found a couple of big live oaks and climbed up in 'em to wait for the full moon. They wasn't the most comfortable accommodations I'd ever enjoyed, but I discovered that by sittin' with my tailbone in a V-shaped fork and layin' my shotgun across two limbs, I could sorta lay back and relax. Zeb did the same in his tree. Then we waited.

"Before long, I fell asleep sprawled out in the fork of that live oak tree. I don't know, maybe the combination of exertion and excitement got to me, but whatever it was, I just flat fell asleep. The next thing I knew, a screech owl had landed on a limb not four feet from my head and let out a blood-curdlin' cry that made me damn near jump outa the tree. Of course, when I startled, the owl took off in a flutter of wings, which apparently startled Zeb awake, too, 'cause he quickly fired off both barrels of his shotgun up into the sky.

"The sound of that explosion echoed through the forest for what seemed like an hour. We scrambled down to the ground, got out in the moon-lit road and continued north at a good pace, hopin' we'd recognize somethin' that would tell us whether we was headed in the right direction or not.

"An hour later, Zeb tapped me on the elbow, pointed to a nearby spot, and whispered, 'Ya see that tree hangin' out over the road? We hid the motorcycle in the woods just beyond that. I'm sure of it. I remember that the tree made sort of a "y" shape stickin' out over the road.'

"'We better be damn careful,' I whispered back. 'That truckload of men we saw earlier makes me think they captured Frank and Paul. They may have a big welcomin' party waitin' for us if Paul and Frank told 'em where we hid the Harley.'

"The moonlight filterin' down through the trees made us see all sorts of weird shapes and things that weren't really there, but somehow we kept our wits about us and moved along. Finally when I sensed we was gettin' close, I put my hand on Zeb's shoulder and motioned for him to stop. We both crouched down and locked our eyes in the direction of where we thought the cycle might be. After watchin' and listenin' for ten minutes or so, I motioned to Zeb for us to move closer, but just then we saw a flicker of light in the woods up ahead.

"Somebody had lit a cigaret. We could see the tip glow bright every time the person took a drag on it. I whispered into Zeb's ear and asked how many shells he had left after the fiasco with the screech owl. He signaled that he had two in his gun and four in his pocket, a total of six, the same number I had.

"We inched forward as silently as a fog bank invadin' the shore. When we got within fifty feet of the smoker, we could hear him talkin' to someone else. He made no effort to whisper. 'They've got to know we caught the other two, as dumb as those two were. Surely the leader and his sidekick have better sense than to come back here. We oughta be knockin' on doors and askin' folks if they've seen 'em.'

"'I'm sorta glad to sit here, myself,' replied a second fella. 'It's better than stumblin' through those saw briers with the rest of the boys, tryin' to keep up with those dang dogs.'

"I pulled Zeb over and whispered, 'Let's make sure there's only two of 'em first. Then maybe we can work our way around behind 'em and get the drop on 'em.'

"We waited for twenty or thirty minutes, bein' very quiet and very still. When we was fairly sure they was alone, I again pulled Zeb over close and whispered a plan. He'd sweep around to the left and I'd go around to the right to make sure there wasn't somebody else waitin' for us besides the men we heard talkin'. If I completed half the circle and he completed half, we'd have a pretty good idea that nobody was there except those two. If one of us didn't show up at the meetin' place behind the two men, we'd know somethin' had gone wrong.

"We split up and headed in opposite directions. I didn't run into any trouble and made it to the meetin' place quick. I don't know if Zeb was more thorough than me or what, but I beat him there by ten minutes. In fact, I'd about decided that somethin' had happened to him, when he finally showed up.

"I moved off to the side just a little bit where I could see the whole profile of both men, then said softly, 'You boys don't move. If ya do, I'll blow ya half in two.' The smoker dropped his cigaret and started to lean forward. 'Don't do that,' I warned. 'I don't wanna kill ya, but I will if ya force me. Now, lay your guns out in front of ya and stand up.' They sat there for a second like they was weighin' the odds against 'em, then set their guns down and slowly stood to their feet.

"Zeb and I edged forward and searched 'em for other weapons, but all they had was a shotgun each.

213

We threw the guns in the motorcycle side car, then ordered the two men to lay flat on their stomachs with their faces to the ground. 'If ya move before we get outa sight, we'll shoot,' I told 'em. Then I cranked up the motorcycle and eased it through the woods.

"We turned north when we hit the main road, and as we did, it looked like somebody set off a fireworks display three hundred yards up ahead. There musta been ten people in the woods on both sides, and all of 'em fired at the same time. If they'd waited another ten seconds, we'd have been close enough for 'em to do us some real harm, but they fired too quickly and we just heard a few scattered shots land nearby. Neither of us got hit, but it scared the livin' daylights outa me, and I whipped around in the middle of the road and took off goin' wide open in the other direction.

"When we passed the place where we'd just left the woods, we saw two figures silhouetted in the moonlight, but they musta been the men we'd disarmed, 'cause they didn't fire at us. I leaned over and yelled in Zeb's ear, 'It's now or never! We're gonna have to go straight through. If there's more people waitin' with guns, they're gonna have to stop us, 'cause I don't plan on slowin' down!' We fairly flew down that dirt road for about a mile, when suddenly another group opened fire on us."

"As we whizzed by, I heard somethin' that sounded like a pistol shot and suddenly felt like I'd been kicked in the nose by a mule. Tears came to my eyes, and blood gushed from the bridge of my nose. I tell ya, nephew, I was bleedin' like a stuck pig. A few seconds later we heard other blasts from behind, but by then we was too far away for the pellets to reach us. My nose hurt like hell, though, so I pulled my handkerchief outa my pocket with my left hand and pressed it across my nose to stop the bleedin'.

"The throttle on the Harley was on the right handle-bar, and I found myself havin' to speed up and slow down as I tried to drive with one hand. After I almost lost control and went off the road a couple of times, I decided if I was gonna get killed, it was gonna be by bullets, not by my own doin'. I stuffed the handkerchief back in my pocket and let the blood flow.

"I was drivin' that old Harley as fast as it would run. So fast, in fact, that it was everything I could do to make the left turn when we got to the road that led to Poplarville. Once we straightened ourselves out, though, I tried to think ahead to what might happen. If those farmers had as much sense as I thought they did, they'd have a second line of defense somewhere up ahead, probably in Poplarville. Those folks didn't fool around, neither. They fired first and asked questions later.

"Since I was pretty sure there wasn't no turn-off before Poplarville, I made up my mind to hold that motorcycle wide open and go straight through the middle of town. If they had a welcomin' party waitin' for us, they was just gonna have to shoot us, and hopefully they wouldn't be no better at guessin' when to fire than the people we'd just come past.

"We was makin' close to fifty miles an hour, which would put us in Poplarville in somethin' like ten or twelve minutes, so I leaned over and yelled to Zeb, 'Ya better say your prayers if ya know any, boy, 'cause I'm expectin' another huntin' party when we get to Poplarville.' He yelled somethin' back, but I couldn't hear what it was. I just put my head down and kept the throttle wide open.

"About three miles outside of town, I stopped to tell Zeb my plan about drivin' right through Poplarville. He agreed that was the only option we had. I also asked him how bad my nose looked, 'cause I couldn't breathe through it at all. I didn't have any teeth loose and I didn't have any other holes in me, but the blood had clotted and blocked air from gettin' through. He said it didn't look none too good, but then I'd always known that. The main thing was that it was still attached to my face.

"Just as I was about to start up again, though, I had an inspiration. 'We've got four shotguns, all of 'em double-barrel and all of 'em loaded,' I told Zeb. 'When we get within about a hundred yards of town, you start firin' off one shot at a time as fast as ya can, whether ya see anybody or not. Shoot straight ahead. I don't want ya to kill nobody, but that'll at least make 'em keep their heads down. It may be the only way we get through.'

"With that, we headed on toward Poplarville. A few minutes later we spotted the white spire of a church, then caught a glimpse of a kerosene lamp. When the sound of the motorcycle carried to the light, however, it went out. That told me and Zeb that they was waitin' for us.

"As we got near the edge of town, he started firin' up ahead of us. Boom! Boom! He'd fire both barrels of one gun, then grab another and do the same. Boom! Boom! To anybody seein' us comin', we musta looked and sounded like somethin' outa hell. It scared 'em so, in fact, that we roared through Poplarville without a single shot bein' fired by the opposition. After that, we didn't stop until it was almost daylight and we'd reached the Alabama state line. From there we turned south toward Mobile. I thought we'd probably be safe if we skirted Mobile and then headed back north, but in the meantime I had to get rid of Zeb. I hadn't told anybody in that crowd where I was from, and I thought it was best if none of 'em knew.

"Somewhere around ten or eleven that mornin', we got to Mobile and stopped at a little stream, where I washed up and took a look at my nose in the mirror of my motorcycle for the first time since gettin' hit. A great big black scab had already formed where ya see the scar today, nephew," he said, pointing out the spot to me, "but I cleaned it up and got it lookin' fairly decent again. Then I laid out the facts to Zeb real plain.

"'If they've wired ahead to Mobile, the police will be lookin' for two fellas on a motorcycle with a side car,' I said. 'I don't want to get *you* in trouble and I don't want ya to get *me* in trouble, so I think we oughta part company right now. No hard feelings, but that's the way it is. They got Frank and Paul, but we don't know what they did to 'em. I don't know about you, but I like it better that way.

"'I'm gonna be honest with ya', I continued on. 'I wish I'd never seen ya, boy. It was a fool thing we did, a damn fool thing, and I'd think it over if I was you. The

217

path you've started down can't bring nothin' but grief. I know, 'cause I've walked it a long time. So if I was you, I'd take that ill-gotten money and get rid of it, then go to work for a livin' and try to make somethin' of myself. That's the best advice I can give ya, the very best.

"'One other thing, Zeb,' I finished. 'If ya happen to get to heaven before I do and you're tellin' the Ol' Man about all the things ya did, be sure to tell him I didn't have to do a lot of talkin' to get ya to rob that cattle barn. Will ya do that for me, boy? I'd be much obliged.'

"And with that, I said goodbye and headed back to Tallapoosa. The next thing I remember, I met Fannie Hawk, and you know about her."

Uncle Will in Love

"Fannie Hawk?" I said. "Who is Fannie Hawk?"

Uncle Will seemed genuinely surprised. "Ya mean ya never heard nobody whisperin' and goin' on about Fannie Hawk? Why, there's been more gossip about what did or didn't happen between me and her than about nearly anything I ever got involved in."

I was thoroughly intrigued by that comment, because Uncle Will had been involved in a lot of wild things in his lifetime. "Was she another bank-robbin' partner?" I asked excitedly.

"Far from it, boy, far from it." He paused here like he always did when he started a new episode of his story, as if he was putting everything in order in his mind, then he proceeded.

"When I got home, I was *more* than ready to settle down and give up my life of crime, so I went over on the Big Tallapoosa River and bought me a farm. I bought a whole land lot, more 'n 200 acres. The Alabama State Line and the Georgia State Line was my property line on two sides. There was a little shack of a house on the property, not much to look at, but nestled there right on the banks of the river, it was an ideal spot. The big shade trees all around it—Spanish Oak, Post Oak, and Red Oak—was so close and so high that I don't think the sun ever touched it in the summertime. And a little bluff behind it kept the cold northers off it in the winter.

"Nephew, ya can't believe how rich I was. I bought that place for $2500 and still had close to $85,000 left. The first thing I did after buyin' the farm was to set about $8000 aside for spendin' and buried the rest in a metal box in the back yard. Back then, which was 1914 or 1915, you could live a long time on the $8000 I kept out. Yes, sir, a long time.

"I hired some local boys to fix up the house a little bit. They painted, put some good weather boardin' on, and even built me a fireplace. I'd go up to Tallapoosa every once in a while or ride over and see Ma and Pa, but mostly I kept to myself a couple of years there except for Fannie."

"Who *was* Fannie?" I interrupted. "Ya haven't told me who she was, yet."

"Patience, boy," Uncle Will said sternly. "I'm tryin' to remember how it was.

"I went up to a carnival one night in Tallapoosa, and there was Fannie. She was a carny girl. She'd had a fight with the man that owned the carnival, and he gave her a great big black eye. But she was a pretty thing, even with a shiner.

"I'll never forget that night. They had one of those little temporary eatin' joints at the carnival where they served a can of pork and beans and charged $1.50 for it. You could eat the same thing at home for fifteen cents, but people would go to a carnival and pay ten times what they ought to, just for the sake of eatin' out. But anyway, we sat down and got to talkin', and it didn't take long to find out that she was bold as brass. I mean, she just came right out and said what she thought, and I sorta liked that in her.

"She told me that the man who owned the carnival had taken advantage of her time after time. She'd thought about quittin', but didn't have anywhere to go. She didn't have any family or friends. In fact, she said she was an orphan. I'd heard Willie talk so many times about how mean they were to ya in the orphanage—and like I say, she was a right pretty thing—that I said, "'Fannie Hawk, how'd ya like to go home with me?'

"'I don't even know ya,' she replied.

"'Well, that makes us even, 'cause I don't know you either,' I answered. 'But I couldn't treat ya no worse than the way you're bein' treated now, and I'll give ya plenty to eat and a warm place to stay. If ya know how to cook, I'll keep plenty of food in the house.'

"I could tell she was considerin' her fate, weighin' me against the man who beat her up. He'd thrown her out, but I think she knew he'd take her back if she begged, which is probably what she usually did. I guess she wasn't in the notion to do that again, though, 'cause after a few minutes she asked, 'What's your name?'

"'Will,' I answered.

"'Well, you've got yourself a deal, Will. Now, how are we gonna get to this place of yours?'

"I carried her over and showed her my Harley Davidson with the side car, and she was ecstatic. 'Why didn't ya tell me about this?' she said. 'It wouldn't have taken me near as long to make up my mind!'

"'I didn't want ya to love me for my money,' I told her, and I meant it.

"Me and Fannie hit it off right good. I carried her over and introduced her to Ma and Pa as my wife. As a matter of fact, I introduced her that way everywhere we went. Since I was known in the family and the community as pretty much a drifter, nobody seemed to take exception. They may have had some doubts about me and Fannie really bein' married, but nobody said anything about it.

"Nephew, I know how the family thinks of me as a murderer. They think I'm cold and don't understand love. But I think I've been more profoundly in love than any of 'em.

"The killings I did was in cold blood they said. But it wasn't cold blood, it was hot blood. I never killed a man not in a fit of passion, with a fire flamin' so high I couldn't abide life another moment unless I did those terrible deeds. But when my rage was done, that was it. That was the end of it, except for the grief and the remorse that have hounded every step I took since.

"I was in love with Fannie Hawk, until I totally took leave of my senses. Let me tell you what we did one Saturday night. We got in my old HarleyDavidson and took a quilt and a couple of bedsheets. We went by the Smithfield Road, where you come in by Phillips' old place, then we walked down Indian Creek along the banks. If you remember, the willows were so thick you could hardly make your way through 'em. I never saw as many willow trees no where in the world as there was on Indian Creek. The willows started at Solomon Phillips place and went all the way to the Tom White Bridge. You remember how thick they was? That's where we watched that old marsh hen, remember that nephew?

"We went down to the old baptizing hole, on the lower side of the old home place, and went skinny-dipping in the baptizing hole.

"You never know'd Fannie. She was a tiny, little thing. Wasn't hardly five feet tall. When she stood straight up in front of me, the top of her head come to that little sunk-in place there in my breast bone. It was almost like she was a child, she was so tiny.

"I know, and I know'd then, that she had known men. I'm talking about 'known' in the biblical sense, nephew, do you know what I mean? I knew she was not no virgin, pure as the driven snow. But at heart, she was the best woman I ever knew.

"The night I am talking about, of course, was fifteen years before you was born, but the baptizing hole is still right where it was then. What we did, about time when it got good and dark—it was hot weather, lord it was hot—we spread that quilt and blanket out and then we put a sheet on top of it.

"As the night critters started calling, we began to see a star pop out here and there, and the lightning bugs were millions. We sat there, it seemed like for hours and didn't say a word. We were just shoulder to shoulder, taking in all of the sounds. Every once in a while during the night, my courage rising, we do our thing and lord it was wonderful.

"Like I said, the baptizing hole was in the same spot then as it was back when you were a kid. If you'll remember, Indian Creek had a big curve in it, and there was a sandbar. The sandbar was on the Bowdon side of the creek. They waded in from the Indian Creek

223

little behind a twitch just as she got in the pussy willows. I know it left some of them Christian ladies with a twinge of envy in their heart. We lost a couple of blankets and a quilt, 'cause I didn't dare go back and get 'em.

"Nephew, that night stands out in my recollection as probably the all time, happiest time in my life. But not long after that, things began to go bad between me and Fannie."

While we continued to talk, Uncle Will started up the old bus and pulled back into the road. I figured we were heading back home, since we'd been gone several hours, and I didn't pay any attention to the course he took. However, suddenly he turned off onto a road I'd never seen before. There was a gate across the road and a large field on the other side.

"Where are we?" I asked. "This is the farm I used to own," he replied. "It's been thirty years since I've been back, but I'm gonna drive down through that pasture and see if I can find the spot where my little house sat."

"Aren't you gonna ask the people who live here now if that's all right?" I asked a little nervously.

"Hell, no, I ain't gonna ask," Uncle Will snapped with typical disdain for law or etiquette. "All I wanna do is go down there and see if I can find the place. I ain't gonna bother nothin'."

The idea of trespassing on someone's property made me very uneasy, but we opened the gate and followed that rough, rut-filled road across the pasture until we eventually drove right up to a river. And there it was, the shack he'd described to me just a little while earlier. The paint was long since gone and the roof had nearly rotted down, but the walls were still standing. As we stepped through what used to be the front door, the floors began to creak and crack as we walked on the old, weathered boards.

"Careful, nephew, don't break a leg," Uncle Will cautioned. "A lot of rain's poured through this roof since I left here, and there's no tellin' how sturdy the floor is."

There was an old fireplace on one side, just like he'd said. Andirons were still sitting in it, with cobwebs stretched from them to the top of the fireplace, creating a crazy patch-work from the hearth all the way up to the mantle board. A half-used box of wooden kitchen matches, their heads melted together by moisture, rested on top of the mantle, along with a Bruton Snuff box that was weathered but still recognizable.

In one corner stood a decaying churn. The ring of the cloth that was once tied around it was still there, though the cloth itself had rotted away, and whatever they'd left in the churn was as hard as a rock. I asked Uncle Will how long he reckoned it'd been since anybody had lived there. "Probably fifteen or twenty years," he responded. "I sold it in the fall of 1918, and the next owners abandoned it during the Depression, from what I heard."

"So you and Fannie lived here four years?"

"Fannie only stayed two," Uncle Will replied as he stared around the delapidated structure he once called home. "They were good years, though. I think we both enjoyed 'em. But she was strong-willed, and so was I. One night after I'd been out with the boys, I came home drunk, and she was gone. No note, no nothin'. She'd just up and left. I never saw her again. I really didn't think we'd been havin' that much trouble. Sure we had a fight every now and then, but that's to be expected. The main problem was that she always thought I was runnin' around with other women.

"Ya know, nephew—of course ya don't know, and I hope ya never do—but when ya drink liquor and do a lot of gamblin', it consumes most of your wakin' hours. Ya ain't got *time* to be chasin' after other women, 'cause ya got more important things to do. But a woman sittin' at home don't understand that. She don't seem to mind the gamblin' and the drinkin', but the thought of ya bein' out at all hours of the night with another woman drives her crazy. That's what she worries about most, when it's really the thing she oughta worry about the least. The true gambler and drinkin' man ain't got time for no whorin'."

As we talked, Uncle Will made his way through an old home-made door that was hanging by one hinge. "This was mine and Fannie's bedroom," he said, motioning to the small room straight ahead. "I remember the night I broke the door down. I came in late, and she put a chair behind the doorknob so I couldn't get in. Well, wasn't no woman gonna keep me outa my own bedroom, and in a drunken rage I kicked the door right off of its hinges. I made kindlin' outa the chair she had propped on the other side, too. Best I recollect, that was the only time I ever hit her. I gave her a shiner about as big as the one she had the first time I ever saw her. She called me a bunch of dirty names and I took out after her, but I musta been drunker than I thought, 'cause I couldn't catch her. The next mornin' when I woke up hung-over, it didn't seem worthwhile to pursue the matter any further. But when I looked at that black eye I'd given her, I felt mighty bad.

"It wasn't too long after that 'til I came home one night in the fall of 1916, and she was gone. When I looked in the chest of drawers and cupboards and saw her things were gone, somehow I knew I'd never see her again. I sat on the bed for a long time that night thinkin' about all the good times we'd had and how Ma and Pa had even come to accept her as a member of the family. Of course, I think they always suspected that we'd never really had a preacher say words over us, but they never once mentioned it.

"I thought about what a good girl Fannie was, too. She cooked and washed and ironed, and in return I kept her in new clothes and plenty of groceries. I also thought about that metal box of money I had buried out in the back yard. Why, I'd been back and forth to that spot so much, I'd left a trail knee-deep. I'd finally moved it to the other side of the yard a month or so earlier, and there was a whole lot less money then than there was the night I first buried it. When ya drink and gamble a lot, money just don't stay around long. After two years of livin' high on the hog, I had less than $10,000 left out of the $80,000.

"I sat on the bed the night Fannie left, and I cried— the first time I'd cried since killin' the Pinkerton man.

I cried 'cause I remembered how when I got drunk enough and I had Fannie there beside me at night, I didn't dream as much about that body tumblin' off the train down into that gorge. Somehow Fannie eased those nightmares. Oh, I had 'em from time to time, even when she was there, and it scared the livin' wits outa her. She said I screamed, screams that would wake the dead and terrify the righteous. Them was her words. And she knew it must be some awful black thing that caused a man to carry on that way in his sleep.

"She asked me a time or two what I dreamed about, but I never told her. I lied instead and said I didn't know.

"Anyway, I cried myself to sleep that night. When I woke up the next mornin', I looked to see if maybe I'd only dreamed that she'd left. But no, she was gone. Long gone."

Moonshinin'

"What'd ya do after that?" I asked, fully expecting him to describe all the pain and misery he suffered.

"I went lookin' for a card game and liquor, that's what I did," he answered quickly. "And I found both at a hangout just below Tallapoosa. I was feelin' mighty low and tryin' to drown my sorrow about Fannie, when suddenly I looked up, and there standin' in the doorway was my old friend, Willie Kilgore! It'd only been a couple of years since I'd seen him, but he looked like he'd aged twenty. His hair had turned white, and he had a scraggly white beard.

"Of course, he'd always been a scrawny little thing, but he looked even skinnier now. Why, he musta lost fifteen or twenty pounds. He'd have to cross in front of the sun twice to make a shadow, he was so thin. None of that really mattered, though, 'cause I needed a friend worse than anything right then. I jumped up, and we had us a huggin' and hand-shakin' reunion on the spot. I let him share my bottle and told him how glad I was to see him. He said the same.

"After a while I got around to askin' what in the world he was doin' in Tallapoosa. He turned real quiet and said he'd married a girl in New Orleans and had a good life with her for a couple of years, but she took sick with T.B. and he'd buried her just a month earlier. He said he'd spent every dime he had on her, so he'd decided to come see if his old friend Will could help him make a new start.

"It was a sad story, one I was sorry to hear. Still, I was glad to see him under any circumstances. I put him in the side car of my motorcycle and carried him out to show him my farm. Of course, it wasn't no bigger than the shack ya see now, but back then it was in a good state of repair."

About that time, Uncle Will stopped and said, "Nephew, let's get outa this damn place. I swear I can almost feel Fannie's presence, and it gives me the heebie-jeebies. There's too many memories here, way too many. Whatta ya say? We'll find a spot on the river and do some fishin', and I'll go on with my story."

We were only fifty or sixty feet from the bank of the river, and he always kept the fishin' gear in the bus, so it woulda been easy enough to throw in a line, but I had my doubts. "Aren't ya gonna ask the folks that own this land about fishing here?" I asked nervously. "Seems like we oughta get somebody's permission so we won't get shot."

"We don't need nobody's permission," Uncle Will snapped. "This is God's river. He made it and He put the fish in it for us to catch." I'd never heard Uncle Will talk about the Almighty quite like that, but it didn't convince me.

"I still think we oughta go up and ask those people if it would be okay. I'd feel a whole lot better about it."

"Okay, nephew," Uncle Will finally replied. "Just so ya won't worry yourself sick about it, I know the people that own this place and I've got a standin' invitation to come over anytime and catch all the fish I want to. Are ya happy now?" I could never tell whether or not Uncle Will was being truthful, but I couldn't think of a way to call his hand on it, so I nodded in agreement.

We picked out a good high spot on the ground and laid the bedrolls out, since it was getting close to dark, then arranged the campfire so that all we'd have to do when it got chilly was strike a match to it. We had everything we needed to cook a mess of fish except the fish, so we both sat down on the bank and tossed in our lines.

I'd always enjoyed fishing. It was such a mystery. You never, ever knew what was going to jump onto the end of that hook. Night fishing was more intriguing than day fishing, because sometimes you couldn't see what you'd caught even after you got it up close to the bank. It could be a turtle or a fish or any number of things.

We sat down in a clean, sandy spot, not expecting to catch anything before it got dark because the fish rarely ever bit in the daytime. We weren't worried, though, since we had some sardines, onions, and light bread we'd brought for the squirrel-hunting trip. Besides, I was really more interested in hearing Uncle Will spin tales about his exploits.

When we finally got settled, he asked as he always did, "Now, where was I?"

"Willie had lost his wife and wanted you to help him get back on his feet."

"Yeah, right. Well, I hated to see Willie that way. He was like a brother to me. In fact, I was still a little bit peeved with him for leavin' me in Richmond, 'cause

I thought we made a pretty good pair. I think I was even madder about him gettin' old so quick. He looked old and tired, and it made me feel old and tired, too. But anyway, we exchanged stories 'til way late into the night. All that time, it seemed like he was shadowboxin'. Somethin' was botherin' him that he wanted to talk about, but he didn't know how.

"Finally when we'd about talked ourselves out, he said, 'Will, did you kill that Pinkerton man, Steve Young?' I was the only person on earth that knew that, and hearin' him ask the question was sorta like bein' slapped in the face by reality.

"'Of course not,' I lied. 'What in the hell makes ya ask somethin' like that?'

"'Well, I passed through Monroe on my way out here, and there was a poster in nearly every store offerin' a $500 reward to anyone who knew his whereabouts. I asked around to find out what was he wanted for, and it turns out that Pinkerton was lookin' for him 'cause he just up and disappeared. They had no idea what happened to him. The last word they had from him, accordin' to a fella I talked to, was that he was leavin' Maine with the two bandits that had robbed the Monroe bank ten years earlier. He was never heard from again. That means me and you was the last people to see him alive, and I never saw him again on the train after ya went in to give him his share of the money.

"'I figured that somehow, some way, ya managed to kill him and get rid of the body without bein' caught. But if ya say ya didn't do it, I'll take your word for it. I do wonder what happened to him, though.'

"In one respect it eased my mind to know Steve Young had telegraphed that he was bringin' us in," Uncle Will said. "That meant he planned to kill us, 'cause he couldn't risk us tellin' anyone about him embezzlin' money. I just beat him to the punch. I thought about tellin' Willie the truth—makin' a confession, so to speak—in hopes of easin' my mind a little. I'd had an even harder time sleepin' since Fannie left, and it took more and more liquor to knock me out at night. But the moment passed, and I never told him.

"Ya know, if people look at that murder—and that's what it was, murder—they'd say I was never punished for it. But let me tell ya, nephew, I been punished over and over and over again. I think it'd be fair to say that I've never once fallen asleep since then without the awful sight of Steve Young fallin' headlong into that canyon. Not one time in all these years.

"Anyway, I carried Willie home with me and let him sleep on an old settee we had there in the livin' room. As I watched him layin' there, sawin' logs, I tried to think of somethin' we could do to make money so he could be self-supportin' in his old age. The next mornin' when we woke up, I put the proposition to him that we start makin' corn liquor. There was talk about the federal government outlawin' alcohol altogether, and I knew enough about human nature to know that if they was ever dumb enough to make liquor illegal, somebody was gonna get awful rich supplyin' it to people who supposedly didn't drink.

"Of course, a World War was goin' on, and there was shortages of all kinds of things. Ya couldn't hardly get sugar, which is one of the main ingredients in makin' good liquor, but there was plenty of sorghum syrup around, so we went down on the creek about 500 yards below my house and set up a little still. We used syrup instead of sugar to make the liquor, and even though it didn't taste the best in the world, boy, it could sure make ya drunk.

"We peddled it around Tallapoosa and over in Muscadine, Alabama. I can't say it was anybody's favorite, but it'd do in a pinch. There was only one small prolem. By the time we'd bought everything we needed and set up the still—not to mention drinkin' all we wanted—I had two thousand dollars less than when we started! Ya can't stay in business long by goin' in the hole two thousand dollars. But things turned around after a while, and we began to make a little profit.

"We went on for the better part of three years, livin' good and drinkin' a lot of liquor. Unfortunately, we was also playin' a lot of poker. Most of the time we played while we was drunk, so we lost any money we made.

"Meanwhile the federal revenue agents started showin' up in swarms. Lots of folks was makin' illegal alcohol, and the revenuers meant to put us outa business. They busted up a lot of stills and arrested so many moonshiners that we began to get scared. Not scared enough to stop, though.

"In fact, early in 1919 we took on a partner in the business. His name was Bud Tillman. Bud wasn't the brightest fella, but he had one of the strongest backs I ever saw. He could tote two hundred pounds of sugar for a mile and never set it down. By then, we could get all the sugar we wanted 'cause the war was over, but we still had to be careful. That's one of the ways they was catchin' the bootleggers—by keepin' an eye on people that bought too much sugar. In fact, just to be on the safe side I'd go far away to buy it where the folks didn't know me.

"With Bud's strong back and my brains, we decided to enlarge the operation, even though the revenuers was gettin' thick in our neck of the woods. Why, they was catchin' somebody almost every day. But business was too good to stop. Often times a fella would get caught, go to jail, make bond, and get caught again while he was out.

"For a while they was tryin' bootleggers in Superior Court, but the Superior Court let 'em off too easy— or at least that's what the federal boys thought—so they moved the trials to Federal Court. The federal judges started handin' down stiffer penalties for bootleggin', 'cause they was serious about stoppin' it.

"Every day it seemed like another trainload of revenuers showed up, until pretty soon everybody got real scared to make liquor. One night, Bud, Willie, and me had a meetin' and agreed that only one person should be at the still at a time. That way, if the revenuers raided it, only one of us would get caught. Meanwhile, the other two would be able to sell the liquor we'd already made and hidden. That was important, 'cause by that time we had nearly three hundred gallons of liquor stored in an old gold mine nearby. Once we sold all that, we'd have enough money to retire for a while. I needed the funds, too, 'cause I was down to less than two thousand dollars. I'd gambled and drank it away. It was gone, nephew, gone."

"In June of 1919, the last batch of liquor we was gonna make was ready to distill. It was my turn that day to watch the still, so I went down to build a fire under the boiler. I was supposed to distill and proof it, then carry it back in the woods to Willie and Bud so they could take it out of the area. I didn't even have the fire hot, though, before the revenuers swooped down on me. They handcuffed me, broke up the still, and took me to jail.

"The revenuers had learned all sorts of tricks. For instance, my property was in Haralson County. I had no property in Carroll County, so they carried me to the Carroll County jail where I couldn't sign my farm over to make bond. That's the way the federal boys did it. They used every trick in the book to force bootleggers outa business.

"As soon as he heard I was in Carrollton, Willie got on my motorcycle and came to see me. My bond had been set at a thousand dollars cash or two thousand in property. Like I say, I still had nearly two thousand hidden at the house, and I told Willie to go dig it up and bring enough for me to make bond.

"When I finally got everything taken care of and left the jail, Willie, Bud, and me went down to a roadhouse just south of Tallapoosa. We was all drinkin' pretty heavy—me to celebrate gettin' outa the hoosegow, them just because they liked to drink, I suppose. Along about four in the afternoon, Willie said he had to go 'cause he had a date with his girlfriend. They was goin' square dancin' that night over at L. M. Skinner's place, he said, and he wanted to sober up a bit. After he left, me and Bud sat there and got drunker and drunker. About an hour before sundown, Bud leaned over to me and said, 'Will, I've been wantin' to tell ya somethin' ever since ya got out, but I don't quite know how to do it. I know ya ain't gonna like it, and I know ya probably ain't gonna believe me, but it's the truth.'

"'What is it?' I asked, surprised by his serious tone.

"'Willie turned ya in to the revenuers. Him and that Nellie Jo he's sweet on are gonna run away and get married, and they needed the money. While you was there tryin' to make bond, he sold all our liquor. He's got the money, and him and Nellie Jo are plannin' on takin' your motorcycle tonight and headin' for Texas. They figure you'll be drunk 'cause ya just got outa jail today and haven't had anything to drink for a week.'

"Of course, I threw a fit. I asked Bud how come he didn't stop them, but he said he didn't know about it himself until that mornin'. Ben Culwell, another friend of Willie's, had told him, and he also knew the fella from Atlanta that bought all the liquor. In fact, Bud claimed, they'd done hauled it out. 'They did it while Willie was gone to get ya,' he said. 'I done been down to the hidin' place in the ol' mine, and I promise you there ain't no liquor there. Would ya like to go see for yourself?'

"We left the roadhouse and headed for the gold mine. Sure enough, there wasn't a drop of liquor in the place when we got there. Of course, I was pretty drunk by then, but there was still somethin' that bothered me. How did Bud know all this stuff? I sat him down, looked him in the eye and said, 'Bud, how do ya know what they're plannin' to do if ya ain't a part of it?'

"Bud's face flushed bright red as he answered, 'I may not be as smart as you, Will, but I knowed as sure as the world you was gonna get drunk this afternoon. And if I knew it, Willie did, too. I also know Nellie Jo's been tellin' her friends that her and Willie are goin' to Texas soon. I don't know for sure that they're leavin' tonight, but I figure as smart as Willie is, he wants to get gone before ya find out what happened.'

"'But Willie never told ya they was plannin' to steal my motorcycle?'

"'No, he didn't tell me, but how else are him and Nellie Jo gonna get out west?'

"'Bud, I love that little son-of-a-bitch,' I said. 'I just don't believe he'd do that to me.'

"'Well, your liquor's gone, Will, or rather, *our* liquor's gone,' he answered, pointin' out the obvious. 'Let's go visit Ben Culwell and see what he has to say.'

"We made our way over to Ben's place and talked for quite a while. I didn't like the way he wouldn't look at me, 'cause it made me wonder if he was hidin' somethin', but he swore that every word Bud told me was the truth. If I'd had a clear head, I mighta been able to sort things out better, but I was mad and drunk.

"After I let Bud back out at the roadhouse, I drove home and got my 12-gage shotgun, loaded it with double-aught shot, and stuck it in the side car. By then it was good dark, and in my drunken stupor I made up my mind that Willie Kilgore, the man I'd trusted with my life time and again, was a dead man. He'd betrayed me, and that was a killin' offense.

"When I got to Skinner's, the banjo players and fiddlers was tunin' up for the big Saturday night square dance. I didn't see Willie or Nellie Jo anywhere, but a fella told me they'd just gone inside a few minutes ago. When I heard that, I pulled that double-barrel shotgun outa the side car and started walkin' slowly toward the front door.

"As I got to the porch, L.M. Skinner, the owner of the place, stepped outside. 'Will, what are ya doin' with that gun?' he asked nervously. 'Ya know that guns and liquor don't mix.'

"'L.M., if you're as smart as I think ya are, you'll stay outa my damn way,' I said through gritted teeth, my words slurred by the liquor. 'I've got business with your sawed-off son-of-a-bitch house guest named Willie. He's got somethin' comin' to him, and I'm here to deliver. Unless ya want some of the same, ya best step aside.'

"And he did. I guess he could tell by lookin' at me that I wasn't in no mood to be fooled with. Ya don't mess with a 12-gage shotgun, not if you've got good sense, anyhow.

"Skinner's house was a big rectangular buildin' with a hallway down the middle and rooms on either side of it. The bedrooms was on the right, and the kitchen, parlor, and dinin' room was on the left. I looked in the parlor first, which was the first room on the left. There was a bunch of folks there—boys and

241

girls gigglin' and talkin', mostly—but no Willie. In the first bedroom, a boy and girl was kissin' and lovin' on each other, but they wasn't the ones I was lookin' for. When they turned and saw me with that shotgun, their eyes about popped outa their heads, but I just shut the door and moved on.

"A moment later I opened the middle bedroom door, and there stood Willie next to the bed. He was alone and just turnin' up a bottle to take a drink when I walked in.

"'Hello, Will,' he said, obviously surprised to see me, his eyes fixed on the shotgun.

"'You little son-of-a-bitch,' I growled. 'I'm gonna blow you half in two.'

"'Put that gun down,' he answered in a shaky voice. 'You're drunk, and ya don't know what you're doin'.'

"'Nobody steals from Big Will,' I said coldly.

"'I know that,' he replied.

"I pulled the hammers back until they clicked and slowly raised the gun. As I did, Willie whirled and started to jump out the window that was behind the bed. Just as he turned his back to me, though, I let fly with both barrels.

"You ain't never seen such a bloody mess," Uncle Will said as he stared off in the distance. "He was dead before he ever hit the bed."

I'd heard all my life about Uncle Will killin' the man who was his best friend, but it was always a distant kind of thing that happened years ago. Sitting there on that river bank in the dark and listening to him describe the actual event like it happened yesterday set my spine ashiverin'. I quietly slipped over and got a blanket out of the bedroll to wrap myself in as he continued to talk.

"Ya know, nephew, in all that excitement, Willie yelled, 'I ain't stole!' as he turned to get away from me. The rest of the words never got outa his mouth. I don't know what he was tryin' to say, but the blackest depression I ever experienced fell over me the moment he tumbled on that bed. I wanted more than anything in the world to know what the rest of that sentence was.

"By now the hallway was full of people, and I suddenly felt awful. I walked back down the hall, out the front door, down the steps, and over to the well near the house to get me a drink of water. I was still drunk, but I don't think any man ever felt worse than I felt at that moment. My motorcycle was parked there and I coulda gotten on it and rode away, but I was too disturbed. I loved Willie like I loved no other human bein' who ever lived, including Ma and Pa, Fannie Hawk, and all the other people in my life. I loved him more than all of 'em put together, and I'd just blown him half in two.

"I sat down by a tree next to the well and leaned my shotgun up against it, then told one of the boys standin' there to go bring the sheriff 'cause I'd just shot the only friend I ever had. As I waited for the sheriff, I went in one more time and looked at Willie's body draped across that bed. Nothin' nobody said or did could make me feel any worse than I did at that moment. I gave L.M. three hundred dollars and told him to see that Willie got a decent burial, which he did. I know that for a fact.

"They scheduled my trial for the next term of court. I couldn't sleep or eat the whole time. Jailhouse food ain't the best in the world anyway, and when you're as depressed as I was, it just seems that much worse. Over and over again, I heard Willie's voice ringin' in my ears, 'I ain't stole...' Night and day I longed to know the rest. 'Willie, the rest of it, say the rest of it,' I'd cry. But he never did.

"I paid a lawyer the last money I had on earth, money I'd come by through robbin' and stealin', to try and get me as light a sentence as possible. I wanted to plead guilty and ask for mercy, but he wouldn't let me. As it turned out, he got me off with a sentence of ten years on the Georgia chain gang, and they sent me to Carrollton to begin serving my sentence.

"Let me tell ya, nephew, the chain gang ain't a good place, to say the least, and when you're big like I am, those little pipsqueak guards can make it awful tough. I didn't have no easy time.

"We'd come in at night from twelve hours of bustin' rocks or other hard labor and go right to supper, but many a night I couldn't eat. Instead, I'd sit there and think. Here I was only thirty years old, and I'd already killed two men. Now I was payin' for it. But as mean and hateful as that chain gang was, it wasn't the worst part. The worst was those endless dreams, first of Steve Young, then of Willie. Willie was my best friend, and I killed him. I'll be haunted until the day I die, prayin' to hear the rest of that sentence, 'I ain't stole...'"

Uncle Will stopped for several minutes, and the silence of the night was deafening. I felt awful for him, but I knew nothing I could say would eliminate the pain of what had happened, so I just sat and respected his sorrow. Finally, he spoke in a softer, fragile voice.

"Pa died while I was in prison," he said. "They carried me back to his funeral under armed guard. The people I grew up with tried not to turn and look, but they couldn't help it. They all watched as the guards took my leg irons off, marched me to the front seat of the church, and sat on either side of me while I listened to the preacher say last words over my daddy.

"Two years later, the same thing happened when my brother was killed. His death was the cruelest of all. He was gassed in a well. They tried to draw him up with a rotten rope, but as they got him to the top, the rope broke and he fell back down on his head and broke his neck. One of the things I kept thinkin' about all the way there and all the way back is that just three dollars of that money I'd stolen—*just three dollars*—coulda bought a good enough rope to save his life. But I'd squandered every last bit of it on nothin' but heartaches."

Puttin' Down Roots

It was black as pitch when Uncle Will finished his story, and I sensed that his mood had grown just as dark. Reliving Willie's murder had obviously been painful for him, and he didn't try to hide it. Luckily, however, the fish began to bite, giving him a chance to refocus his attention.

"Let's catch enough while they're bitin' so we'll have some for breakfast in the mornin'," he suggested. "We'll leave 'em on the string overnight to keep 'em fresh." That sounded great to me, and pretty soon we had a mess of catfish. As usual, I started the fire while he skinned our catch, and we fried them to perfection.

Despite the wonderful meal, Uncle Will still seemed quiet and subdued, so I didn't really know if I ought to question him any further. But sitting there by the warm campfire with a full stomach and him smoking on his old corncob pipe, I finally said, "I'd like to hear more, Uncle Will."

"Well, nephew, there ain't a whole lot that's interestin' about a chain gang," he replied. "They made me a trusty after a while, which gave me a little more freedom than other prisoners. After a year or two, a trusty don't have to wear a ball and chain, and that was a big help. I also behaved myself, which helped even more. I didn't give nobody a hard time.

"Ya know, it's a funny thing to me, though," he continued. "People had lots rather pick on a big fella that can't fight back than a little one who can't. Some of the guards was especially mean to me just because of my size. I guess it made 'em feel big to boss me around. But the chain gang gave me a chance to reflect back on my life, and I must say that I never got anything I didn't richly deserve.

"Every once in a while I'd run across some good liquor and get drunk at night in the cell, but that didn't happen very often. For the most part, I kept my nose clean.

"In fact, I got out on parole in March, 1929, some six months before my sentence was up. They handed me fifty dollars cash and a suit of clothes that went out of style in the 1800s, and I headed back to Tallapoosa.

"When I got to the little house where Fannie and I'd lived, a sign posted on the door said it would be auctioned off the first Tuesday in May for nonpayment of taxes. I knew they could sell a piece of property for the taxes owed on it, but not once durin' my stay in prison did it occur to me that they'd actually do it. I didn't even know how much tax I owed, so I went up to the courthouse at Buchanan and checked the land records. After addin' up everything I owed, it came to six hundred dollars. That's what it would take to get my land free and clear. Now, where in the world is an ex-convict gonna get six hundred dollars?

"Times was good, though, and I decided to try and sell the land, 'cause I really had no interest in it anymore. Somehow I associated it with Willie and Fannie, and all I wanted to do was get enough money out of it so I could move on.

"I had about six weeks to raise the money, but first I needed a way to travel, so I got a friend to carry me over to L.M. Skinner's place. When I walked in, it looked almost like it did the night I left. L.M. had eighty dollars left from Willie's funeral, and he also still had my ol' motorcycle with the side car on it. I went out and pushed the kick-start, and, nephew, I've never been so surprised in my life. The thing cranked up just like it did the last night I drove it nine years before! I went in and told L.M. it was nothin' short of a miracle.

"'Oh, I cranked it up every two or three months while you was gone, 'cause I figured you'd come back for it some day,' he explained.

"'I'm much obliged to ya, L.M.,' I replied. 'Ya wouldn't by any chance know anybody that might wanna buy that land I've got down on the Big Tallapoosa, would ya?'

"'I might be interested in it if you've got it priced right,' he said. 'How much are ya askin' for it?'

"I had no idea how much land was worth. I did know that times was pretty good, though. The stock market was goin' crazy, and folks seemed to have more money than they ever did before. 'Would ten thousand be too much for it?' I asked.

"'It's more than I'd give,' he answered. 'I couldn't pay but half that. But ask around and see. If ya can do better, there'll be no harm and no hard feelings. If not, I'll buy it for five thousand if you're agreeable.'

"With L.M.'s offer in mind, I climbed on my motorcycle and rode back to my farm down on the river. It was a cold, bleak, lonely place that held nothin' but heartaches for me. There was just too many damn memories, so I drove over to Ma's house.

"I didn't know what to expect from her, but she made me just as welcome as the day I left. She didn't have much to eat, but she fixed me some pot liquor, buttermilk, and a slice of raw onion. It tasted good, just like I remembered it. As I sat and looked across the table at Ma, who was now old and nearly blind, I couldn't help but feel a terrible remorse for all those wasted years when I was stuck in prison. I hadn't given a thought to how she lived alone, without anyone to look after her after Pa died. All I thought about was me. I asked her about it, and she said, 'I growed a few stalks of corn, tobacco, and turnip greens. It was hard, but I got by.' That night, I made a vow that I was gonna help her no matter what it took. I mean, here I was forty years old and I hadn't spent the night in my ma's house in 25 years. I felt like a stranger.

"I got that same sad, haunted feelin' everywhere I went. I was a stranger who didn't belong nowhere.

"That night after Ma went to bed, I sat for a long time askin' myself, 'Where do I belong? Where do I belong?' Ya know, nephew, I still don't have the answer today. I ain't never found the place where I fit.

"The next day, I went back to see L.M. and told him I'd deed him the farm if he'd settle up the taxes and give me $4400. He agreed, and we made the deal. Then I went to town and bought Ma all the groceries I could haul in the side car of the motorcycle, which was a whole lot. I laid her in a good supply of food, brought in firewood and stove wood, and decided to do whatever I could to make up for the things I hadn't done for her through the years.

"I also asked about the taxes on the little farm Pa had left her. She said she hadn't been able to pay 'em in several years and didn't know how much she owed. 'I always had a horror of dyin' at the poor farm,' she said, 'but it looks like that's gonna be my lot.' The idea of my own ma dyin' poor, without a roof overhead, bothered me somethin' fierce, and I went to the courthouse the next day to settle up her taxes. I knew that once I paid 'em, they couldn't sell her property for another seven years, 'cause that was the law in Georgia.

"I stayed around for several days, tryin' to be the son she'd never really had, but it wasn't long 'til I began to get on Ma's nerves and she began to get on mine. She still treated me like I was fifteen years old, just like Pa did when I returned home with Willie years ago, and pretty soon I knew I'd have to move on. But I decided to do one more thing before I left. I counted out five hundred dollars and told her to hide it somewhere and to use it only when she really needed somethin'. An old peddler came by every once in a while, I knew, and she could buy all the necessities from him. After makin' sure she had everything she needed, I climbed on my Harley and took to the road again.

"Since I'd been west already, I decided to try north this time, and before long I was drivin' through northeast Alabama. It was beautiful country, green and fertile, not like that ol' dead-lookin' red clay we had so much of in Carroll County. In fact, I was so impressed with it that I stopped in the town of Sand Mountain to find out more about the area.

"I started chattin' with a fella at the general store and asked if there was any land for sale at a reasonable price. 'The widow Crow's tryin' to sell her little spread,' he answered. 'Her husband died a few months ago, and she's tryin' to raise enough money to get out west where her daughter lives. She's got a nice, tight little house on fifteen acres of land about two miles from here, and I heard she's askin' fifteen hundred for it.' That price sounded fine, especially to a man with only four thousand dollars left to his name, so I got directions from the man and went to pay widow Crow a call.

"It turned out that the house was just right for someone like me. It had two small bedrooms, a cook room, a dinin' room, and a parlor—more than adequate for a bachelor. The widow Crow seemed eager to part with it, too, so I bought it for fifteen hundred right on the spot. She asked me when I wanted to take possession of it, and I said, 'Well, I bought it, and I want it.'

"'The soonest I can leave is a day or two,' she replied. 'In the meantime, you can stay in the spare room if you'd like.' It was a funny thing. Here I'd just bought the place, but she was tellin' me where I could sleep! That didn't bother me, though. 'Any place is fine,' I told her. 'All I need is a place to lay down my head.'

"'I don't think the neighbors will talk, not since you've bought the place and I'm fixin' to leave,' she said, 'But if they do, they do. I'm not spendin' good money to stay somewhere else, and apparently you ain't either. You own the place now. Just be sure ya behave yourself.'

"'Yes ma'am,' I responded, sorta tickled that she thought I'd be interested in an old woman like her. 'By the way, do ya know where the property lines are?'

"'Yeah, the road is the west boundary and the little creek is the south boundary. There are metal pins to mark the north and east boundaries.'

"'I'll get out and scout 'em tomorrow so's in case I can't find 'em, you can show 'em to me before ya get on your way.'

"'I guess it's just my busybody nosiness,' she said, 'but you seem to be travelin' awful light for a man your age. Don't ya have any family? It ain't often we see a motorcycle around here, especially with a man your age drivin' it.'

"'I suppose I just never did grow up,' I answered more honestly than usual. 'That motorcycle is fifteen years old, but I didn't get on it for ten of those years. Now I'm not sure I ever wanna get rid of it. Besides that, the side car is a real handy little item. You can haul belongings in it, or ya can haul people.'

"'That's just what I was thinkin',' she replied. 'Since I've sold you the place and everything goes with it, all I'm gonna have when I leave here is two suitcases. I wonder if you'd consider takin' me up to Chattanooga? That's where I was plannin' on leaving from. I've got a sister up there, and I wanted to spend a couple of nights with her before I head out west. As a matter of fact, I could leave tomorrow if you'd carry me to her place. Then you'd have the house all to yourself.

"'It's about forty miles to Chattanooga, and I'll need to stop one time before we get there,' she continued. 'I've got real good friends about three miles up the road I wanna say goodbye to. Then we'll go to my sister's, and I'll leave ya in peace. Do ya mind doin' that?'

"'No, ma'am, that's fine,' I said.

"'In that case we need to leave pretty early in the mornin' to give ya plenty of time to get back before dark, so I'll start packin' my things and takin' a final look around,' she said with tears in her voice."

"The next mornin' after cookin' us a hearty breakfast, she collected her things and announced she was ready to go. As we reached the door, she turned and looked with sad eyes at the little house. 'I've lived in this house for forty years,' she said. 'I raised three children here and buried my husband here, and leavin' it's a bit like cuttin' a piece of my heart out. But I'm fast approachin' the time when I can't look after myself, and I'm goin' where my younguns can take care of me in my old age.

"'Do you have any children?' she asked. I told her I didn't. 'Well, that's too bad, 'cause they're a joy. You don't know what you've missed.'

"I couldn't help but think if I'd had kids and they'd turned out like I did, they wouldn't have been a whole lot of pleasure to me. I know I was never much pleasure to my kin. But I didn't say anything to the widow. I just picked up her suitcases and went out to tie them on the back of the motorcycle.

"When she walked out and climbed in the side car, tears was flowin' freely down her cheeks, and she

253

actually waved goodbye to that little house. It sent a chill down my spine, 'cause in a strange way I knew how she felt. I think I'd have experienced the same feelin' the night I rode off on Pa's mule if I'd known that was the last time I'd spend any time in that house.

"After one more glance over her shoulder, she said, 'Let's go,' and we started up the road. When we'd come to a fork in the road, she'd reach over and hit me on the arm to get my attention and point which way we was supposed to turn. Fifteen minutes later, we drove up to a beautiful farmhouse. You could tell by all the buildings and machinery that it was a prosperous place. When the widow knocked on the door, a young, attractive woman close to six feet tall answered and invited us in.

"'Is your Ma around, Beth?' asked the widow.

"'Yes ma'am, I'll get her,' the young woman replied. 'In the meantime, can I get ya a cup of coffee or somethin' to eat?' Mrs. Crow said no, that she was headin' west to be with her family and just wanted to thank Beth's mother for bein' such a wonderful friend through the years.

"All the time Mrs. Crow and Mrs. Parker was talkin', this Beth was up doin' things, gettin' the cups and carryin' on a conversation. She was a bit too tall and somewhat ungainly, but there was a little turn about her that was real appealin' to me, and I knew I wouldn't soon forget her.

"Mrs. Crow said her goodbyes quickly, and we headed back on the road as Beth Parker and her Ma stood on the front porch wavin'. If you've ever ridden much on a motorcycle, nephew, ya know ya can't carry on a whole lot of conversation. But I leaned over and asked Mrs. Crow if Beth was married. 'No, she's an old maid,' she yelled.

"'How old?' I yelled back.

"'I don't know for sure. Maybe thirty or a little over.'

"Like I say, it's awful hard to carry on a conversation on a motorcycle, so I just made a mental note of where the Parkers lived and decided I'd make it my business to find out more about this old maid in the days to come. Meanwhile, I delivered Mrs. Crow to her sister in Chattanooga and headed back to my new home in Sand Mountain.

"Like the man at the store told me, it was a tight little house. It also had a nice garden, a barn out in back, and enough cleared land for a fella to make a livin'. If the fella had a mule, he wouldn't want for nothin', especially since the place was paid for. He wouldn't want for nothin', that is, except a woman. I didn't have me a woman, and I really wanted one. The more I sat around the house that summer and fall, the more I thought about Beth Parker. The more I thought about her, the more I wanted to know about her. So one day in late September I just up and went to pay a call.

"When Beth came to the door, I said, 'Miss Parker, I don't reckon ya remember me. I'm the fella who brought the widow Crow by here on her way to Chattanooga a few weeks ago, and I just thought I'd drop by and sit a spell with ya again if it's all right.' She sorta flushed and started straightenin' her dress and actin' self-conscious, lookin' down to see if everythin' was the way it was supposed to be. You know how girls do sometimes, nephew, especially when they get flustered. Well, maybe ya don't know yet, but ya soon will.

"Anyway, she invited me into the parlor and we took an almost instant likin' to each other, I think. She was probably interested because people look at womenfolk funny if they ain't married by the time they're twenty-three or twenty-four. She was well past that age, but she was still young as far as I was concerned, 'cause I was done on the shady side of forty myself.

"We sat together until an hour before sundown, and then I had to leave 'cause I needed to give myself plenty of time to get home. You don't know nothin' about how bad it was drivin' at night then, nephew. We have sealed-beam headlights nowadays that let ya can drive at night as well as ya can in the daytime. But before we had 'em, drivin' at night was sorta like tryin' to thread a sewin' machine needle with the machine runnin'. By the time ya saw somethin' up ahead, you was there. So ya tried to do all your travelin' in the daytime.

"Before I left I asked Beth if there was anything goin' on in the neighborhood where young folks could get together for parties and such. I'd been off of liquor for several months, and I didn't want to go back to it 'cause I always seemed to get in trouble when I drank. I thought if I settled down with some nice girl and stayed off of liquor, my life oughta be more productive in my last forty years than it was in my first forty. Liquor might not have been totally to blame, but I still sorta thought it never did do me a whole lotta good.

"She said they was havin' a square dance at a neighbor's house that Saturday night. When I heard that, I thought about the last square dance I went to. It cost me ten years in the penitentiary for killin' my best friend. I asked her was there a lot of drinkin' and the like goin' on, and she said no, that they had a little problem with drinkin' at the dances a few years ago, but they got together and decided that if anybody showed up drunk at a dance, they'd ask 'em to leave. 'Folks around here pretty well don't drink anyway, though,' she explained. 'It's a sober, God-fearin' crowd that farms Sand Mountain.'

"I decided that was where I needed to be—with a sober, God-fearin' crowd—and she accepted my invitation to the dance. She even asked me to go to church with her come Sunday. I was so taken with her that before I realized what I was doin', I said yes.

"Then I got to thinkin'. I hadn't been in church except for funerals since I was fourteen or fifteen years old. It'd be strange sittin' in a church all dressed up, holdin' hands with a girl and listenin' to the preacher. So strange, in fact, that I got cold feet. But I'd done give her my word, and I didn't wanna back out for no reason. Finally, I said, 'I'll tell ya what. The only transportation I've got is that motorcycle and side car, and there ain't no top on either one. As long as it ain't rainin', I'll pick ya up Sunday, okay?'

"'Daddy's got a car,' she replied. 'I'll come by and pick ya up if it's rainin'.' I was trapped! I couldn't think of a way out, so I said, 'All right. Rain or shine, we'll go to church Sunday.'

"Well, as sure as the world a storm blew in Sunday, but I'd told her I'd go no matter what. About ten o'clock she came drivin' up to carry me to church, and ya know, it wasn't half bad. After church she carried me to her home for Sunday dinner. I met her Pa, and he seemed like a right nice fella. We sat around and talked the better part of the afternoon before she carried me back home.

"When we got to my place, I asked her in to look over the house. I took a jug of kerosene and some kindlin' and started us up a blazin' fire in the hearth, and we sat on the davenport and enjoyed the warmth. She sat closer to me than I expected and didn't resist much when I slipped my arm around her shoulder. But then we sorta froze in that position 'cause I really didn't know how to treat nice girls. Fannie Hawk was nice, but not in the same way Beth was. Fannie had been around the world, and she knew pretty much what the world was all about. It was obvious that Beth didn't, so I was at a bit of a loss as to what to do next. I know that sounds silly with me on the shady side of forty at the time, nephew, but that's the way it was. Finally, not knowin' what else to do, I reached over through the buttons of her dress and put my hand on her breast.

"For a moment I thought she relaxed a little and snuggled closer. But then, wham! She slapped me so hard, it jarred my grandma.

"'Will, keep your hands to yourself!' she said angrily.

"'So this is the difference between nice girls and the girls I know about,' I thought to myself. 'Well, at least now I know.'

"After a few minutes, she got up and cooked me a bit of supper, told me how much she'd enjoyed the day, and left.

"Nephew, for the first time in my whole life I found myself feelin' like a dumb-struck teenager. I'd always liked women and used women, but often-times they just seemed like a necessary evil, so to speak. Now suddenly I was feelin' what I'd always heard described as love. It was a new, scary, wonderful thing.

"I took my time with it, though. Over the next three years I saw a lot of Beth, and I grew very, very fond of her. We went once or twice a month to church or to a square dance or somethin', and I got invited over to the Parker house from time to time, too. I got on right well with her folks, and I think they liked me. Of course, I was careful not to tell 'em much about my past. Several times durin' those years, I nearly asked Beth to marry me, but some little somethin' would happen and I wouldn't do it. Then on the way home I'd kick myself and say, 'Well, maybe next time.'"

Scene of the Crime

"In October of '29, the terrible stock market crash hit. I read in the newspaper about people jumpin' outa skyscrapers and that sorta thing in New York City, and there was even a few people over in Chattanooga that lost everything. Not me, though. I'd made a little money on crops and had right at two thousand dollars hidden in the safest place I knew—right under my mattress.

"But by the spring of '32, things began to fall apart everywhere. Jobs was harder and harder to come by, and ya just couldn't go out and sell your crops for what you'd been able to before. Money got awful tight, and I got depressed as a result 'cause I was used to havin' plenty of it. One day I got to thinkin' about my situation. It'd been over three years since I'd taken a drink of liquor, and they'd been pretty good years. I'd met Beth and was serious about her, but I never could get up the courage to just come out and ask for her hand. I was pretty sure she'd say yes if I asked, but I never got up the nerve to do that. So I decided to get away and ponder things for a while.

"I took a thousand dollars with me, went to Chattanooga, and checked in to the best hotel I could find. Then I asked around about the shady side of life in Chattanooga—women, gamblin', drinkin', and the like. At first everybody was afraid to talk to me 'cause they thought I was some sort of lawman, but after I was there a week or so, they told me where I could find anything a man might desire.

"One night I sat in on a poker game they'd told me about. It was not the gentleman kind of game I'd played in Bar Harbor. No, sir. This was a bunch of real cutthroats. Why, they was such professional cheats that even *I* was amazed by some of the things they could do with the cards. I wasn't drinkin' when I got in the game, 'cause I knew one thing for sure: I couldn't play in that game if I was drunk, not with everybody at the table bein' a card mechanic. After sittin' there for thirty minutes and watchin' all the shenanigans those fellas pulled, I finally said, 'Is there an honest game around anywhere?' Not everyone could ask a question like that and get away with it, but since I was the biggest man at the table, nobody took offense. In fact, the whole table broke up with laughter.

"They said their game existed for big-shot salesmen from outa town. It was their patriotic duty, they felt, to make sure those fellas didn't carry any Chattanooga money back to New York or Philadelphia or wherever, and usually they was highly successful in that endeavor. After sittin' there watchin' them for a half hour, I could believe it. If you weren't pretty knowl-edgeable about a deck of cards, you could be separated from your hard-earned money mighty quick.

"But with one of their own kind, which they recognized I was right off, they was a friendly bunch. They told me where I could find a more or less 'honest' game, and I set out for the place. Sure enough, there was only one cardshark in the joint, and he didn't look to be that good. At least, I'd seen better in my day. The liquor was good and flowin' freely, and pretty soon I began to relax and bet more and more on the hands. Yes sir, it was just like ol' times.

"The next thing I knew, it was mornin' and I couldn't remember a thing after the third or fourth drink the night before. And God, I had a hangover I couldn't believe. My first thought was that they poisoned my liquor. I'd apparently drove myself back to the motel, since my motorcycle was parked out in front, but I sure didn't recall doin' it.

"Suddenly it occurred to me to check my money. I rolled outa bed and searched my pockets, but there wasn't nothin' there. Not a dime. I'd lost a thousand dollars in one night.

"After crawlin' back into bed to sleep a while longer, I got dressed and went downstairs to where my Harley was parked. There was plenty of gas in it to get me back to Sand Mountain, so despite the fact that my head felt as big as a full-grown pumpkin, I climbed aboard and headed home. When I got there I took my other thousand dollars and went lookin' for bootleggers. Here I'd been in Sand Mountain for two and a half years, and I didn't know any bootleggers. That was unusual for me.

"It didn't take long to find one, though. In less than an hour I bought me two gallons of good corn liquor, put it in the side car, and carried it back home.

"Three days later, I woke up for the first time. It looked like I couldn't catch up for all those months I'd gone without drinkin'. Instead of drinkin' and bein' satisfied, it seemed like I couldn't get enough. When those first two gallons was gone, I went back and bought me five more from the same fella. The next time I knew I was in the world, Beth had a bath cloth and was washin' and shavin' me. Then she broke some raw eggs in sweet milk and forced me to drink it. Over the course of the next two or three days, the little green men, the pink elephants, and all of those things—not to mention Ol' Ebo—chased me up and down the fields of the bed clothes. But I finally came back to my senses and swore I'd never touch another drop of that rotgut stuff as long as I lived. That's what I told Beth, anyway. I thanked her for bein' so kind and told her I'd be fine after that, so she left and headed home.

"Meanwhile, I was broke and couldn't get a job killin' a snake. I was so ashamed of myself that I decided to get on that ol' ragged motorcycle of mine and go back out west. Times was supposedly better out there. I went by to tell Beth goodbye, but in a moment of weakness, and for the lack of anything else to say, I blurted out, 'Beth, the next time I see ya, girl, I'm gonna ask ya to marry me. I promise ya that.' My face flushed with embarrassment as the words tumbled out, and I hopped on my motorcycle and took off before she could reply.

"For the next week I slept on the ground almost every night. About all I had was a bedroll and an old sleepin' bag, but by hook or by crook I managed to make it to Louisiana. Once I was there, I couldn't resist the temptation of goin' by to take a look at Monroe, where my life of crime had started. Some towns change so fast they don't look the same from one day to the next, but not Monroe. It looked like it'd been frozen in time. Nothin' had changed at all, at least nothin' at all I could see.

"I stopped in the middle of town and stared for a minute or two at the bank that Willie and I'd robbed some thirty years earlier. From the looks of things, it'd been empty for a good while, but there was still a bench sittin' on the porch in front of it. As I walked up and sat down, an old gray-haired gentleman with a walkin' cane came by. 'Say, mister, seems to me like this used to be a bank,' I said. 'Is that so?'

"'Yeah, the Farmer's and Merchant's Bank,' he answered. I asked if he'd lived in town long, and he said all of his life.

"'My daddy was a travelin' salesman,' I lied, ' and he was here one day back in '04 or '05 when the bank got robbed. He said it was an excitin' day. Do you remember that?'

"'Of course, I remember it,' the old man said. 'Everyone does. It was 1903, though, not '04 or '05. That bank robbery set off some real strange events that never made a whole lot of sense to anybody.

"'It's funny you should ask,' he continued, 'because I was just thinkin' about that this mornin'. The fella that was vice president of the bank at the time was engaged to marry my daughter. She was a beautiful woman—still is, for that matter. But when she was a girl of 18, she was as pretty as the pink on a gourd vine. She was engaged to this fella named Steve Young, and they was gonna get married the followin' year.

"'Then the robbery happened, and Steve Young became a hero overnight in these parts. Ya see, he somehow figured out how the bandits was gonna escape from town and almost captured them. After that, he became so famous and so popular that he didn't have time for my baby any more. In fact, he never came to see her again. She pined away around the house and cried every time anyone looked at her, poor thing.

"'In the meantime, Steve Young got himself a job with the Pinkerton Agency. Them's the folks that hunt down bank robbers and big-time crooks. He also married a rich widow over at Crossville, but he wasn't with her more than a year or two before she died. Some said it was the flu, some said it was consumption, and some even said her death was suspicious. No one ever knew for sure. But my baby never married. Bless her heart, she's an old maid near fifty years old now.

"'The strange thing I started to tell you is this,' the old man went on. 'About ten years after the bank robbery, my baby got a telegram that said, "Am bringing in two men that robbed Monroe Bank. STOP. Meet me at railroad station. Will send another telegram as to arrival time. STOP. I love you and want to marry you as soon as I arrive. STOP. Steve."

"'Lordy, she was beside herself! Here she was close to thirty years old, resigned to the idea of bein' an old maid all her life, and suddenly she gets a proposal from the man she'd always loved. I think she was probably the happiest woman in the world. But as time went on and she didn't hear nothin' else from him, she began to get worried, so she went to the police. They'd received a telegram sayin' the same thing about him bringin' back the two bandits from Ellsworth, Maine.

"'Now, here's the really strange part of the whole business. When she didn't hear anything else from him for six weeks, she took a train to Ellsworth to talk to the police there. They remembered Steve Young and the fact that he was very much interested in a murder that'd been committed on an island nearby. A young giant from down south had murdered a fella on the island, and Steve Young went to investigate because he thought the killer might be the same man he'd been followin' for years.

"'A terrible storm came up that night and lasted the better part of forty-eight hours, though, and after that, no one ever saw him again. It was as if he just vanished from the face of the earth. Rumor had it that Young got his man and headed home with him by train, but no one could ever verify that. The closest my baby came to findin' out what happened was an ol' porter who thought he remembered sellin' a bottle of liquor for a hundred dollars to a giant of a man who was travelin' with a midget and another fella. The porter recalled the giant and the midget gettin' off in Buffalo, but he never saw the other fella again.'

"At that point the old gentleman stopped and said, 'I've laid a lot of words on ya, stranger, but you ain't said nothin'. Do ya have an interest in that bank robbery?'

"'No, ol' timer,' I replied. 'I was just sittin' here thinkin' about somethin' I read one time that said everyone at some time in their life will sit at a banquet of circumstances. I'm not sure I knew what the fella meant when I read it, but after listenin' to your story, I think I understand.'

"I walked out to my old motorcycle and looked back at the old bank. I've heard all my life that in his dyin' moments, a man's whole life will flash before his eyes. I don't think it has to be a dyin' moment, though, because my past raced through my brain at that instant. I couldn't help thinkin' about that poor old maid goin' to bed lonely night after night, cryin' for her man. And Willie, Steve Young, Fannie, Beth—they all marched through in such rapid succession that a great weariness came over me.

"I sat there a long time before crankin' up the Harley and headin' on west. As I drove along, I saw sharecroppers pullin' pitiful wagonloads of ragtag odds and ends. Things was worse out west, not better. When I crossed into Texas, it was late spring of 1933. The engine in my motorcycle had been makin' some queer noises for a couple of days, and finally the piston rod came right through the bottom of the crank case. She died somewhere in east Texas.

"After that, I started walkin'. Just before dark I came to a railroad track runnin' north and south. Summer was comin' and I wanted to go south, so I pitched my little bedroll right there and waited for the first train headin' that direction. I hoped to wind up somewhere in the Rio Grande Valley and maybe get a job in the orange groves. As luck would have it, that's what I did."

Breakin' Out

"I hoboed that freight all the way to the Rio Grande Valley where they grow oranges, grapefruit, and such, and I got a job pickin' oranges for forty cents a day. Most of the folks that worked in the orchards was short little Mexicans, and at six-foot-six I could reach a lot higher up in the trees and pick the oranges that they couldn't get. Pretty soon I was in big demand around there. The livin' conditions wasn't that great—we slept in an ol' warehouse that stunk to high heaven 'cause of all the smelly bodies—but at least I was makin' a little money.

"I didn't work long at forty cents a day, though, 'til my gifts for makin' corn liquor began assertin' themselves, so I got me a partner and started up a still. Unfortunately, I didn't know the ropes in south Texas the way I should have. I made one run and got about $35, which was good money in those days, and was ready to make another one when a sleek black car drove up in the middle of the night and shined its lights on the front of the warehouse where we was all sleepin'.

"'Big Will, come on out here,' a big boomin' voice rang out. 'We got business with ya.' I had no idea what anyone could want with me, but I stumbled outa bed and stepped outside into them blindin' headlights.

"There was four or five men standin' there with clubs and rifles, which told me right away that they wasn't payin' a social call. Finally the fella with the loud voice said, 'Ya just come in here a total stranger, and without even askin', ya start makin' corn liquor on your own and stealin' customers that we been servin' for years. Well, we think ya need to know how it is in the orange groves. Horse stealin' is a hangin' offense in these parts, and I've got a horse missin' and a witness that says you took him. But I ain't gonna report that to the sheriff, not if ya up and disappear from the valley. Ya best do it by mornin', though, or we're gonna have us a necktie party. Ya hear me?'

"I could see it wouldn't do no good to try and fight a gang of crooks like that, so I yelled back, 'I hear ya,' and packed my things and headed north.

"When I got to the outskirts of Houston a few days later, I found me a saloon where there was a card game goin' on. I still had most of the $35 from my bootleggin' operation, and I sat down and told 'em to deal me in. It was against the law to buy liquor at the time, but everybody else at the table had a bottle, so I ordered me one, too.

"I got into the game just before sunset that day, and by nine that evenin' I coulda gone into the bankin' business. I tell ya, I was on a roll like most folks only dream of. In fact, I was so hot that the other players started grumblin' about me cheatin', but I swear to ya, boy, I never cheated once in that poker game. The cards was just fallin' my way.

"Somewhere along around midnight I had one drink too many, though, and the next thing I knowed I woke up in the calaboose with four other fellas and an awful feelin' that I was in big trouble for somethin' I couldn't even remember. Then one of the guards broke the news: I was accused of killin' a man. But nephew, may God strike me dead, the last thing I recall was the fella across the table from me dealin' stud poker. I had an ace in the hole and two showin', and I didn't see how I could lose. That's the last thing I remember 'til I woke up in jail.

"Three days later they brought all five of us into court to hear the charges. It seems a fine upstandin' citizen of Houston had gotten himself killed in a brawl that night in the bar, and someone had to pay for it. I never did know what the man looked like. I don't know if I ever even seen him. To hear the witnesses talk about the dear departed, though, you'd think he shoulda been preachin' revival services instead of hangin' around a barroom, he was such a saint. I figured he musta been a friend of the judge. But he got himself killed, and there was five of us accused of bein' involved.

"Nobody knew for sure who stuck the knife in him, but they said I struck the blow that started the fight, so a lot of the testimony was directed at me. I always thought they was just lookin' for a scapegoat, and since I was an outsider, they decided to pin it all on me. But like I say, I have no idea what really happened in the bar that night.

"All day long we heard about how sorry I was and how good the deceased was, then the jury went out for fifteen minutes and came back with a verdict that I was guilty of second degree murder. The judge sentenced me to five years in the Texas state penitentiary and let the others go.

"Now, the Texas penitentiary is the worst place on the face of the earth, nephew. The inmates is mean and hard, and the guards is usually worse. I knew the moment I walked through the gates that I intended to get away from there as soon as possible, one way or the other.

"In those days, people didn't carry a lot of identification around with them like they do today. Unless they knew otherwise, the authorities had to take your word on who ya was and where ya was from, and I had the good sense to lie from the moment I was arrested. I told 'em I was Will Summer from Maryville, Tennessee. That's one of the few intelligent things I ever did in my life.

"I started my prison sentence sometime in early May. Texas, like most states in the south, put a ball and chain on its prisoners, and after only a few months in that hot, humid southeast Texas climate, the area on my ankles where the irons rubbed was solid sores. I picked up and carried the ball to lessen the pain as much as possible, but the irons still tormented me somethin' awful.

"By July I was havin' trouble even walkin'. I was startin' to wonder if I'd ever make it outa prison alive, when an almost miraculous thing happened. The man us convicts knew as the 'whippin' boss' called me over one afternoon and said he was gonna remove my leg irons long enough for my ankles to heal. I'd been a model prisoner up to then, and the whippin' boss let me know that was the only reason he was treatin' me so kindly.

"'Will,' he said as the irons was bein' broken off, 'if ya decide to run, chances are I'll end up servin' your sentence if I don't catch ya. I know it's hell in here most of the time, but I got a wife and kids at home that depend on me, so if ya got any decency at all, you'll repay my kindness by stayin' put.'

"And I intended to do just that, nephew. At first I was so thankful to get the irons off that I had no thought of runnin'. But as the days passed and I started feelin' better, I knew I wouldn't survive five years in the Texas pen, so I began plottin' my escape.

"To give myself time to make a good plan, I peeled the scabs off my legs every few days so the healin' would take longer. However, one mornin' a couple of weeks later the whippin' boss told me the irons was goin' back on soon, and I knew I'd have to make my break.

"That same day, we was cuttin' off ditch banks just north of Houston on what is now Highway 45. That's the highway that runs north–south through Porter, Humble, Cleveland, and on into Huntsville where the main branch of the Texas penitentiary is located. There was about twenty men in my work detail, guarded by two men with sawed-off shotguns.

"At about two in the afternoon, a big thunderhead began boilin' up in the west. Lookin' across those wooded hills, we could see a wall of lightnin' and showers headin' toward us, and as it did I slowly started easin' my way away from the main detail, swingin' my bush blade as hard as I could so I'd look like I was just heavy into my work. Every once in a while I glanced back to see if the guards was showin' any signs of gettin' suspicious, but they was enjoyin' the shade of a huge live oak tree too much to notice.

"Suddenly a fierce bolt of lightnin' struck within a quarter mile of where we was, followed by a deafenin' crash of thunder. Everyone stopped and watched as the sky grew almost black, then opened up and began rainin' a flood of water down on us. The guards started yellin' and wavin' their arms wildly, motionin' everyone to load up the old prison bus sittin' nearby, and I knew right then it was now or never.

"I threw down my bush blade," Uncle Will said with the fire of excitement in his eyes, as if reliving the very moment, "and run like I ain't never run before. I heard a double-barrel shotgun blast and waited for it to tear me in half, but I was far enough away that it just stung the back of my legs.

"Not another shot was fired," he continued. "I looked back over my shoulder to see what was happenin' as I raced away, and it looked like the other prisoners was tryin' to help me by takin' their own sweet time gettin' to the bus. That kept the guards busy tryin' to be sure nobody else got away.

"It was rainin' so hard that I couldn't see no further than a few yards ahead of me, but when I finally came to a crossroad, I turned to the right and headed east— toward Georgia and everything that was dear to me. As the ditches and roads began to fill up and become almost like a lake, it got harder and harder to run, but I just kept on, ignorin' my sore ankles and burnin' lungs.

"After half an hour, I came across a sharecropper's shack. Behind it at the edge of a small garden stood a stretch of rope with some fresh-washed clothes hangin' on it. Without slowin' my pace one bit, I raced past the clothesline, grabbed a man's shirt and a pair of overalls, then returned to the road and continued east. Fifteen minutes down the road, I made my first stop since the moment I broke for freedom, pausin' just long enough to tear off my clothes and put on the overalls and blue denim shirt.

"The pants was eighteen inches too short," Uncle Will laughed, "but at least they wasn't convict clothes. In fact, nothin' had felt that good in a long, long time.

"I kept on for hours, sometimes runnin', sometimes walkin'. The rain fell steadily until just before sundown, then gradually began taperin' off a bit. When the clouds finally did break up to reveal the sky, it was nearly dark, but I decided to move on into the woods instead of stay on the road 'cause I felt sure they'd come lookin' for me as soon as the rain stopped.

"For five days and nights I made my way east, stealin' food from fields and gardens to satisfy my hunger and relievin' yet another farmer of a better-fittin' set of clothes. I did most of my travelin' at night, since it was safer and cooler. Durin' the day I hid out in the woods and slept.

"Early on the sixth mornin', I came upon a sign that read, 'Twenty miles to Lake Charles, Louisiana,' and a surge of joy went through me, 'cause although I still had a long way to go, I felt I'd be a whole lot safer once I was outa Texas.

"My sense of well-bein' was short-lived, however. Less than twenty-four hours later, I reached a country store and post office at Araby, Louisiana. As I cased the store shortly before dawn, my eye caught a poster that turned my blood cold. 'Wanted by the Texas Rangers,' said the announcement in big letters. '$100 reward for information leading to the capture of this dangerous convict.' Below the words was my picture. The Texas Rangers wasn't givin' up as easily as I'd hoped.

"After sleepin' most of the mornin', I decided to use the daylight hours to make tracks. That afternoon while walkin' in the woods alongside an east-bound dirt road, I heard a car comin' in the distance. Moments later a brand new Model A Ford carryin' two people passed by and turned on a narrow side road up ahead marked 'Cajun Fish Camp.' It was the most beautiful automobile I'd ever seen, nephew, a bright green convertible tourin' car with the top down.

"I couldn't imagine why the well-dressed couple in the car, a man in his mid-forties and a woman who couldn't be more than twenty, would be goin' to a fish camp, but my curiosity got the best of me and I followed the road they'd taken. About a mile down the way I came to a small turn-around off to the side, and there in the shade of a grove of trees sat that beautiful Model A.

"I approached cautiously, but no one seemed to be around. As I slipped quietly up to the car and looked inside, I saw two sets of clothin', underwear and all, lyin' on the back seat. But where was the couple? In the stillness of the woods I heard a woman's faint laugh and made my way through fifty yards or so of grass and undergrowth until I saw the glimmer of sun on a pool of water. Easin' up closer, I saw the man and woman splashin' and swimmin' together, both naked as jaybirds.

"Under different circumstances, I mighta stayed to watch," Uncle Will said as he winked at me, "but that day I hurried back to the car. The gas gage showed full, and never one to look a gift horse in the mouth, I climbed into the driver's seat, cranked up the car, and headed back toward the main road as fast as that little car would go."

"For the next several hours, I put as many miles as I could between myself and the couple at the pond," Uncle Will continued. "Normally a person who didn't know the territory well could stop and ask directions now and then along the way, but I was afraid someone might recognize the car and become suspicious, so I just kept goin' north and east as long as possible.

"As I drove along, I thought back to that man and woman. If I had to guess, I'd bet they wasn't married—not to each other, anyway—and a question came to mind: How in the world would they make it back to town without benefit of clothes or a car? Nephew, there was just somethin' funny about the picture that created, and for the first time in what seemed like forever, I laughed long and hard.

"Of course, I had other things on my mind, too, not the least of which was where I was gonna come up with money for gas to get home. The full tank I started with, compliments of the previous owners, wouldn't take me nearly far enough. In fact, after drivin' maybe a hundred miles or so, the fuel gage showed just under half a tank left.

"A few minutes later I came to a road I judged to be runnin' east and west. Turnin' right, away from the sun, I continued to drive at a hard pace. However, within moments I had my first real scare. As I came around a sharp left curve, a Louisiana State Highway Trooper passed me goin' the opposite direction.

"That trooper nearly broke his neck cranin' to get a look at the Model A as it whizzed by," Will said, "and I got the most awful sinkin' feelin' in the pit of my stomach. I just knew the car had been reported stolen and that trooper was gonna be comin' after me, so I pulled off on the first side road I saw and backed into the bushes to hide.

"I stayed there for nearly half an hour, my heart racin' as I waited for the sound of another vehicle, but the trooper had apparently kept goin'. Finally I eased back onto the main road and headed east again, soon passin' a sign that read, 'Natchez, Mississippi, 130 miles.' A wave of excitement swept over me as I thought for the first time I might really make it home.

"At about six o'clock, with less than a quarter tank of gas left, I found another side road and pulled over to stop for the night. In the mornin' I'd drive on toward Natchez until the car hit empty, then start walkin' again. As I crawled into the back seat, though, the sight of the couples' clothes lyin' there suddenly reminded me that I hadn't even looked at 'em since I'd stolen the car earlier in the day.

"Holdin' up the man's pants to see how good a fit they might be, I noticed a lump in the pocket and pulled out a thick wallet. Inside it was three 20-dollar bills, three 10s, three 5s, and seven ones—$112 in all. It was a miser's fortune! If I hadn't been hidin' from the law, I'd have shouted for joy. But the other papers in the wallet sobered me up mighty quick, 'cause they identified the man I'd left naked and carless as none other than the 42-year-old sheriff of Bogalusa Parish, Louisiana. His companion, whose purse contained nothin' but a few coins, was nineteen, just old enough for the sheriff to avoid being brought up on a morals charge.

"I knew immediately that if that sheriff ever got hold of me, I'd wish I was back in the Texas penitentiary, so I climbed back in the driver's seat and took off again. Luckily, it wasn't long before I found a country store and filled up with gas. As I paid for the gas and a small sack of groceries, I asked the ol' man waitin' on me how far it was to Mississippi.

"'Forty miles as the crow flies,' he replied.

"'What if the crow is drivin' a Model A Ford?' I said.

"'He'd probably be there by dark if he stepped on it.'

"And I did just that, drivin' like a madman for three more hours. As night began to fall, I saw a store with a light in the window and pulled in to ask how much further it was to Mississippi.

"'This is it,' the clerk replied. 'Washington, Mississippi.'

"I was thrilled, to say the least. 'I don't suppose ya ever heard of Sand Mountain, Alabama, did ya?' I asked excitedly.

"'Sure have. Why? You headed there?'

"'Yeah, I'm hopin' there's a girl there waitin' for me.'

"'Well,' the man answered, 'there ain't no easy way to get there, but if ya just keep leanin' to the north and the east for another four hundred miles or so and stop to ask directions now and then, ya should be able to make it in a couple of days.'

"I took his advice, and at ten in the mornin' on a Friday, I pulled into Beth's front yard, honked the horn, and told her I'd come to get hitched. She looked right pleased."

I sat back as Will recounted his tale and remembered the day I first met him and Beth at Ma's house when I was three years old. I didn't know it then, but he must have been freshly married and only two or three weeks AWOL from the Texas penitentiary.

"I been out of state, boy," he had said mysteriously that afternoon when I asked him, and I recall thinking what a wonderful ring that phrase had to it. If I'd known just *where* he'd been and how he'd gotten back, I probably wouldn't have been nearly as impressed.

Comin' Home to Die

"There's one thing ya haven't told me," I said one night after I'm sure he thought he'd told me everything. "There was a stretch of time durin' the war when ya just up and disappeared. Then one day ya came drivin' up in the ol' bus like you'd never been gone. Where'd ya go durin' that time? Were ya fightin' the Germans?"

"Hell, no!" he laughed at my ignorance. "They wouldn't let a codger like me in the Army. But ya know, boy, you're the first one in the family to even wonder about that. The others probably wish I'd never come back." I suppose it would've been the polite thing to deny that, but the truth is he was probably right, so I didn't respond.

"My leavin' had to do with Beth," he went on. "Ya asked once what happened to her, and I didn't tell ya 'cause I didn't want anybody knowin' about it. But now I guess it don't matter any more.

"Remember when she made me pay ya that money for helpin' cut and haul our firewood?"

I nodded.

"Well, that was the last straw for her, I guess. Up 'til then I think she believed I had a little good in me, but when I tried to get out of payin' ya the money I'd promised—money we had right there in the house— well, that was too much. I came home drunk after takin' ya back to your Pa's house, and we had a real scrap.

280

"'How could ya look that boy in the face and lie?' she yelled with fire in her eyes. 'Ya knew good and well the money was under the clock!'

"'Yeah, and if you'd kept your trap shut, it'd still be there!' I spit right back at her. 'We needed that money for food.'

"'Food?' she says. 'Ha! Ya mean liquor, don't ya? That's all our money goes for anyway, to keep you soused.' I raised my hand to smack her—somethin' I'd never done before—but she picked up a chair and threat-ened to break it over my head, so I just said, 'Forget you, woman,' and stumbled into bed to sleep it off. The next afternoon when I came to, she'd taken her things and left."

"What'd ya do then?"

"I sat around the house for a couple of days, waitin' to see if she'd come back, but I guess I knew all along she wouldn't. Beth was one tough ol' woman. When she made up her mind about somethin', she stuck with it. I figure that's the only reason she stayed around as long as she did. She vowed 'til death do us part, and to her it meant just that. But when she saw what I tried to pull on ya, that's somethin' she just couldn't put up with.

"When I was sure she was gone for good, I packed up my stuff and left, too. The farm wasn't doin' no good anyway. We was always livin' hand to mouth. So I just walked out and hitched the first ride I could find goin' north. My plan was to head on up to Tennessee. I'd gone on a good drunk in Chattanooga when Beth and I was courtin', and I decided that was as good a place as any. But halfway there I heard a fella say somethin' about Fort Knox, Kentucky, and I changed my mind.

"Ya know about Fort Knox, don't ya? That's where they keep all the gold. Well, durin' the war a lot of other countries was sendin' their gold there for safe-keepin', too. Anybody with one eye and half a brain knew that there was bound to be soldiers guardin' it, and I figured there oughta be some way to make a livin' off those boys in blue. I thought of settin' up a crooked poker game nearby where I could relieve 'em of their money every payday, but as it turned out I spent nearly three whole years at as near-honest work as I ever did in my entire life.

"It was at a place called the Busy Bee Bar and Grill. There was a back-room poker game that'd gone on for years and years, and I got hired as the house man to keep it all above board, if ya can believe that. The soldier boys would come in to drink, then step in the back for a few hands of poker. It was my job to see that no card mechanics got in the game to cheat 'em. They could lose all the hard-earned cash they wanted to honestly, but the owner of the place didn't want 'em cheated out of it. I was good at what I did, too, especially as long as I didn't drink. The only problem was that I couldn't go very long without liquor.

"I finally worked me out a system. I didn't drink any at all Friday night and Saturday, 'cause that was when we did the most business. Then after we closed up at two o'clock Sunday mornin', I'd get drunk and stay drunk all day Sunday and Monday. Sometimes it'd even be Tuesday before I sobered up, but that was

okay with the owner 'cause those was slow days anyway. The rest of the week was pretty much touch and
go. Sometimes I'd be sober as a judge, and sometimes
I'd be so sick I couldn't hold my head up."

"If drinkin' was that bad on ya, what on earth did
ya do it for?" I asked with a mixture of anger and
sympathy.

"Now that's the sixty-four dollar question," he
replied. "And the answer to it is I don't know, and I
don't think anybody else knows. Sometimes I'd pour
me a glass and just dread takin' the first drink 'cause
I knew what was gonna happen. But I'd do it anyway.
It don't make no sense, but many's the time I'd walk a
rotten log through hell to get a drink of liquor.

"Anyway, I kept this card game straight for several
years and got paid right good for it. I even got me a
place to stay. I could sleep in a room at the back of the
Busy Bee, fix my own meals—I had it made. None of
the family had any idea where I was, either. I suspect
most of 'em were glad of it. I never was a whole lot of
fun, a whole lot of help, or a whole lot of comfort to my
kin. And after Ma died, there wasn't nothin' much
around home for me."

By now Uncle Will's emphysema had hold of him,
and he had to stop to catch his breath. I'm not sure why
I said it, except that it seemed logical at the time, but
I asked "Well, what'd ya come back for, then?"

"To die, boy," he answered softly but matter-of-
factly. "Just like the ol' bull elephant that roams the
whole world over, then goes back home when his time
is up, I come home to die."

"I don't want ya to die!" I blurted out, my voice choked slightly like something had hold of my Adam's apple.

"Oh, I ain't gonna die, boy. Not today, anyway. But soon. And ya know what? You're probably the only one in the whole damn state that cares one way or the other. I must say it's a bit of a comfort to know that somebody cares. I'm sure Pearl and Hoyt wishes I'd go ahead and get it over with." Pearl and Hoyt were the niece and nephew with whom he split his time when he wasn't living in his old bus. He'd spend a few nights with one, sleep a few days in the bus, then spend a few nights with the other one. Both of them had children, and I think maybe the children resented him coming and going so much.

"I'll tell ya somethin', though, nephew. I read a book one time—I don't remember the name of it, but it was about Vikings, I think—where one of the characters made the statement that as long as somebody says your name once a year, your soul won't die. No matter how bad ya been, he claimed, your soul won't die as along as somebody says your name. So, nephew, I'm gonna ask ya a favor. You're young and healthy. As long as ya plod this ball of dirt, remember from time to time to say my name."

I couldn't speak for a while, but when I found my voice again I said, "I'll do that, Uncle Will. I promise."

Two months later they called from the hospital to tell me he was dead.

•

It'd been nearly three hours since I sat down in the barn to grieve over the loss of Uncle Will. The only interruption had come when Daddy stepped in to check on me, but as soon as he saw me crying he just said they'd save me some supper and went back to the house.

I quickly finished milking the old cow, then hung the milk bucket on a big nail in the hall of the barn and backed up in the feed trough to watch the raindrops dance in puddles around the front of the barn.

For a moment I was very angry toward the people who came to the funeral to make sure Uncle Will was dead. Many faces marched by that open coffin, and in my mind I saw a smirk or a smile on every one. Maybe I saw something that wasn't there, but to me the people at the funeral seemed entirely too light-hearted for such a solemn occasion. Even members of my own family seemed to be relieved, though in his last years Uncle Will was certainly no threat to anybody. He could barely breathe, much less hurt anyone.

The sadness and anger I felt that evening didn't linger long. As a vigorous man, my thoughts soon turned to other things, but a sense of emptiness still touched my heart at certain moments. A special smell in the woods or a pinch of crimped-cut Prince Albert tobacco burning in an open pipe would momentarily rekindle the memories of me sitting astride a log in the Tallapoosa woodlands, listening to Uncle Will recount the experiences of his youth.

Sometimes even now if I awake in the middle of the night, I think of "Ol' Ebo" and the spirits of Willie and Steve Young paying their nightly, ghostly visit to his troubled sleep.

Now I find myself rapidly approaching the time, at least in years of age, when Uncle Will crossed over to that mysterious other world—a world that had aroused in him no small mixture of anticipation, dread, and outright fear. Only today am I beginning to understand his reasons.

"Up there is writ every mean, stinkin', low-down thing I ever did," he said. "Someday I'm gonna have to explain it all, and boy, I won't be done by the time ya get there."

Well, I've now walked a bit of that rocky road myself, Uncle Will. And if you're still explaining things to the Almighty when I get there, I'll help you as much as I can.